ISBN 978-1-332-60732-7
PIBN 10144940

English
Français
Deutsche
Italiano
Español
Português

www.forgottenbooks.com

Mythology Photography **Fiction**
Fishing Christianity **Art** Cooking
Essays Buddhism Freemasonry
Medicine **Biology** Music **Ancient
Egypt** Evolution Carpentry Physics
Dance Geology **Mathematics** Fitness
Shakespeare **Folklore** Yoga Marketing
Confidence Immortality Biographies
Poetry **Psychology** Witchcraft
Electronics Chemistry History **Law**
Accounting **Philosophy** Anthropology
Alchemy Drama Quantum Mechanics
Atheism Sexual Health **Ancient History**
Entrepreneurship Languages Sport
Paleontology Needlework Islam
Metaphysics Investment Archaeology
Parenting Statistics Criminology
Motivational

JUSTICE AND CODIFICATIO

PETITIONS.

Justice and Codification

PETITIONS:

BEING

FORMS PROPOSED FOR *SIGNATURE*

BY ALL PERSONS WHOSE DESIRE IT IS TO SEE

JUSTICE

NO LONGER SOLD, DELAYED, OR DENIED:

AND

TO OBTAIN A POSSIBILITY OF THAT *2617*

KNOWLEDGE OF THE LAW,

IN PROPORTION TO THE WANT OF WHICH THEY ARE SUBJECTED TO

UNJUST PUNISHMENTS,

AND *370.547*

DEPRIVED *of the Benefit of their* RIGHTS.

DRAFTS FOR THE ABOVE PROPOSED PETITIONS, BY

JEREMY BENTHAM.

LONDON:

PRINTED BY C. AND W. REYNELL, BROAD STREET,

CONTENTS.

I. Advertisement.

II. Preliminary Explanations necessary.

III. Full-length Petition for Justice.

IV. Abridged Petition for Justice.

V. More Abridged Petition for Justice.

VI. Supplement to any of the above Petitions.

VII. Petition for Codification.

ADVERTISEMENT.

Contained in the present publication are three Papers :—

Paper the first, Proposed Petition for JUSTICE, at *full length.*

Paper the second, Proposed Petition for JUSTICE in an *abridged* form.

Paper the third, Proposed Petition for CODIFICA-TION.

Petition for JUSTICE at *full length.* Parts of it these.

Part I. *Case made :*—Grounds of the hereby proposed application to the House of Commons: inaptitude, to wit, of the existing system of judicial *procedure,* with reference to its alleged and supposed ends, as also of the judicial *establishment* occupied in the application of it: proofs, the several heads and instances of abuse and imperfection, which are accordingly brought and held, up to view.

Part II. *Prayer consequent :* — Remedy proposed, for the disorder composed of those same abuses and imperfections.

Prayer, its parts,—

Part 1. Outline of the proposed *judicial esta-blishment.*

Part 2. Outline of the proposed system of *pro-cedure.* Model, the *domestic* system: that, to wit, which is pursued of course by every intelligent father of a family, without any such idea as that of its constituting the matter of an art or science: sole difference the necessary enlargement and di-versification, correspondent to the difference in magnitude between the two theatres.

II. Petition for JUSTICE in an *abridged* form. Parts of it these.

Part I. Abridgment of the *case* part of the full-length Petition.

Part II. *Prayer* part. Matter of it the same, word for word, as that of the full-length Petition: reference accordingly sufficient; repetition, need-less.

Reasons for the two different forms, these:

1. In the full-length Petition, number of the pages, as will be seen 207. Cumbrous would an instrument of this length be, if presented in the only *form* in which it would be received,—cum-brous, and *that* to such a degree, that its bulk might of itself be found an insurmountable ob-stacle to its being carried about for signature. This form is—that of a roll of parchment, com-

posed of skins tacked on, one to another; length, whatever is necessary for receiving the signatures, in addition to the matter of the Petition.

2. Compared with that of the abridged instrument, the expense of the operation of engrossing would of itself be a serious obstacle.

3. *Readers* in greater numbers—*readers* and thence *signers*, may of course be expected for the shorter than for the longer instrument: to each reader the two will here present themselves for choice.

For *reading*, the instrument presented to a person looked to as disposed to promote the design, will be of course a printed copy of this work. In this way it is perusable by any number of persons at the same time; while, if there was no other copy than the above mentioned roll, years might elapse before this instrument could pass through the number of hands in succession, to each of whom a single day might suffice for the perusal of a copy of it.

III. Petition for CODIFICATION. Intimately connected is the subject-matter of this Petition with that of the Petition for *Justice*. No otherwise than by codification can the reform here prayed for—or any effectual reform in any shape,—be carried into effect. A Petition, in the terms here seen, having been honoured by the approbation of greatest number obtainable in the same, so supremely and all-comprehensively important service.

Nor to this purpose is the same sanction of authority altogether wanting. By implication at any rate, codification has in its favour the declared opinion, and recommendation of the real property commissioners: witness the questions circulated by them. Sufficiently manifest at any rate is the recommendation; while, in pursuance of their labours, something should be done. But by Parliament, whatever it be, either by codification or not at all, will it have been done: and whatever be the length to which this indispensable operation has been carried—why it should stop there or any where short of completion, is a question to which it rests with any declared opponent of codification to find, if it be in his power, anything like a rational answer: by his refusal to answer it, or his silence, in relation to it, judgment of inconsistency against him will be signed.

These things considered, requisite assurances are not wanting, that as soon as the press of more urgent business admits, the matter of both petitions will, by appropriate motions, be brought to the view of the Honourable House.

Instructions as to the mode of proceeding for obtaining signatures.

Provide a skin of parchment, tack to it one after another others in sufficient number to contain the matter of the petition, with the addition of signatures in such number as you expect to obtain for it. A thing desirable is, that all persons who join in the petition may be distinguished, each one from any other: for this purpose, let each subscriber add to his name at length an indication of the place of his abode. If it be where there is a town, the name of the county and the parish will be the proper mode of designation: if in a town, the name of the town, with that of the street or other mode of address, employed in sending a letter by the *post:* To save bulk and expense,— divide the roll into parallel columns, each of them wide enough to receive a signature of an average length, in which case, when it exceeds that length, two lines will always be necessary, though commonly sufficient. To each signature prefix a number expressive of the order in which it stands.

As to the instrument thus employed—in general, if not exclusively—it will be the *abridged* petition: the *full-length* petition being much too large, and the transcription of it too expensive, for general use. To any person disposed to use his endeavours to obtain signatures for the longer petition; should it present itself as being too long, an easy operation it will be to strike out of it such parts as, it seems to him, can best be spared. Where any *abridged* petition is the one employed —in this case, a copy of the petition at length, as printed, should be left with the person applied to, that he may peruse it, if so inclined, before the roll is put into his hands for signature.

Of the opposition which every such coadjutor has reason to expect, it is material that he should be sufficiently aware. From all persons to whom any change in the existing system would be an object of regret, such is the reception which should of course be looked for and provided against : and in this number are included of course all those by whom, to any amount, in any shape, in any way, direct or indirect, profit is derived, or thought by them to be derived, from any abuse or imperfection, to which, by the proposed draught, a remedy is endeavoured to be applied : more particularly all attornies or solicitors, as of late years they have been called, and persons specially connected with them by any tie of interest or relationship, not to speak of judges, other persons belonging to the judicial establishment, and barristers.

Nor as to the whole class, and its several ramifications, let it ever be out of mind, that, on their own principles, by their own shewing, being incontestably interested, they are, one and all, in relation to this matter, not to speak of so many other matters, to use their own language, so many incompetent, incredible, and altogether inadmissible witnesses.

Of this publication one natural effect is the producing addresses, in one way or other, to the author, from correspondents, to the number of whom no certain limits can be predicted, and which, if precautions were not taken, might be such as to be oppressive. For, so it is, that whatever probability there may be of the presentation of *petitions*, or though it were no more than a single petition, in the course of the present session, the like probability may continue during an indefinite length of ulterior time: but for the arrangement thus requested, this publication might therefore have for one of its effects the imposing upon the author a charge to an indefinite amount, and not terminating but with his life.

On this account it is requested that no communication be addressed to the author but through the medium of the bookseller: nor to the bookseller, but either post paid, or accompanied with an order for a copy of the work.

Lastly, as to the usefulness of this production, and the endurance of which it is susceptible. To those whom the design may be fortunate enough to number amongst its well-wishers, and the production among its approvers, a consideration that cannot fail to be more or less agreeable, is—that, whatsoever may be its capacity for attracting signatures, the same may remain to it during an indefinite length of time: and that, so long as the remembrance of this publication lasts, no one to whom the existing self-stiled instrument of security is a source and instrument—of depredation, of oppression, in a word, of *injury* in any shape, can be in want of a ready vehicle for the communication of his complaints.

CORRIGENDA.

Page viii, last line, *for* that is—of, *read* that of.
iv, line 17, *for* questiun, *read* question.
v, 13, *for* another, *read* the other.
21, line 21, *for* altercation, *read* alteration.
35, 21, *for* in request, out of, *read* in request,—out of.
35, 23, *for* Say each one for another, *read* Each one after another.
37, 3, *for* primee, *read* prime.
41, 9, *for* member as in every, *read* member in every.
41, 12, *for* achdemics, *read* academics.
43, 28, *for* rewards, the, *read* rewards in the.
44, 23, *for* joined, *read* concurred with.
48, 16, *for* and the practice, *read* and so far the practice.
48, 29, *for* his profits, *read* the profits.
48, 32, *for* This service, *read* This series.
50, 20, *for* whose testimony, were he admitted, *read* who being tendered for admission.
54, 12, *for* creditor, *read* Creditor.
55, 8, *for* conveyances, in, *read* conveyances, or in.
57, 8, *after* evidence, *insert*—in cases styled civil.
62, 12, *for* adoption, *read* adopters.
62, 17, *for* opposite is to be, *read* opposite, to be.
65, 24, *for* In no one instance endurance, *read* Scarcely more than one instance of endurance.
66, 19, *for* In no known, *read* In scarcely more than one known.
67, 17, *for* meaning now the benefit, *read* meaning the benefit.
70, 26, *for* one effect : so far therefore of the oaths—one effect. *Dele* so far, &c.
73, 7, *for* no such endurance, *read* scarcely endurance.
86, 17, *for* mode which, *read* mode by which.
87, 15, *for* this suitor, *read* him.
88, 14, *for* established, *read* and established.
88, 18, *for* other had, *read* other hand.
93, 22, *for* operation, *read* operations.
99, 35, the blank between sittings, and days, is unnecessary.
101, 9, *for* was the equivalent, *read* was anything like an adequate equivalent.
103, 17, *for* took the commencement, *read* took commencement.
104, *for* in London, *read* or London.
108, 18, *for* in possession, *read* in his possession.
113, 15, *for* plaintiff's, *read* plaintiff.
113, 16, *for* defendant's, *read* defendant.
114, 1, *for* entire system, *read* entirely new system.
115, 15, *for* writing : it is to be, *read* writing, is to be.

Page 131, line 12, *for* even the whole field of law, *read* over the whole field of law.

132,   31, *for* any wards, *read* any ward.

135,   30, *for* the act supposes a blow, *read* the act, suppose a blow.

137,   24, *for* unmoveables, *read* immoveables.

139,   17, *for* a negative act, *read* commonly a negative act.

143,   34, *for* give it, fulfilment effected ; unless he, *read* give it, unless he.

146, last line, *for* cause, *read* case.

147,   21, *for* that story it is, *read* that it is.

147,   25, As to the story's being a lie, that's no concern of yours, *dele*.

149,   23, for *omission insertion*, read *omission* put *insertion*.

150,   4, *for* thus kept destined, *read* thus kept distinct.

150,   19, *after* for *insert* the ; *after* to be *insert* thus.

151,   1, *for* one mischievous, *read* the mischievous.

151,   16, *for* an, *read* or.

153,   7, *for* conscience, read *conscience*.

153,   25, *for* done then, *read* done, then.

156,   8, *for* the first instance, *read* the next instance.

159,   18, *for* 20*l*. 1826: *read* 20*l*. in the year of our Lord 1826.

159,   24, *for* four-and-sixty, *read* a hundred and sixty-five.

163,   4, *for* barbarity and impotence, *read* barbarity, and impotence.

166,   34, *for* sheriff of the courts, *read* sheriff of the county.

173,   34, *for* day, *read* days.

182,   31, *for* having been, *read* has been.

182, last line, *for* being capable, *read* be capable.

183,   27, *for* these three lines, *read* these lines.

184,   13, *for* judicature,—in all cases, *read* judicature, in all cases.

191,   5, *for* distinct dependency, *read* distant dependency.

193,   18, *for* in which imposition may be from a degree, *read* which imposition may have place in a degree.

198,   12, *for* oppropriate, *read* appropriate.

203,   21, *for* charge, *read* scale.

ABRIDGED PETITION.

Page   1, line 17, *for* expense without, *read* expense, without.

2,   23, *for* of from nine-tenths, *read* of nine tenths.

6,   1, *for* unintelligiblized, *read* unintelligibilised.

7,   1, *omit* and.

11,   25, *omit* correspondent.

11,   26, *before* service, *insert* correspondent.

12,   28, *after* declaration, *omit the* comma.

14,   29, *after* mendacity, *insert* a dash.

14,   30, *after* mind, *insert* a dash.

16,   1, *for* matter a fact, *read* matter of fact.

16,   29, *for* new, *read* now.

19,   19, *for* endless, *read* needless.

19,   28, *for* excepted, in, *read* excepted. In.

20,   22, *for* Is, *read* In.

24,   29, *for* The, *read* To the.

24,   30, *for* indispensable, *read* the indispensable.

30,   33, *for* system established, as, *read* system, established as-

31,   1, *for* necessitated ; and, *read* necessitated, and.

Page 31, line 2, *for* time, adequate, *read* time adequate.
    31,   2, *for* need, delay, *read* need : delay.
    31,   3, *for* is made, *read* is thus made.
    32,   3, *for* For, *read* To.
    33,   2, *for* self-differing, *read* self-disserving.
    39,   29, *for* solicitors, *read* solicitor.
    40,   6, *for* the, *read* that.
    43,   18, *after* wisdom, *insert* a dash.
    51,   18, *for* far, *read* as to.
    51,   25, *omit* included.
    68,   2, *for* usurpation) alone excepted, *read* usurpation alone ex-
                 cepted.)
    74,   17, *after* side, *omit* the comma.
    81,   28, *for* would, *read* could.
    83,   26, *for* of which, *read* which.

MORE ABRIDGED PETITION.

Page 2, line 14, *for* services, *read* service.
     2,   25, *for* (as by salary, money in the shape of) *read* (as by money
              in the shape of salary.)
     6,   22, *for* it is a favourable case, *read* it is a favourable case for
              her :
     8,   32, *for* vexation, but, *read* vexation,—but.
     9,   16, *for* at any rule, *read* at any rate.
   11,   17, *for* statute law, *read* statute law.)
   12,   2, *for* abrogation, *read* for its abrogation.
   12,   25, *for* comfort ; condition, *read* comfort, condition.
   13,   25, *for* to fear, he has, *read* to fear,—he has.
   14,   11, *for* humbly *insert*, *read* humbly *insist*.

SUPPLEMENT.

Page 2, line 6, *for* hundreds of thousands, *read* tens of thousands.
     3,   23, *for* exposed; are— *read* exposed, are—
     3,   25, *for* shape, *read* shapes.
   10,   31, *for* amelioration, *read* melioration.
   15,   20, *for* instance, *read* instances.
   16,   27, exemplification of the crime-licensing system,—*dele*.
   18,   28, *for* applyed, *read* applied.
   19, last line, *for* subordination, *read* subornation.

PRELIMINARY EXPLANATIONS

---

1. In the Introductory Advertisement will have been seen, the consideration which gave birth to the proposed Abridged Petition for Justice, in addition to the Full-length Petition.

2. When that advertisement went to the press, the drawing up of the Abridged Petition had proceeded about half way: and, from the progress at that time made had been deduced an assurance, delusive as it has proved, of completing it within the desired compass: the compass, both as to *time* and *space*.

3. From that time, the further this part of the work went on, the less apposite was perceived to be the appellative *Abridged*, by which it had been originally designated : till, at length, instead of the one operation *abridgment*, four distinguishable ones—subtraction, addition, repetition, substitu-

b

tion,—were the operations found to have been performed.

4. Of this variety of operations,—imperfection, in respect of clearness, conciseness, and methodical order, on the part of the draft, considered as a literary composition, has been the indispensable consequence.   But,. should it be seen, as the author trusts it will be, that without detriment to the practical purpose, no different course could have been pursued,—no material dissatisfaction on the part of the reader will, it is hoped, have place.

5. Practical *end* or purpose,—change for the better: *means* employed,—maximising the number of the persons known to entertain the desire of seeing such change take place : *mode* of making this desire known,—attachment of each one's signature to some copy of a petition praying for such change.

6. Now, then' for maximising the number of signatures, one means is—the maximising the number of copies, offered for the reception of those same signatures. But, by the bulkiness of the aggregate mass of the matter by which the *reasons* for the change stand expressed, will the end and purpose be obstructed? No: it will be promoted. How so? *Answer :* Because the instrument may be cut into smaller instruments, in any

number; to each of which, signatures may be found obtainable, from persons from whom this expression of concurrence would not have been obtainable for any one other of these same component parts, much less for the whole.

.7. Now, then, as to the particular use and purpose of the two here-proposed instruments—Fulllength and Abridged Petitions—taken together. This was—the maximising the number of the arrangements in the existing system, seen by the several readers to be adverse to the ends of justice; to which end a means manifestly conducive was— the tying up, as it were, of those same arrangements into bundles, characterised and distinguished from each other by appropriate names. This, accordingly, is what has been done by the list of *Devices*.

. 8. Considerations, showing the course actually pursued to have been the most conducive that *could* have been pursued, the following:—

9.—I. In proportion as the operation went on,— matters of detail, deemed, all of them, contributory to the common ends, but which had not, all of them, presented themselves at the time of drawing up the first-drawn Petition,—came into view. By exclusion put upon any of these additional grounds and inducements, would the chance for the attainment of the common end have been increased? No, surely.

10. True it is—that, in the ordinary case of an abridgment,—between clearness and conciseness, a mutual repugnancy has place : as conciseness is increased, clearness is diminished, But, in the present case, happily no such repugnancy has place : no mutual counteraction but what is capable of being effectually got rid of. Decomposition, as above, is the operation by which this reconcilia- tion is capable of being effected ; and is accordingly here proposed to be effected.

11. Now as to the course which may be seen *actually* taken, as above, in pursuance of the *design* of abbreviation. *First* came *condensation* ; as in the ordinary case of an abridgment : *then*, simple *elimination*, or say *subtraction*, applied to certain *paragraphs* belonging to the device in questiun : lastly, *elimination* applied to the *whole* of the matters contained under the head of a Device. In this last way may be seen dealt with three devices ; namely, Device XI. *Decision on grounds avowedly foreign to the merits;* Device XII. *Juries subdued and subjugated :* and Device XIV. *Result of the fissure* (in Device XIII mentioned) *ground- less arrestation for debt.* As the pressure produced by the influx of additional matter increased, these more and more efficient modes of reduction may be seen successively employed.

12. The two drafts taken together being in this state, comes now the question—of the com-

pound mass—any and what portion is there, that can with truth be pronounced useless? Answer, Yes: namely the aggregate of the paragraphs reprinted without variation.

After this deduction, every other assignable portion of the matter may be stated as having its use.

13. The case in which, if at all, the correctness of this proposition will be most questionable, is that, in which, of two paragraphs, the one is, as above, but a *condensation* of the other: but, even in this case, so it may be, that the one of them may be the most apt in the eyes of one set of proposed subscribers; another, in the eyes of another such set.

14. In the disposition made of the matter of the *original* draft,—and thereafter of that of the *abridged* draft,—a *method*, as serviceable as it was in the author's power to give, has been given to it. But now—take the worst case that can have place. Suppose nothing to have place that can have any claim to the appellation of *method :*—the whole matter—is it useless, and the labour thrown away? By no means.

15. For, the purpose being to prevail upon the constituted authorities to take the whole of the mass of existing law in question for the subject matter of consideration—and this for the purpose of reform and amendment,—of no blemish in any

shape, can any indication, in any language or form, be given, that will not be more or less contributory and conducive to the purpose.

16. Upon the whole,—proposed for the choice of all persons, disposed to be contributory to the proposed design, by framing drafts for circulation, for the purpose of obtaining signatures, will be—the *options*, examples of which are the following:—

i. To employ the *full length* draft, without alteration, as it stands.

ii. To employ the *abridged* draft, without alteration, as it stands.

iii. To employ either draft, with amendments, such as may appear meet: amendments, whether additive, subtractive, or substitutive.

iv. To form drafts of their own; composed of matter—none of it contained under any of the heads employed in the above drafts.

v. To form drafts, composed of matter of their own, with or without use made of those same heads, and with or without insertion, *declaredly* given to more or less of the matter contained under them.

vi. To frame drafts composed of matters exclusively their own, without reference made to, or use in any way made of, any part of the matter contained in either of these same drafts.

17. Of these several options; (to which others might have been added) the one last mentioned (it will of course be supposed) is not of the number of those which the author expects to see embraced. But, even supposing it were,—whatsoever be the number of the drafts, thus framed, and, with attached signatures, presented to the constituted authorities,—correspondent will be the service rendered to the cause of reform and improvement by these pages.

18. A lottery (suppose) set up; and paragraphs of the Abridged Petition, some or all of them, drawn out of it, and written down on the roll in the order assigned to them by *fortune*,—even in this case, a Petition, so framed and thereupon signed, would not be altogether without its use.

19. So long as that most' all-comprehensive, most grinding, and most crying of all grievances—the tyranny of judge-made law—continues unredressed,—the correspondent public service unperformed—so long as the torrent of human misery, flowing from it, keeps running on;—be the number of 'ages' during which it will have continued ever so great, never will the use, whatever it be, which the matter of these proposed Petitions is capable of being put to, be at an end.

20. To the care of posterity, should the time

not be yet ripe, the author will recommend this matchless service with his dying breath.

21. Hapless individual! whoever you may be, whose lot it is to behold your means of subsistence torn from you, and plunged into the gulph called by a cruel mockery a *court of equity*, there to be devoured by the appointed sharks,—in these pages you may at all times see samples—samples ready made—of the only sort of *instrument*, which it is in your power to make application of, in the character of a remedy :—with this in hand, you may go about, and look about, for assistants and coadjutors, in those companions in misery, whom in such deplorable abundance, you will behold presenting themselves all around.

22. Nor, while for companions in misery you look sideways, forget to look upwards, for the authors—cruel hypocrites, in pretence alleviators—in reality, preservers—of all parts of it anxious and industrious preservers, when neither creators nor exacerbators.

23. But (says somebody) is there not one still better course left, which you might have taken, and which is still left open to you to take? From the matter of the original Full-length Petition and the Abridged Petition taken together, might not you have drawn up—might not you even now draw up—a new draft, consigning to the flames *both* the

existing ones? *Answer:* By *time* and *expense* taken together, intimation is given of two objections, the first of which might of itself be conclusive : considering that, during the time thus occupied in an operation little better than mechanical, all other works, of greater usefulness in this same time, would be at a stand.

24. But, another answer still more conclusive, and it is hoped satisfactory, is this. By no means, by any such ulterior and amended abridgment, would the purpose of it be answered. For, while for the purpose of it, a survey were taking of the field, fresh weeds would be seen springing up, and pressing themselves upon the extirpating hand. In this way, after enlarged as well as abridged editions, in any number—each superseding all former ones,—still the demand for another and another would be presenting itself : nor, for the consumption of labour, time, and money, would the demand cease, till the work, of which an *outline*, and nothing more, is here professed to be presented, had been brought to a state regarded as a state of completeness.

25. Suppose it now in that state, the following is the form in which it would present itself to view: of the here-proposed system, the part called the *Prayer*, in the very *words*, or as lawyers say, *tenor* of it, occupying the foremost places : but, by

the side of it, all along, a delineation, of the several correspondent features of alleged inaptitude; ascribed to the existing systems : to the principal *text* would thus be subjoined a sort of *perpetual commentary* thus composed.

26. In conclusion, a word or two as to the *numerical figures*, which, in the abridged petition, stand prefixed to the paragraphs : in the abridged petition only ; in the original one not ; the demand for that help to reference not having as yet presented itself to view.

27. For all but the two *first* of the above proposed six options, indisputable assuredly is the facility that will be found afforded by this little additament. Witness, sad experience of the result of the non-employment of them. By means of these instruments, (than which nothing can be more familiar or indispensably useful,—or, even, by the constituted authorities themselves, more universally applied to portions of the matter of law,— except where the production of uncertainty and mistake is among the objects aimed at) reference is, in the concisest manner possible, made, to any assemblage of words whatsoever, without danger of mistake :—without them, mistake and uncertainty may, to any amount, be produced.

28. Accordingly, wherever, in relation to a law or a body of laws, to maximize the execution and

affect given to it is really an object of desire;—numerical figures, prefixt, to the several portions of discourse, are the instruments employed. Witness the practice in every civilized part of the globe; England — lawyer-ridden England — alone excepted.

29. On the other hand, wherever the design entertained, is,—the giving increase to such uncertainty, with its attendant miseries,—objects in view. the benefit of the lawyer class, and those connected with it by any community of sinister interest,—the use of this, together with so many other instruments of certainty, is pertinaciously and inexorably abstained from : imitated thus the fabled barbarity of Mezentius : kept bound up in the closest contact with careases in an ambiguous state between life and death, is the whole stock of those statutes, which are still designed, as well as destined, to be employed as living ones. Witness the latest of the string of *Bills*, framed exactly as if they had for their object, on pretence of diminution, the augmentation and perpetuation of depredation and oppression. "Repealed—such an Act, (thereupon designated by its long and woolly title) and such an Act, (designated in the same conception-confounding manner) and *so much* of such an act—in like manner designated."—So much ? How much ? Learned sir ! Right Honorable

sir! whichever be your right name—render it possible for us to know *how much :* instead of consigning to complete ruin, by alleged mistake as to the *how much,* on the part of a wretch, who has been half ruined, by some petty tyrant, clothed in the authority of a justice of the peace, at whose charge, on the faith of parliament, that compensation has been *sought,* which would not have been promised, but for the foreknowledge that it would never be granted.—" *So much?*"—Once more, *how much ?*—Till of late, followed upon the words " *so much*" the words " *as relates to* the subject of.... :" whereupon came some sort of designation given of it. Now, even this clue is refused, and the passage evaporates in nonsense.

30. To these figures,—when the question was as to the mode of preparing drafts for receiving signatures,—an objection was made on the ground of *unusualness.* To the quarter from whence the objection came, nothing short of the most respectful attention could be paid. But the use, to which on that occasion it was destined, was no other than that of being applied to an instrument which was then actually in a state for receiving signatures : and to which accordingly, references, for any such purpose as the one then in question were not intended to be made. Of these instruments of clarification, the use and purpose here in question

is—the subjecting to decomposition the supposed too bulky bodies,—that out of them, other bodies in any required number, *polype* like, might be framed. But, in the case here alluded to, no such decomposition was contemplated.

Comes now another use, of these small but effective instruments of precision: call it for example, the *argumentative* or argument-assisting use: calling, for distinction sake, the one first mentioned the *simply indicative.* Of these same little instruments is constituted a support—and that a matchless one—for *close reasoning.*

32. Pitiable, in good truth, will be seen to be the condition of the disingenuous opponent, who, casting an eye on a body of argument which he stands engaged to encounter and attack, beholds it armed with them. Thus distributed into so many articulate parts,—for the clear, correct and complete designation of each of which, a single word is effectually sufficient,—the discourse, be it what it may, presents to him, in each part of it, a determinate and never misapprehensible object and standard of reference. " Here, sir, is proposition the first. What say you to it? has it your assent? has it your dissent? if your dissent, for what reason or reasons? Unapprised of the existence of these defences,—he comes (suppose) with his quiver full of *devices* borrowed from the *Book of*

Fallacies. See then the condition, in which he finds himself. Instead of doing as he had flattered himself with doing,—instead of shooting fallacies into the middle of the discourse at random,—or enveloping the whole expanse of it as it were in a net,—he feels himself pinned down, under the pressure of a most distressing alternative. Taking in hand the chain of discourse,—either he must grapple with the links which it is thus composed of, one after another,—or remain motionless :— remain motionless ; and thus, by a token more unequivocal and demonstrative than it is in the power of words to be, acknowledge the object of his hostility to be unassailable.

Nothing can he say—(for such is the supposition, and this is a supposition which may continually be seen verified)—nothing can he say, but what is to be found in this or that chapter, section, and article, of the *Book of Fallacies :* some article, in and by which, before he ever took this device of his in hand, it may be seen ready confuted. Looking at the mark,—nothing can he find to hit it with, but some witticism—some well worn piece of nothingness—some *vague generality*— which,—like a cloud,—dark or more or less brilliant,—hanging in the air,—is seen to have no substance—nothing that can be brought to bear upon the object of his warfare.

33. " Well, sir,"—(says now to him the master of fair and close reasoning:)—" here sir, is the proposition: what say you to it?"—What! nothing? a·man—for ingenuity and promptitude so highly distinguished, kept mute by prudence, because unable to find anything which a man could utter without shame?—What? still silent? Well then: the demonstration is complete: the proposition uncontrovertible. Yes, altogether uncontrovertible; since you, sir, even you, can find nothing to object to it.

34. Think now, once more, of the condition of the disingenuous and self-condemned would-be assailant,—when, by every fresh proposition, he beholds a fresh triumph over him thus secured.

☞ After writing what is above, came the conception and the hope, that an additional optional Petition might have its use: and that,—by the same observations, by which *explanation* and *justification* have been given to the two first,—the like service might in a sufficient degree be rendered to this third: by the title of the *More Abridged Petition*, it is accordingly subjoined.

PETITION FOR JUSTICE.

---

*To the Honorable the House of Commons
in Parliament assembled.*

JUSTICE! justice! accessible justice! Justice, not for the few alone, but for all! No longer nominal, but at length real justice! In these few words stands expressed the sum and substance of the humble petition, which we, the undersigned, in behalf of ourselves and all other his Majesty's long-suffering subjects, now at length have become emboldened to address to the Honorable House.

At present, to all men, justice, or what goes by that name, is either denied or sold; denied to the immense many—sold to the favoured few; nor to these, but at an extensively ruinous price. Such is the *grievance*.

As to the cause, it is undeniable. Power to judges to pay themselves—to pay themselves what they please, so it be at the expense of suitors.

The denial and the sale follow of necessity. Be the pay in each instance but a farthing, to all that cannot pay the farthing, justice is denied; to all those who can and do pay the farthing, sold.

B

And the persons on whom alone this burthen
is imposed, who are they? Who, but the very
persons, who alone, were the exemption possible,
should be exempted—altogether exempted from
it. Distinguished from all other persons are
suitors, by the *vexation* which, as such, they
endure. The security, whatever it be, which,
by this vexation, these so dearly pay for, all
others enjoy without it; and on each man, the
greater the vexation in other shapes, the higher
(it will be seen) is the tax; for the longer, and
thence the more vexatious, the suit, the more
numerous are the occasions on which payment of
this species of tax comes to be exacted.

What if this faculty of setting, in the same
way, their own price upon their own service,
were given—(and why might it not as well be
given?)—to functionaries in other departments?—
say, for example, the military. The business of
military functionaries is to give security against
external, of judiciary functionaries against internal
adversaries. What if to the army power were
given to exact whatever contributions it pleased,
so it were from those alone who had been sufferers from hostile inroads? By those military
functionaries this power has not ever been received;
by judiciary functionaries it not only has been
received, but, to this day, continues to be exercised.

The tax called *ship-money* found a Hampden to
oppose it; to oppose it at the expense, first of his
money, then of his life. Neither in its principle
was that same *ship-money* so absurd, nor in its
worst natural consequences would it have been,
by a vast amount, so mischievous, as this *justice-
money*, for so, with not less propriety, might it be

called. *Ship-money* produced its Hampden: the Hampden for *justice-money* is yet to seek.

Taxes, imposed on suitors at the instance of ministers were bad enough; but they are not, by a great deal, so bad as those imposed by judges. Ministers cannot, without the sanction of Parliament, give increase to taxes imposed at their instance. Judges can, and do give increase, at pleasure, to taxes imposed for their own emolument, by themselves.

Out of our torments they extract their own comfort; and in the way in which they proceed, for each particle of comfort extracted for themselves, they, of necessity, heap an unmeasurable load of torment upon us. By every fee imposed, men, in countless multitudes, are, for want of money to commence or carry on a suit, deprived of rights to any amount, and left to suffer, without redress, wrongs to any amount: others made to suffer at the hands of judges, for want of the money necessary to enable them to defend themselves against unjust suits.

In all other cases, the presumption is, that, if left to himself, man will, upon each occasion, sacrifice to his own, every other interest; and upon this supposition are all laws grounded: what is there in irresistible power, wrapt in impunity, that should make it—what is there in an English judge that should make him—an exception to this rule?

Such being the grievance, and such the cause of it, now as to the remedy. *The cause* we said, for shortness; *the causes*, we should have said, for there is a chain of them; nor till the whole chain has been brought to view can any tolerably adequate conception be entertained of the sole

effectual remedy—the natural substituted to the
existing technical system of procedure. Cause
of the oppositeness of the system to the ends of'
justice, the sinister interest on the part of the
judges,' with whom it originated. Cause of this
sinister interest, the mode of their remuneration:
instead of salary paid by government, fees exacted
from suitors. Cause of this mode of remuneration, want of settled revenue in a pecuniary
shape: for military and other purposes, personal
service rendered to government, being paid for,
not in money but in land. Cause of this mode
of payment, rude state of society in these early
times.

But for the Norman conquest, no such sinister
interest, in conjunction with the power, of giving
effect to it, would have had place. At the time
of that disastrous revolution, the local field of
judicature was found divided into small districts,
each with its appropriate judicatory; still remaining, with small parcels, or faint shades of the
power, are the denominations of those judicatories,
county courts, for example, hundred courts,
courts leet, courts baron. In each such district,
in the powers of judicature, sharers (in form and
extent not exactly known) the whole body of the
freeholders. Form of procedure, the natural, the
domestic; natural—that is to say, clear of all
those forms by which the existing system—pro-
duct of sinister *art*, and thence so appositely
termed the *technical*—stands distinguished from
it: forms, all of them subservient, of course, to
the ends of judicature; all of them opposite, as
will be seen, to the ends of justice.

Let not any such charge as that of unwarrant-
able presumption attach on the views, which we,·

your petitioners, venture thus respectfully to submit to the Honorable House. Be the occasion
what it may,—when by numerous and promiscuous
multitudes, expression is given to the same opinions,
as well as to the same wishes, unavoidably different
are the sources from which those opinions and
those wishes are derived: in some reflection made
by themselves; in others, confidence reposed in
associates. Among those in whom, on the present
occasion, the necessary confidence is reposed, are
those, the whole adult part of whose lives the study
of the subject has found devoted to it.

History and description will now proceed hand-
in-hand. As it was in the beginning, so is it now.
How things are will be seen by its being seen how
they came to be so. To the arrangements, by
which the existing system has been rendered thus
adverse to the ends of justice, will be given the
denomination of *devices:* devices, having for their
purposes the above mentioned actual ends of judicature: and under the head of each device, in
such order as circumstances may in each instance
appear to require, the attention of the Honorable
House is solicited for the considerations following—1. Mischievousness of the device to the public in respect of the adverseness of the arrangement to the ends of justice.

2. Subserviency of the device to the purposes
of the authors—that is to say, the judges, and other,
partakers with them in the sinister interests.

3. Impossibility that this adverseness and this
subserviency should not have been seen by the
authors.

4. Impossibility, after this exposure, that that
same adverseness should not now be seen by those
to whom the device is a source of profit.

5. Incidentally, originally-established apt, arrangements, superseded and excluded by the device.

. The ends of justice—we must unavoidably *remind*, (we will not say *inform*) the Honorable House—the ends of justice are,—1. The giving execution and effect to the rule of action; this the main end: 2. The doing so with the least expense, delay, and vexation possible; the collateral end.

In the main end require to be distinguished two branches: 1. Exclusion of *misdecision:* 2. Exclusion of *non-decision.* Non-decision is either from *non-demand* or *after demand.* The first case is that of simple denial of justice: the other case is that of denial of justice, aggravated by treachery and depredation to the amount of the expense: of the collateral end, the three branches, delay, expense, and vexation, have been already mentioned.

To these same ends of justice, correspondent and opposite will be seen to be the ends—the originally and still pursued actual ends—of judicature: from past misdecision, comes succeeding uncertainty; from the uncertainty, litigation: from the litigation, under the existing fee-gathering system, judge's profit: from the expense, in the more immediate way, that same sinister profit: from the delay, increase to expense and thence to that same profit: from the expense and the delay vexation: this not indeed the purposed but the unheeded and thence recklessly increased result. Of the non-decision and the delay, ease at the expense of duty will moreover, in vast proportion, be seen to be the intended, and but too successfully cultivated, fruit.

Manner, in which this mode of payment took place, this. Originally, king officiated not only as commander-in-chief, but as judge. From this reality came the still existing fiction, which places him on his own bench in Westminster-hall, present at every cause.

At the early period in question, in the instruments still extant under the name of *writs*, king addresses himself to judge and says, " These people are troublesome to me with their noise : see what is the matter with them and quiet them— *ne amplius clamorum audiamus*."

Thus far explicitly and in words. Implication added a postscript: " This will be some trouble to you; but the labourer is worthy of his hire."

Nothing better could judge have wished for. All mankind to whom, and all by whom injury had been done or supposed to be done, were thus placed at his mercy : upon the use of his power, he had but to put what price he pleased. To every one who regarded himself as injured, his assistance was indispensable : and proportioned to plaintiff's assurance of getting back from defendant the price of such assistance, would be his (the plaintiff's) readiness to part with it. To the defendant, permission to defend himself was not less indispensable. As to pay, all the judge had to choose was between high fees and low fees. High fees left at any rate most ease ; but the higher they were, the less numerous : the lower, the more numerous the hands by which they could be paid. Thus it was that, by kings, what was called justice, was administered at next to no expense to themselves, the only person, by whom the burthen was borne, being the already afflicted. Bad enough this ; but in France it was still worse. Independently of the taxes, imposed under that name directly, on the proceedings, profit by sale of the power of exacting

the judge's fees, was made a source of revenue:
and hence, instead of four benches with one judge,
or at most four or five judges on a bench, arose all
over the country large assembly rooms full of
judges, under the name of *Parliaments.*

Of the *devices* to which we shall now intreat the
attention of the Honourable House, the following
are the results :—

  I. Parties excluded from judges' presence.
  II. Language rendered unintelligible.
  III. Written instruments, where worse than use-
    less, necessitated.
  IV. Mendacity licensed, rewarded, necessitated,
    and by judge himself practised.
  V. Oaths, for the establishment of the men-
    dacity, necessitated.
  VI. Delay in groundless and boundless lengths,
    established.
  VII. Precipitation necessitated.
  VIII. Blind fixation of times for judicial opera-
    tions.
  IX. Mechanical, substituted to mental judica-
    ture.
  X. Mischievous transference and bandying of
    suits.
  XI. Decision on grounds avowedly foreign to the
    merits.
  XII. Juries subdued and subjugated.
  XIII. Jurisdiction, where it should be entire, split
    and spliced.
  XIV. Result of the fissure—groundless arrests for
    debt.

Explanations (we are sensible) are requisite:
explanations follow.

I.—*Device the first. Parties excluded from judges' presence.* Demandant not admitted to state his demand; nor defendant his defence : admitted then only, when and because they cannot be shut out : admitted, just as strangers are : admitted without the power of acting for themselves.

In this device may be seen the *hinge,* on which all the others turn : in every other, an instrument for giving either existence or effect, or continuance to this indispensable one.

Only by indirect means could an arrangement so glaringly adverse to the ends of justice have been established : these means (it will be seen), were the *unintelligible* language and the *written pleadings.*

At the very outset of the business, the door shut against the best evidence : evidence in the best form, from the best sources. No light let in, but through a combination of mediums, by which some rays would be absorbed, others refracted and distorted.

No information let in but through the hands of middle men, whose interest it is that redress should be as expensive, and for the sake of their share in the expense, as tardy as possible.

For what purpose, but the production of deception by exclusion put upon truth, and admission given to falsehood, could any such arrangement have been so much as imagined ?

For terminating a dispute in a family, was ever father mad enough to betake himself to any such course ? Better ground for a commission of lunacy would not be desired ; no, not by any one of the judges, by whom the profit from this device is so largely reaped.

Upon each occasion, the father's wish is to come

at the truth : to come at it, whatever be the purpose: giving right, giving reward, administering
compensation or administering punishment. The
father's wish is to come at the truth: and the
judge's wish—what else ought it to be? For coming
at the truth, the means the father employs are the
promptest as well as surest in his power: what
less effectual means should be those employed by
the judge ?.

Forget not here to observe how necessary the
thus inhibited interview is to the ends of justice—
how necessary accordingly the prevention of it to
the actual ends of judicature.

Where the parties are at once allowed and
obliged, each, at the earliest point of time, to appear in the presence of the judge, and eventually
of each other; where this is the case (and in small
debt courts it is the case), the demandant of course
brings to view every fact and every evidence that
in his view makes for his interest: and the defendant, on his first appearance, does the like. If
the demand has been admitted, demandant applies
himself to the extraction of admission from defendant, defendant from demandant. Original demands—cross demands—demands on the one side
—demands on the other side—relevant facts on one
side—relevant facts on the other side—evidence on
the one side—evidence on the other side—all these
grounds for decision are thus at the earliest point
of time brought to the view of the judge; and, by
anticipation, a picture of whatsoever, if anything,
remains of the suit, pourtrayed in its genuine, most
unadulterated, and most instructive colours.

Of the goodness or badness of each suitor's
cause, of the correctness or incorrectness of his
statements; all such evidence is presented to the

judge's view, as it is in the nature of *oral* discourse, gesture, and deportment, to afford.

As to *mendacity*, say, in the language of reproach, *lying*, licence for it could no more be granted to a party, in this supposed state of things, than to a witness it is in the existing state of things.

Continue the supposition. For the truth of whatever is said, every man by whom it is said is responsible. From the very first, being in the presence, he is in the power of the judge. Moreover, for continuing such his responsibility as long as the suit renders it needful, a mode of communication with him may be settled in such sort, that, for the purpose of subsequent operations, every missive, addressed to him in that mode, may, unless the contrary be proved, be acted upon as if duly received.

In the judicatory of a justice of peace, acting singly, and in a small debt court, conducted in this way, many and many a suit is ended almost as soon as begun: many a suit, which, in a common-law court, would have absorbed pounds by hundreds, and time by years; and, after that, or without that, in an *equity court*, pounds by thousands, and time by tens of years; as often as, upon the demandant's own showing, the demand is groundless, to him, who, under the present system, would be defendant, all the expense, all the vexation, attached to that calamitous situation, would be saved.

To go back to the primeval period, which gave rise to this device, where, in a countless swarm, fee-fed assistants and they alone had to do the business with their partner in trade, the fee-fed judge, the reverse of this took place; and continues to have place of course. Everything was and is kept back as long as possible : operation was and is made to follow operation—instrument, instrument—that each operation and each instrument may have its fees. On the one hand, *notices*, rendered as expensive as possible, are sent for the purpose of their not being received : on the other hand, notices that have been received, the receipt is left unacknowledged or even denied, and in either case assumed not to have place.

True it is, states of things there are, in which, either at the outset, or at this or that time thereafter, neither in the instance of both parties, nor even of either party, can the appearance in question have place. For a time longer or shorter, by distance, or by infirmity, bodily or mental, a party may stand debarred altogether from making his appearance before the judge; or, though appearing, the aid of an apt assistant may be necessary to him. When the party interested is a body corporate, or other numerous class, composed of individuals assignable or unassignable, of agents, and other trustees of all sorts, the attendance may, at the outset or at some later period, be necessary, with or without that of their respective parties.

But, whatever be the best course, the impracticability of it, in one instance, is it a reason for not pursuing it, as far as practicable, in any other?

Under the system in its present state, certain sorts of suits there are, to which the exclusion does not apply itself. What are they? They are suits in which, if thus far justice were not admitted, the exclusionists might themselves be sufferers : suits for murder, theft, robbery, house-breaking, and so forth. Judges, whether they have bowels or no, have bodies : judges have houses and goods.

A year or two at common-law, ten or twenty years in equity, would be too long to wait, before the criminal could be apprehended. But, that purpose accomplished, off flies justice: six months or twelve months, as it may happen, the accused lies in jail, if guilty; just so long does he, if innocent. But, of this, under the head of *Delays.*

But (says somebody) why say *excluded?* When, in any one of these courts, a suitor makes his appearance, is the door of the court shut against him? Did no instance ever happen, of a suitor standing up in court, and addressing himself to the judge? Oh, yes: once in a term or so; scarce oftener. And why not oftener? Even because, as every man sees, nothing better than vexation is to be got by it. And, if at any, at what period can this be? Not at the outset: not till the suit has run out an indefinite part of its destined length: the judge being in by far the greatest number of individual suits, from first to last, invisible: nor yet an invisible agent, but an invisible *non-agent:* mechanical, as will be explained; mechanical from the outset being the mode, to a truly admirable length, substituted to mental judicature. But suppose the unhappy outcast in court, proceedings, by the devices that will now immediately be explained—proceedings, and even language, have been rendered (he finds) unintelligible to him. Even if he has counsel, of whom, besides one for use, he must have at least one, and may be made to have half-a-dozen for show; if, though it be but one of them has opened his mouth, the mouth of the unhappy client is not indirectly as above, but directly, and with the most shameless effrontery, inexorably closed. The one in whom all his confidence is reposed, may, by treachery or negligence, or craving for greater gain elsewhere, have forfeited it. Three hundred guineas have been given with a brief, the fee left unearned, and restitution refused. If, in such circumstances, a counsel though it be one who, not expecting to be needed is unprepared, has but opened his lips; *no* (says the judge), counsel has spoken for you, you shall not speak for yourself. A plaintiff, had he ever such full license to speak, could he compel the appearance of a defendant? Not he, indeed. If both were in court together, by accident, could either compel answer to a question put to the other? As little.

II. *Device the second.—Language rendered unintelligible.*—It was by this device that, in the first instance, the exclusion was effected.

To Saxon judicature succeeded that of Norman conquerors: to Saxon liberalism, Norman absolutism. In Saxon times reigned, in adequate number, local judicatories: not only county-shires, but, so to speak, still lesser judge-shires: hundred courts, courts leet, courts baron, and others.

Then and there, people or lawyers made no difference; language was the same. From the presence of the judge, in any one of these small and adequately numerous tribunals, directly or indirectly, was suitor ever excluded? No more than in a private family, contending children from the presence of their fathers.

Under the Norman kings grew up Norman French speaking lawyers. Whether in the metropolis or elsewhere, along with his horses and their grooms, one train of these domestics was always in attendance about the person of the king. To this train was given the cognizance of all such suits as, from such varied distances, so various and some of them so long, could be made to come to it.

Quartering himself upon vassal after vassal, the king was perpetually on the move: in his train moved a judge or judges.

To this train, whatever part of the country he had to come from, every man, who had anything to complain of, had to add himself. To the place, wherever it was, that the train happened to be at, the defendant had to be dragged. When there, these same suitors there found a judge or judges, who, speaking a different language, could not, or would not, understand what they said.

· The language of the Normandy-bred lawyers was a sort of French. The language of the country from whence they came, these lawyers spoke: the language of the country into which they were come, they disdained to speak. The rules, such as they were, by which the procedure of these foreign despots, in so far as memory served, and self-regarding interest permitted, could be guided, would of course be such as their own language gave expression to: rules which, as well as the rest of the language, were, to the vast majority of the suitors, unintelligible: meaning by suitors, on this occasion, not only those who were actually so, but those who, but for this obstacle, would have been, but could not be so. *Justiciables* they are called in French. In British India this state of things may, with a particular degree of facility be conceivable.

Here then by a plaintiff, if he would have his demand attended to, by a defendant if he could be admitted to contest it—here were two sorts and sets of helpmates to be hired; interpreters to convey what passed between parties and their advocates,

and between witnesses and judge; and advocates
to plead the cause on both sides.

Between advocates and judges the connection
was most intimate. Like robbers acting together in
gangs and without licence,—these licenced, irresistible, and unpunishable depredators, linked
together by one common interest, acted as *brothers,*
and stiled one another by that name.

Thus circumstanced, they had but to take measure of the disposable property of the suitors,
and divide it among one another, as they could
agree.

In and by this confederacy, in a language, intelligible seldom to both parties, most commonly
to neither; or, what was worse, to one alone, was
the matter talked over and settled. As to the
truth of what was said, how much was true, how
much false, was not worth thinking about; means
of ascertaining it there were none. Parties while
exhausting themselves in fees, either looked on
and stared, or seeing that by attendance nothing
was to be got but vexation, staid away. At an
early period minutes of these conversations came
to be taken by authority, and continued so to be
till the end of the reign of Henry the VIIIth,
Ao. 1546, from which time under the auspices of
chance, they have been continued down to the
present. Under the name of the *Year-books,* from
the commencement of the reign of Edward the Ist,
Ao. 1272,, they are, in greater or less proportion,
extant in print, having been printed, Ao. 1678.

By this one all-powerful judicatory (*metropolitan*
it might have been stiled, had the place of it been
fixed), by this one great French-speaking judicatory, the little local English-speaking judicatories
were swallowed up. Remains to be shown how
this was managed.

A suit, from which, if given *for* him, a man saw he should reap no benefit, would not be commenced by him. When, in a local judicatory, in which the plaintiff's demand being so clearly just, the defendant would have been sure to lose, a suit was depending, the judges on each occasion, at the instance of the defendant, sent to the, howsoever distant, judicatory an order to proceed no further, and to the defendant an order to come and, along with the plaintiff, add himself to the train, as above. This having been made the practice and been extensively felt and universally seen to be so; thus, all over the kingdom was an end put to the business of all these English-speaking and justice-administering judicatories.

If a man, who was rich enough, beheld within the jurisdiction of one of those judicatories, another whom, by enmity or any other cause, he was disposed to ruin, all he had to do was to commence a suit either in the great travelling judicatory, or in the first instance in the little first judicatory, and thence call it up into this all-devouring one.

Appeal, on such occasions, does good service; this practice (*evocation,* in French, it is called) was, anybody may see to how great a degree, an improvement upon it.

If, from all these judgeshires, howsoever denominated and empowered—county courts, hundred courts, courts leet and courts baron,—appeals had been receivable, this would have done much, but this would not have done every thing. Some indeed would have passed through the strainer, and yielded fees. But by far the greater part would have stuck by the way, and have thus been useless. Upon the vulgar modes of appeal, evocation was no small improvement. On an appeal,

c

misdecision on the part of the inferior authority,
required to be proved.   Presumption is shorter
than proof.   By an evocation this presumption
was regularly made, and being made, acted upon.

III.—*Device the Third.— Written instruments, where worse than useless, necessitated.*

So far from being worse than useless, indispensable to perfect judicature is the art of writing, in
so far as properly applied.   Properly applied it is
to three things ; instrument of demand under the
appropriate heads ; instrument of defence under
appropriate heads ; and on both sides *evidence*.   To
no one of these three heads belong the so much
worse than useless written instruments, stiled
pleadings.   Behold, in the first place, the use and
demand there was for instruments of this sort ;
meaning always with reference to the sinister
interests of Judge and Co., then afterwards their
particular nature.

By the unintelligibility given to the language,
absolutely considered, not inconsiderable was the
profit gained ; comparatively speaking, relation
had to what could be done, and was done accordingly, very little.

Of the French language, the usefulness to Judge
and Co., was wearing out.   Not to speak of ami-
cable and commercial intercourse, *war* was, ever
and anon, sending Englishmen into France, lower
and higher orders together, by tens of thousands
at a time.   Under Edward the IIIrd, a hundred
thousand at one time made that fruitless visit to
the walls of Paris.

While the use of the French language was thus
spreading itself, so was the art of writing, and with
it the use of the Latin language ; among the

priesthood it was common; and amongst the earliest lawyers were priests.

Now was come the time for pressing pre-eminently useful art, and not altogether useless eru-
dition, into the service of discourse. Written
pleadings were added to oral ones; added, not
substituted; prefixt, being interposed between the
delivery of the original scraps of parchment, and
the debate in court. French the spoken matter,
preceded by Latin, and that written; thus was
darkness doubled, and difficulty trebled. Of this
darkness the Latin part continued, unimpaired by
any the faintest ray of light, till towards the middle of the last century. By statute of the 4th of
George II, Ao. 1731, the darkness invisible, trans-
figured into the existing darkness visible.

Contemplating it, the all but failure, Blackstone
cannot hold his exultation.

Notice to dishonest men, in general, was then
given by the fee-fed judges. Is there any man
whose property, or any part of it, you would like
to have? Any man you would like to ruin, if you
can drop pence with them into my *till*, till they
are tired, do what you like, and if they call upon
me to help them, stand fast; they shall have their
labour for their pains. Or, if you cannot come at
them, I will do the thing for you. This was
neither cried, nor sung, nor said. But when acts
speak, words are needless. Such was the language then, such is the language now.

As to the uses—the advantage obtained through
mendacity will be brought to view under the next
head: even supposing the line of truth ever so
rigidly adhered to, still the advantage could not
fail to be considerable. To no inconsiderable
extent, incapacity, especially in that rude state

of society, would do the work of sinister art.
Only by the capacity of paying on the one part
for it, would any bounds be set to the extent to
which, without aiming at excess, a rambling story
might be spun out on either part.

Even from the first, to the purpose of giving the
proposed defendant to understand he was expected
to make his appearance, on a certain day, at a
certain place, on pain that should follow, was
applied (it should seem), a scrap of parchment
(paper as yet unknown), with a scrap of writing
written upon it. Of the writing, *Latin* was the
language; by anything so vulgar as the conquered
language, conquerors disdained to sully hands,
lips, or ears. It was between this *writ* (so it came
afterwards to be called) between this *writ* and the
viva voce discussion that the pleadings were interposed.

On the occasion of each suit, four things there
are, to distinguish which clearly from each other
was, and still continues to be found a task of no
inconsiderable difficulty: these are—1. The service demanded of the judge at the charge of the
proposed defendants, say in one word *the demand*:
—2. The portion of law on which the demand was
grounded :— 3. The individual matter of fact,
which, it is alleged, has brought the individual
case within the sort of case, for which the provision has been made by the law :—4. The evidence,
or say the proof, by which the existence of these
same facts was required and expected to be made
manifest: not to speak of the *law*, where there not
being any really existing portion of law bearing on
the sort of case, the existence of a portion of law
adapted to the plaintiff's purpose must of necessity be assumed : assumed—that is to say, created

by imagination, in a form, adjusted in some way or other to the demand. Correspondent was the course necessary to be taken on the defendant's side.

As to the *demand*, next to nothing was the information given in relation to it by the *writ*. Remained therefore to be given by the pleadings the particular nature of the service, as above demanded, together with a statement of the *facts*, on which the demand was grounded, with which was chemically combined, a dram of the portion of Common alias Judge-made law, which this same demand took for its ground.

Signal was the service rendered to the inventors by this decree. 1. Spoken words could not be sold at so much a dozen : the written words could be and were; so much for the profit account : 2. Of the word of mouth alterations, not a syllable could be uttered, which the judge did not sit condemned to hear : all labour, without profit : different the case when this preliminary written altercation came to be added : once commenced, then on it went of itself, like a pump set a going by a steam-engine : the judge receiving his share of the profit on it, neither his ears nor his eyes being any part of the time troubled with it : so much for the *ease* account. But of this further, under the head of mechanical *vice* mental judicature.

Yet another use : The additional and so unhappily permanent, served thus as the subject matter and groundwork for the subsequent and evanescent mass of profit yielding surplusage.

By the plaintiff, his story had to be told to a sort of agent called, in process of time, an *attorney*, a word which meant a *substitute* : from this

statement, the attorney had to draw up a *case* :
from this *case* an advocate, stiled a *sergeant contour*,
afterwards simply sergeant, (originally stiled *ap-
prentices*, barristers were not hatched) had to draw
up the pleadings, commencing with that stiled, as
above, the *declaration* : attached to each of these
learned persons was his clerk : masters and clerks,
by each one of them was received his fees.

Father of a family ! when you have a dispute to
settle between two of your children, do you ever
begin by driving them from your presence? do
you send them to attorney, special pleader, sergeant, or barrister? Think you that by any
such assistance, any better chance would be afforded you for coming at the truth, than by hearing what the parties had to say for themselves ?

Page upon page, and process upon process,
each process with fees upon fees,—all these for
the production of no other effect than what is
every day produced all over the country, by a
line or two in the shape of a summons or a warrant from a justice of the peace ; a hundred-horse
steam engine for driving a cork out of a bottle.

" Tell Thomas to come here," or " bring
Thomas here :" this is what a father, when his
wish is to see his son Thomas, says to his son
John. Father of a family, if your power of endurance is equal to the task, wade through this
mass of predatory trash, and imagine, if you can,
the state your family would be in, if by no one of
your children you could ever get anything done,
without the utterance of it. Well then : exactly
as necessary—exactly as contributive is it to the
giving execution and effect to an ordinance of the
king in parliament, as it would be to the giving

execution and effect to an order addressed by you, on the most ordinary occasion to any child of your's.

The judge was in a word, a shopkeeper. A spurious article, stampt with the name of *justice*, the commodity he dealt in. By hearing the applicant—the would-be plaintiff in person, nothing was to be got: by serving the scrap of parchment, a fee was to be got: one fee, and that one, like the queen bee, mother of a swarm of others.

To conclude this same subject of written pleadings, and the use of it to lawyercraft. Well might Blackstone thus triumph as above : well might he felicitate himself and his partners in the firm. To his Analysis is subjoined an *Appendix*, in x numbers, the vii. last of which are precedents of, contract or procedure, chiefly procedure, still in use. Numbers vii. divided into sections 22 : and, in each of several of the sections, distinct instruments more than one. An exhibition more eminently and inexcusably disgraceful to the head or heart of man, scarcely would it be in the power of reward to bring into existence. Not one of these instances is there, in which, in an honest, intelligible and straitforward way, the purpose might not with facility be accomplished : in not one of them, in any such way is the purpose actually aimed at. In every one of them, the matter of it is a jargon of the vilest kind, composed of a mixture of lies and absurdity in the grossest forms. In maleficence, much worse than simple nonsense. By nonsense, no conception of anything being presented by it to anybody, no deception would have been produced : by this matter, to every eye but that of a lawyer, a false conception is pre-

the judge, will cause seizure and sale to be made
of the defendant's goods; and the proceeds, to the
amount in question, delivered to the plaintiff.
What the dishonest plaintiff knew from the first
was—that for no *lie*, by which he gave, as above,
commencement to the suit, would he be punishable: here, then, was the *allowance*, or say *licence*:
what he also knew was—that, if the first tissue of
lies failed of being, in appointed time, answered
by the defendant in correspondently mendacious
prescribed form,—he, the dishonest plaintiff, thus
rendered so by the judge, by the invitation virtually
given to him and every body by this his hired instrument and accomplice,—would receive the contemplated reward for his dishonesty: here, then, comes
the remuneration and the compulsion: the remuneration thus given by the judge to the dishonest plaintiff: the compulsion thus applied by the judge to
the defendant; and so on through any number of
links in the chain of pleadings.

Had justice been the end aimed at, would this
have been the course? No: but a very different
one. No sale of dear bought strips of parchment,
befouled by judge's lies. From the very first, no
suit commenced but by an interview between the
suitor and the judge. No ear would the judge
have lent to any person in the character of plaintiff, but on condition, that, in case of mendacity,
he should be subjected to punishment, including,
in case of damage to an individual, burthen of compensation. Thus, then, vanishes the distinction
between *pleadings* and *evidence;* and of the dishonest suits that then were, and now are, born
and triumph, a vast proportion would have been
killed in embryo. Of whatever, on this occasion,
were said by the applicant, not a syllable that

would not be received and set down as *evidence*; received, exactly as if from a stranger to the suit; and so in the case of the defendant. Wherever it were worth while, in the thus written evidence, the now written, and above described unpunishably mendacious, pleadings would have their so uncontrovertibly beneficial substitute.

Now for Mendacity practised.—By mendacity is understood the quality exemplified by any discourses by which wilful falsehood is uttered: habit of mendacity, the habit of uttering such discourse.

. Uttered by men at large, wilful falsehood is termed wilful falsehood: uttered by a judge as such, it is termed fiction: understand *judicial fiction.*

Poetical fiction is one thing: judicial fiction, another. Poetical fiction has for its purpose delectation: producing, in an appropriate shape, pleasure: the purpose here a good one, or no other is so. To a bad purpose it is indeed capable of being applied, as discourse in every shape is. But in its general nature, when given for what it is, it is innoxious, and in proportion to the pleasure it affords, beneficent: no deception does it produce, or aim at producing. So much for poetical fiction, now for judicial.

In every instance, it had and has for its purpose, pillage: object, the gaining power; means, deception. It is a portion of wilful falsehood, uttered by a judge, for the purpose of producing deception; and, by that deception, acquiescence or exercise given by him to power not belonging to him by law.

If, by a lie, be understood a wilful falsehood, uttered for an evil purpose, to what species of discourse could it be applied with more indisputable propriety, than to the discourse of a judge, uttered for an evil purpose?

How much to be regretted, that for the designation of the sweet and innocent on the one hand, the caustic and poisonous on the other, the same appellation should be continually in use; it is as if the two substances, sugar and arsenic, were neither of them known by any other name than *sugar!* But the abuse made of this recommendatory word is itself a *device:* an introductory one, stuck upon the principal one.

So much for the delusion, now for the criminality.

Obtaining money by false pretences is a crime: a crime which, except where licensed by public functionaries, or uttered by them, to and for the benefit of one another, is punished with infamous punishment. Power, in so far as obtained by fiction, is power obtained by some false pretence: and what judicial fiction, that was ever uttered, was uttered for any other purpose? What judicial fiction, by which its purpose has been answered, has failed of being productive of this effect?

If obtaining money by false pretences is an immoral practice, can obtaining power by false pretences be anything less so? If silver and gold are to be had the one for the other, so can power and money; if then either has value, has not the other likewise?

If obtaining, or endeavouring to obtain money by false pretences is an act presenting a well-grounded demand for legal punishment, so in its origin, at any rate, was not the act of obtaining, or endeavouring to obtain, by those same means, power? power, whether in its own shape, or in this, or that other shape?

. As to the period—the time at which this device had its commencement in practice can scarcely have been so early as the original period so often mentioned: lies are the instruments rather of weakness, than of strength; they who had all power in their hands, had little need of lies for the obtaining of it.

On every occasion, on which any one of these lies was for the first time uttered and applied to use, persons of two or three distinguishable classes may be seen, to whom, in different shapes, wrong was thus done: the functionary or functionaries, whose power was, by and in proportion to the power thus gained, invaded and diminished: and the people at large, in so far as they became sufferers by the use made of it: which is what, in almost every instance, not to say in every instance, upon examination, they would be seen to be.

In the present instance, functionaries, or say authorities of two classes, are discernible.

The authority, from which the power was thus filched, was either that of the sovereign, their common superordinate—or the co-ordinate authority, viz. that of some judge or judges, co-ordinate with that of the stealers. In a certain way, by the deception thus put upon him, the sovereign was a party wronged, in so far as power was taken from any judge to whom it had by him been given. But this was a wrong little if at all felt: the only wrong felt certainly and in any considerable degree, was that done to another judge or set of judges.

. Say *stealing*, or what is equivalent, as being

shorter than to say obtaining under false pretences.
In each instance, if deception, and by means of
it power-stealing, was not the object of the lie,
object it had none ; it was an effect without a
cause.

By a man in a high situation, a lie told for the
purpose of getting what he had already, or could
get without difficulty without a lie—such conduct is not in human nature.

As to sufferings, nominal only, as above observed, were they on the part of the supreme
and omnipotent functionary ; here, supposing
them real, no sooner had they been felt, than they
would have been made to cease, and no memorial
of them would have reached us.

Not so in the case of learned brethren : stealing
power from them, was stealing fees. Accordingly,
when, towards the close of the seventeenth century, a theft in this shape had been committed,
war broke out in Westminster-hall, and fictions,
money-snatching lies, were the weapons.   But
of this under the head of *jurisdiction-splitting*.

There, all the while on his throne sat the king:
that king, Charles the IInd.   But, to a Charles
the IInd, not to speak of a king in the abstract,
war between judge and judge for fees, was war
between dog and dog for a bone.

Now come the real sufferers—the people.   Subjection to arbitrary power is an evil, or nothing
is ; an evil, and that an all-comprehensive one.

Now, every power thus acquired is in its
essence arbitrary ; for, if to the purpose of obtaining anything valuable—call it money, call it
power—allowance is given to a man, on any
occasion, at pleasure, to come out with a lie ;
which done, the power becomes his, what is it

he cannot do? For where is the occasion on which a lie cannot be told? And, in particular, on the whole expanse of the field of law, no limits being assigned, where is the lie which, if, in his conception, any purpose of his, whatever it be, will be answered by it, may not be told?

Accordingly, wilful falsehoods, more palpably repugnant to truth, were never uttered, than may, by all who choose to see it, be seen to have been uttered, and for the purpose of obtaining power, by English judges.

Take for example the common recovery fiction; a tissue of lies, such, that to convey to a non-lawyer any comprehensive conception of it, would require an indefinite multitude of pages, after the reading of which it would be conceived confusedly or not at all. But what belongs to the present purpose will be as intelligible as it is undeniable.

1. Descriptions of persons stolen from, three. 1. Children, in whose favour a mass of immoveable property had been intended to be made secure against alienation; eventual subject-matter of this property, no less than the soil of all England. 2. Landowners, by whom, by payment of the fees exacted from them, was purchased of the judges of the court in question—the Common Pleas—that power of alienation which they ought to have gratis, or not at all. 3. Professional men, —conveyancers, (the whole fraternity of them) despoiled, in this way of a share of such their business, by the intrusion of these judges.

Now for the falsehood—the artful and shameless predatory falsehood—by which all these exploits were performed. Officiating at all times in the court in which these judges were sitting, was a functionary, styled *the cryer of the court;*

his function; calling individuals, in proportion as
their attendance was required, into the presence of
the judges. Sole source and means of his subsistence, fees ; in magnitude, the aggregate of
them correspondent to the nature of his function.
Behold now the fiction. A quantity of parchment
having been soiled by a compound of absurdities
and falsehoods, prepared for the purpose, and fees
in proportion received for the same, a decision
was by these same judges pronounced, declaring
the restriction taken off, and the proprietors so
far free to alienate : to the parties respectively
despoiled, a pretended equivalent being given, of
which presently. Persons whom it was wanted
for—(not to speak of persons not yet. *in esse,*
and in whose instance accordingly disappointment
might be prevented from taking place) young persons in existence in indefinite multitudes, from
whom, on the several occasions in question, their
property, though as yet but in expectancy, was
thus taken—taken by these same judges, whose
duty it was to secure it to them. Now for the equivalent. To all persons thus circumstanced, it was
thought meet to administer satisfaction : it was
by a speech to the following effect, that the heal-
ing balm was applied. " Children, we take your
estate from you, but for the loss of it, you will not
be the worse. Here is Mr *Moreland,*" (that was
always the gentleman's name) " he happens to
have an estate of exactly the same value : this
we will take from him, and it shall be your's."
Exactly in this way, on one and the same day,
were estates in any number disposed of at the appointed price by these supposed, and by suitors
intituled, ministers of justice. Such was the proceeding then : and such it continues to this day.

There we have one fiction : now for a parallel to it.   Once upon a time, in Fairy land, in the court of a certain judge, under the seat of the crier of the court, was a gold mine.   On a touch given to the seat by a wand, kept for the purpose by the judge, out flowed at any time a quantity of gold ready melted, into an appropriate recep- tacle, and on the turning of a cock, stopt.   Here we have a fiction, which, if it be a silly, is at any rate an innocent one.   Be it ever so silly, is there any thing in it more palpably repugnant to truth than in that predatory and flagitious one.

Two points, could they be but settled, might here afford to curiosity its aliment.

1. Point the first.   Those fictions, such as they are, in what number could they be picked up like toad-stools, in the field of common law !   By dozens at any rate, or by scores, to go no further, they might be counted.

Roman lawyers too, have theirs.   But for every Rome-bred fiction, a dozen English-bred ones, to speak within compass, might be found.

2. Point the second : birth-day of the fiction —latest hatched and let fly to prey upon the people—Was it the day next before that of the first newspaper ?   Was it that of the last witch burnt or hanged ?   Be the species of imposition what it may —be the field of deception what it may, a time there will always be, after which new impostures will not grow on it.   But, as to the time when those which have root at present will be weeded out, this question is a very different one.

By the operation here in question, good (will it be said ?) good, in a certain shape, was done ? good, for example, of the nature of that which it belongs to political economy and constitutional law to give indication? Be it so. But, be it ever so great, good, considered as actually resulting, is on this occasion, nothing to the purpose : only lest it should be thought to be overlooked, is mention thus made of it : the only good. which is to. the purpose is the good intended.

Lastly, as to certain ulterior uses of this species of poetry to the reverend and learned poets. Those of the coarsest and most obvious sort—power-stealing and money-stealing — having been already brought to view.

To complete the catalogue, require to be added, —1. Benefit from the double fountain, constituted as above. 2. Benefit from the thickening thus given to confusion.

1. First, as to the double fountain. A juggler there was, and a fountain he had, out of which at command flowed wine, red or white, without mixture. This reality, for such it is, may help to explain one use, and that a universally applying one ; the purpose, whatever it be, is it by the truth that it is best served ? The argument is drawn from the truth side. Is it by the fiction ? Side from which the argument is drawn, the falsehood.

Such being the emblem, now for the application. Be the mess what it may, truth is always the substance of it; lies, how coarse and gross soever, but the *seasoning*. The purpose, whatever it be—is it by the fiction that it is best served? From the fiction side it is that the argument is drawn : is it by the truth alone that the purpose can be served? It is to the truth, with whatsoever reluctance, that recourse is had. Thus *quacunque via data*, as the law Latin phrase has it, the point is gained.

2. Lastly, as to the benefit from the confusion that, proportioned to the extent to which non-con-

ception, or what is so much better, misconception in regard to the rule of action, has place on the part of those who are made to suffer, in proportion to their non-compliance with it, the particular interest of Judge and Co. is served: these are propositions, of which the whole substance of this our humble Petition is one continual proof. That the giving to these two so intimately connected states of things the whole policy of this class of politicians has from first to last been universally directed, is another proposition, to which the same proof applies itself with the same force. But to say that by and in proportion to the degree of confusion that has place in the aggregate mass of ideas produced by the aggregate mass of discourse, expressed in relation to the subject and received, this same purpose is answered, is but to say the same thing in other words.

If, to the intelligibility of that which is here said about unintelligibility, any addition can be made by the sort of imagery so much in request, out of each one of Judge and Co.'s double fountains, rises at all times a thick fog. Say each one for another will be brought to view, namely, under the head of device the eleventh—*Decision on grounds foreign to the merits.*

V.—*Device the fifth. Oaths, for the establishment of the mendacity, necessitated.*

That the ceremony of an oath is the instrument by means of which the licence to commit mendacity is effected, has just been stated. Now as to the mode of applying the instrument to this purpose. Nothing can be more simple. On the occasion of any statement, about to be made, on a juridical occasion, or for an eventually juridical purpose, is it your wish (you being a judge) that mendacity should *not* have place, you cause the individual by whom the statement is made, to have, just before the making of it, borne his part in this same ceremony: on the occasion of any statement so made, is it your wish that mendacity *should* have place, you abstain from requiring the performance of this same ceremony : and, at the same time, you give to the naked statement so made, whatsoever effect it suits your purpose to give to it.

Not that it was for this purpose that the ceremony itself was invented : for, along with the *time,* the *cause* of its invention is lost in the darkness of the early ages : all that, on this occasion, is meant is—that it is for the purpose of organizing mendacity, and giving to that vice every practicable encrease, that the ceremony, being found already in use, was taken advantage of.

Properties, which we shall now present to the view of the Honourable House this instrument as possessing, are the following : they consist in its being,

1. *Needless ;* to wit, for the purpose of repressing mendacity on judicial occasions or for a judicial purpose.

2. *Inefficacious,* on these same occasions.

3. *Mischievous,* to an enormous extent in a variety of ways.

4. *Inconsistent* with the received notions belonging to *natural religion.*

5. *Anti-scriptural.*

6. *Useful to Judge and Co.,* eminently subservient to their particular and sinister interest; and as such cherished by them.

First as to needlessness.   For the needlessness

of this ceremony, on the sort of occasion or for the sort of purpose in question, we humbly call to witness your Honourable House : primee in legislation is in effect the part borne by you. In your hands is the public purse : with you, with few and casual exceptions, laws originate. Take any law whatsoever, in the scale of importance what, in comparison with the power of making that same law, is the power of exercising, in relation to it, an act of judicature, reversable of course at pleasure by the powers by which the law was enacted? Well then—when at the instance of the Honourable House a law has been enacted—this same law, was it passed upon determinate grounds, or was it *groundless*? To stile it *groundless*, would be to pass condemnation on it. It having determinate grounds, and those grounds appropriate, of what then are those same grounds composed?

Answer. Of matters of fact, and nothing else ; for nothing else is there of which they can be composed. On the occasion in question, these same matters of fact, whatsoever they may be, will respectively either be considered as already sufficiently notorious, or not : if not, then will the existence of them, for the purpose of this same act of legislation, as for the purpose of any act of judicature, be considered as requiring to be established by evidence. No otherwise than in as far as thus grounded and warranted, can any law whatever be anything better than an act of wanton despotism. Most laudable accordingly—unmatched in any other country upon earth, is the scrutinizing attention and perseverance, so constantly employed by your Honourable House, in the collection of appropriate witnesses, and the elicitation of their testimony. Of their testimony? and in what

shape? in that which is the very best possible:
oral examination, subject to counter-interrogation
from all quarters, re-examination at any time, and
with the maximum of correctness secured to it by
being minuted down as elicited, and subjected afterwards to correction by the individual from whom
it emanated. Behold here a mode of proceeding,
dictated by a real desire to elicit true, and appropriately complete, information: the desire accompanied with a thorough knowledge of the most effectual means for the accomplishment of it.

Well then. For securing to each article of information thus elicited, the same character of truth
at the hands of each witness, putting out of the
question the spiritual motive, what are the temporal motives which, in the shape of eventual
punishment, in case of mendacity, your Honourable House makes application of? Answer: in a
direct shape, imprisonment only; with or without
fine: in an unimmediate and indirect shape, fine,
for the extraction of which the imprisonment is
the only instrument.

Now then, as to the ceremony called *swearing*,
or *taking an oath.* Whether it be for want of
power, whether it be for want of will,—(the single
case of election judicature excepted, and *that* no
otherwise than in pursuance of a special act of
parliament) no use does your Honourable House
ever make of this same ceremony. What follows?
Does mendacity find the Honourable House impotent? On the contrary: much more effectual is
its power against this vice than that of ordinary
judicature, with its expensive prosecution and se-
verer punishment. Why? because, while the
mode of elicitation employed is such as needs not
the assistance of the ceremony, its mode of proce-

·dure is such, as is able to cause the punishment
·to follow instantaneously upon the offence. Yet,
has it as yet a weakness, to which consistency will
one day, it is hoped, apply the obvious remedy.
Standing at the highest pitch at the commencement of each parliament, it sinks, (this indispensable power,) ·as the parliament advances in age,
till, at last, it is sunk in utter decrepitude.

After such a demonstration of the needlessness
of this ceremony, but for the importance and no-
velty of the subject, other proofs might be put
aside, as being themselves needless: important
the subject may well be stiled, or no other is so:
for, so long as this ceremony has place, justice, to
the prodigious extent that will be seen, is absolutely incapable of having place.

To the benefit of the testimony of Quakers, ever'
since the year 1696, justice has, without the benefit of this ceremony, by various statutes, been admitted, in cases called *civil* cases: and now, by a
statute of 1828, in cases called *criminal* and *penal*
cases. If, then, as a security against mendacity,·
the ceremony is indispensable in the case of all
other men, can it be needless or safely omitted in
the case of these?

Moreover, on any one of these occasions, what
is there to hinder a non-Quaker from personating a
Quaker? Clothed in the habit, and speaking the
language of a Quaker, suppose a non-Quaker, by
·his evidence, giving success to Doe, in a case in
which, otherwise, it would have gone to Roe.
The imposture afterwards discovered, would success change hands?

On the evidence of an impostor of this sort,
suppose a man convicted of murder and executed.
The imposture being afterwards discovered, would

the felony be transmuted into a non-felony, and the hanging operation be, in law language, declared void?

Not only in the case of a class of men so well known as this of *Quakers*, but in the case of a class comparatively so little known as that of *Moravians*, has justice been in possession of this same benefit, ever since the year 1749, by statute 22 Geo. II. ch. 30.

Of detriment to justice from this allowance, in what instance was any suspicion ever entertained? Was not the assuredness of the absence of all increased danger of mendacity, from this admission, in *civil* cases,—was not *this* the cause of the extension given to it in criminal cases?

So much for *needlessness*.

2. Now as to *inefficiency*. Considered with reference to the purpose here in question, oaths stand distinguished into *assertory* and *promissory*: but, in both cases, the sanction is precisely the same. Take then, for example, oaths of the *promissory* sort: because these stand clear of various points of contestation, which have place in the case of *assertory* oaths: whereas in the case of a promissory oath, if violation has place, seldom does the fact of the violation stand exposed to doubt.

Now then for the examples. Example the first. Protestant sees in Ireland, bishops 22: archbishops 4: together 26. Previously to investiture, oath taken by every bishop, promising to see that in every parish within his diocese, a school of a certain description shall have place. Of the aggregate of these oaths, what in the year 1825, was the aggregate fruit? Performances 782: perjuries 480. When received and communicated, (so at least says the solemn office)—when received and communicated, behold the preservative power of the Holy Ghost in these minds against perjury.

Example the second. In England, through the university of Oxford, pass one half of the 12,000 or 13,000 church of England clergy; through the university of Cambridge the other half. In *Oxford*, preeminent in uselessness and frivolousness, a volume of statutes, receives at entrance from each member as in every article of it, a security for observance, an appropriate promissory oath.

Now for the effect. On no day does any one of these academies tread on the pavement of that same holy city, without trampling upon some one or more of these oaths. Held up to the inexorably conniving eyes of the constituted authorities, has been the contempt thus put upon this ceremony,—held up, not by strangers only, but by members—not by lay-members only, but by clerical members :—for more than the last half century, by a clerical member—Vicesimus Knox—in a work, editions of which, in number between 20 and 30 are in circulation.

So much for promissory oaths. To come back to assertory oaths. Stand forward *Custom-house oaths*. For demonstration of the inefficiency—the uncontested and incontestible inefficiency—these two words supersede volumes : exacted to a vast extent the assertion of facts, of which in the nature of things it is not possible that the assertor should have had any knowledge. How prodigious the benefit to finance and trade if *asseveration*, with appropriate punishment in case of mendacity, were substituted, and by adverse interrogation, a defendant made subjectible to a limited loss, as by equity interrogation he is to loss of all he has! Thus simple is the arrangement, by which

without the illusory assistance of the thus universally contemned ceremony, finance might be made
to assume a new and healthful face; trade be
made. to receive changes in great variety, generally regarded as beneficial; and pounds, by hundreds of thousands a year—not to say millions, be
saved.

So much for needlessness and inefficaciousness.

3. Now as to *mischievousness*. Of the immense
mass of evil constantly flowing from this source,
a part, and but a part—has as yet been presented
to the view of the Honorable House :—namely,
under the last head, the head of *mendacity*.

1. By so simple a process as the declining to
act a part in this ceremony,—any man, who has
been the sole percipient witness to a crime may,
whatever be that crime, murder, or still worse,—
after appearing as summoned, give impunity to it :
without the trouble or formality, producing thus
the effect of pardon : sharing thus with his majesty this branch of the prerogative, and even in
cases, in which his said majesty stands debarred
from exercising it.

2. By the same easy process, in a case called
civil, may any man give to any man any estate of
any other man.

Not quite so easy, (says somebody.) For would
not this be a contempt? and would he not of course
be committed?

May be so : But when the murderer has been
let off, or the man in the right had lost his cause,
would the commitment last for life? In a word
what would become of it?

But to no such peril need he expose himself.
A process there is which is still easier. "*I am
an atheist.*" He need but pronounce these four

words. The pardon is sealed : or Doe's estate is given to Roe.

But of this, more presently.

Behold now perjury established by law : established on the most extensive—established on an all-comprehensive scale : established by impunity, coupled with remuneration altogether irresistible. Such is the effect of *test oaths.* Of these oaths, some are or may be assertory, some promissory, some assertory and promissory in one : declaration of opinions entertained : declaration of course of actions determined to be pursued, or of opinion determined to be entertained : to be entertained, spite of all conviction and persuasion to the contrary. For perjury in this shape, premium the highest given—for good desert in any shape; for appropriate aptitude, in the official situations, the most richly remunerated. Of the whole of the expenditure of government, a vast proportion thus employed in raising annual and continually increasing crops of perjuries ; and while such is the reward, impunity is absolute and secure.

Oh the admirable security! A man who, with or without pecuniary reward has, for any number of years together, as above, been leading a life of perjury, is to be regarded—not only as capable, but as almost sure, of being stopt from giving his acceptance to any of the very richest rewards, the king's gift : stopt by the fear of no more than what if anything, may follow from one single instance of perjury, and that a compleatly unpunishable one—made to refuse for example, an archbishoprick of Canterbury, with its 25,000*l.* a year, and its *et cæteras* upon *et cæteras ! ! !*

Sowing oaths and reaping perjuries is a mode of husbandry, in a particular instance, affected to be disapproved by Blackstone. But in that instance, compared with this, the scale is that of a garden-pot to that of a field.

Bidding thus high for perjury, is it possible that of the self-same man it should be the sincere wish to prevent it?'

What then (says somebody) the fear of punishment at the hands of the Almighty,—is that to be set down as nothing? The answer is, yes; on this particular occasion, as amounting absolutely to nothing: but of this presently.

By the inducting of these same reverend, right reverend, and most reverend, self-styled perjurers, (for so they are specially declared to be by these their own statutes,) has been established the national school of church of England orthodoxy.

These things considered, and the use made of oaths on judicial occasions,—Westminster Hall, not to mention its near neighbourhood, may it not be styled the great *National School* of perjury?

What then (says somebody) are all *tests* meant to be thus condemned? Oh, no; tests, for declarations of the party joined, by a man, on this or that occasion, may be useful: useful, and even necessary; and at any rate unexceptionable: in some cases by acceptance, in other cases by non-acceptance, useful indications may be afforded. On an occasion of this sort, who are they whom you choose to be considered as siding with? This is the question, propounded by the call to join in the declaration; and in this case no mendacity need have place.

4. So much for needlessness, inefficiency, and mischievousness. Now as to repugnance to natural religion.

This supposed punishment for the profanation,

on whom is the infliction of it supposed to depend?
On the Almighty? No; but, in the first instance,
at any rate, on man alone. No oath tendered, no
offence is committed: no offence committed, on
no man punishment inflicted. According to the
oath-employing theory, man is the master, the
Almighty the servant. In respect to the treatment to be given to the supposed liar, the
Almighty is not left to his own choice. In the
event in question, at the requisition of the human,
the divine functionary is made to inflict an extra
punishment. Exactly of a piece with the authority exercised by a chief justice of the King's
Bench over the sheriff of a county, is the authority
there, by every man who has purchased it, pretended to be exercised over the Almighty. In
Westminster Hall procedure, the chief justice is
the magisterial officer; the sheriff of the county in
question a ministerial officer, acting under him:
a written instrument, called *a writ*, the medium
of communication, through which, to the subordinate, the command of his superordinate is
signified.

In the case of the *oath*, the man by whom the
oath is administered performs the part of the chief
justice; the Almighty that of the sheriff acting
under him; and the kiss given to the book performs the service of the writ.

Is it by a country attorney, dignified by the
title of master extraordinary in Chancery—is it
by this personage that the oath is administered?
In this case, it is the attorney that the Almighty
has for his master now; and by the shilling paid
to the attorney—by this shilling it is that the
Almighty is hired.

On the expectation of the addition thus to be

produced to the spiritual punishment appointed by the Almighty of himself for mendacity—on this alone depends the whole of the molehill of advantage, if any such there be, capable of being set against the mountain of evil that has just been brought to view.

Of mendacity, variable is the maleficence, on a scale corresponding to that of the maleficent act, of which it is made; or endeavoured to be made, the instrument: of the profanation of the ceremony, the guilt, if any, is one and the same.

Infinitely diversified in respect of degree of importance, are the purposes to which this instrument, such as it is, is wont to be applied. Does it, in its nature, possess any capacity of being, by its variability in quantity, and thence in form, accommodated to these several purposes? Not any.

The punishment, if any, the infliction of which is expected, is in every instance the same, for which the attorney, for his shilling, draws upon the Almighty. This draught, will it be honoured?

But (says somebody) for binding a man's attention to the importance of the occasion, some mark of distinction between an assertion that *is*, and one that is *not* intended to be legally operative—may it not be of use? Yes, doubtless. But for this purpose, no such preposterous pretended assumption of authority over the Creator by the creature, is either necessary, or in any degree useful. By the word *asseveration*, the appropriate extraordinary application of the faculty of attention is already sufficiently indicated.

On occasions of the sort in question, in the instance of the people called Quakers, by special allowance from the legislature, already in use is the word *affirmation.* This word might not improperly serve. But the word *asseveration* is, perhaps, in some degree, preferable; since it presents to view more assuredly than does the word *affirmation,* the idea of a special degree of attention and decision beyond what has place on ordinary and comparatively unimportant occasions.

5. Now, as to repugnancy to Scripture. " Thou shalt not take the name of the Lord thy God in vain." So says the second of the ten commandments. " *Swear not at all.*" These are the words of Jesus, as reported in the gospels: " *Above all things, swear not.*" These are the words of St James, in his Epistle. But for texts of Scripture, when troublesome, there are rules of interpretation: one of them is, the rule of contraries.

Says God to man,—thou shalt not perform any such ceremony. Says man to God—I do perform this ceremony, and thou shalt punish every instance of disregard to it. Suppose the Almighty prepared to punish every or any instance of disregard to this ceremony, you suppose him employed in sanctioning disobedience to his own express commandments.

If, to the compellers of such oaths, punishment, in a life to come, were at all an object of consideration, the punishment attached to disobedience— to commandments thus plain and positive, would produce in their minds an impression rather more efficacious, than what has been seen produced, as above, by the punishment supposed to be attached to a disregard for the purely human and recently invented ceremony.

But, for the use of so useful an instrument of profitable maleficence, no punishment is too great to be encountered. " The punishment" (say they,).

" what matters it ? Turning aside from it, we extinguish it."

The thus imagined supernatural punishment, has it really any efficiency in the character of an auxiliary to human punishment, and a security against maleficence in its several shapes? If yes, why thus narrow the benefit producible by it? Why not make out at once a complete list of maleficent acts of all sorts, fit to be, in due form of law, converted into offences? This done, collectively or upon occasion severally, the promissory declaration may be attached to them, and the book kissed.

This done, and not before, consistency will take the place of its opposite; and the practice of swearing, against conviction, cease.

6. So much for needlessness, inefficiency, repugnancy to natural religion, repugnancy to revealed religion, as well as abundancy in mischievousness. Now for use to Judge and Co.—Multifarious and extensive is this use. The capital use, establishment of the mendacity-licence, with the increase given to the profit by written pleadings, keeps pace with the mischievousness of the practice, and has been already brought to view.

But the use of oaths to the partnership does not stop here. The greater the quantity of immorality, in all shapes, but more particularly in that of injustice, the greater the quantity of his profits: for, the more immorality, the more transgressions; the more transgressions, the more suits; the more suits, the more fees. This service presents a *clue*, or say a *key*, which comes to the same thing, to all the arrangements which enter into the composition of judge-made law.

By the confusion with which the field of law

has thus been covered, observance of oaths, or breach of oaths, according as countenanced by a judge, being regarded as a merit and a duty, thus it is that judges have come to be regarded as invested with the power of converting *right* into *wrong*, and *wrong* into *right:* right and wrong following continually the finger (as the phrase is,) of the law.

Decency, as well as that inadequate degree of efficiency which their own particular interest requires to be given to those parts of the law on which personal security depends, join in necessitating, as above, some restraint on mendacity in certain cases: at the same time, their official and professional interest requires that, to a vast extent, that same security should be inefficient. By a compromise between these two antagonising interests has been produced the form of the prosecution for perjury.

Not applying the temporal punishment but in the comparatively small number of instances in which it has been preceded by this ceremony, and the application of it requiring a separate suit, with two witnesses to give effect to it—a suit, of which the expense to the prosecutor is great; and the advantage, in case of success, limited to the few cases in which it has for its effect the reversal of the judgment grounded on the false testimony, they thus make a show, and no more than a show, of wishing to extinguish the vice, to the propagation of which, so far as profitable to them, their endeavours have been so diligently and successfully directed. Bating this rare case, ere any such prosecution can have been instituted, signal must have been the triumph of passion over prudence. Among ten thousand perjuries committed, is there

E

so much as one punished? For *ten* might have been put a hundred, or for a hundred a thousand.

Built originally for feasting, Westminster-hall is thus become the great national school for perjury.

Picking out men, in whose breasts the aversion to mendacity is strongest and most incontestible—picking out these men, and expelling them from the witness's box, with ignominy stampt on their characters—is another service extracted by Judge and Co. from this ceremony.

In the instance of one half of that order of men, who are so richly paid for professing to impress morality, in all its shapes, upon the conduct of the rest of the community, the universality of habitual, perjury has been already brought to view.

One of those suits, which the existing system engenders in such multitudes—a suit in which one of the parties is conscious of being in the wrong, has (suppose) place. One percipient witness there is, whose testimony, were he admitted as a narrating witness, is on good grounds believed by this dishonest suitor to be an atheist. But, atheist as he is, nothing does it happen to him to have, or to be so much as supposed to have, to bias him, and warp his testimony one way or the other: and no man is maleficent without a motive.

Answering to his call, this man places himself in the witness's box. The learned counsel has his instructions. Sir, (says he) do you believe in a God? What follows? Answering falsely, the proposed witness is admitted: he can not be rejected: answering truly, he is silenced, and turned out with ignominy. The martyr to virtue, the martyr to veracity, receives the treatment given to a convicted felon.

The atheist was unseen and silent. These lawyers drag him into broad daylight, and force into the public mind the poison from this confessing and thus corrupting tongue.

What will not the advocate do—what will not the fee-fed judge support him in doing—for their fees? An inquisition, this high commission court, all over. For the purpose of thus punishing the offence, they create it: themselves accessaries before the fact: themselves suborners.

Individuals they thus invest with the power of pardon — thus do these sworn guardians of the king's prerogative. Individuals? and what individuals? In the first place, these same atheists; in the next place, all Christians and other theists, whom they have succeeded in rendering mendacious enough to pretend to be Atheists.

A murderer (suppose) is on his trial: necessary to his conviction is the testimony of an individual, who has just mounted the box. Before the oath is tendered, "First (may it please your lordship,) let me ask this man a question," says the counsel for the murderer. Thereupon comes the dialogue. Counsel—"Sir! Do you believe in a God?" Proposed witness—"No, sir." Judge—"Away with him; his evidence is inadmissible." Out walk they, arm-in-arm, murderer and atheist together, laughing: murderer, to commit other murders, pregnant with other fees.

Robbers in gangs go about (suppose), and to suppress testimony, murdering all whom they rob, and all who are supposed by them to have seen or to be about to see them rob. On being taken, one of them (suppose) turns king's evidence. Question by prisoner or prisoner's counsel—Do you believe in a God? Answer in the negative: off goes the witness, and off with him goes the prisoner. Will

it be said, that the condition, not having been performed, that is to say, the procurement of the defendant's conviction, the pardon will not be granted,
and the accomplice will be hanged? Not he, indeed. No sooner does any one of these murderers
enter the witness box, than, by Judge and Co., if
not an atheist already, he is thus converted to atheism. The consequence is—the necessary evidence
being thus excluded, the virtual pardon of the
whole gang—this man along with the rest—takes
place of course.

Another use to Judge and Co., from the all-cor-
rupting ceremony: the shilling per oath received
for the administration thereof: the shillings in
front, with pounds, in many cases, in the back
ground. Hence, patronage, with reference to the
situations in which this profit is received. Considerations these, by no means to be neglected.
What is there that is ever overlooked in the account of fees?

Another case. An instrument in the hand of
hypocrisy—an instrument to cajole a jury with—
is another character in which the ceremony is of
special use to a judge. It forms a charm, by the
fence of which, transgression in every shape is
rendered impossible to him. Gentlemen of the
jury, you are upon your oaths: I am upon mine.
Mine calls upon me to do so and so, quoth the
ermined hypocrite: out comes thereupon whatever happens to suit his purpose. On any adequately great occasion, appropriate gesture—application of hand to bosom, might give increase to
stage effect. Speaking of a noble lord, as having
been saying so and so—" My lords," (said a judge
once) " he smote that sacred tabernacle of truth,
his bosom." Your oath? What oath? Who ever

saw it? Where is it to be seen, unless it be on the back of the roll on which is written the body of your common law? One of three things. Either you never took any such oath at all, or if you did, it was either a nugatory or a maleficent one.: a promise, for example, on all occasions to make sacrifice of all other interests to the interest of the ruling one. An old printed book there is, intituled The Book of Oaths: and of one or other of these two descriptions are the several oaths therein stated as taken by judges. At any rate, whatever oath you took, if any, in no one's presence was it taken but that of him by whom it was administered. In what better light, therefore, than that of a fresh act of mendacity and imposture, can any such mention of an oath be ever regarded by a reflecting juryman?

So much for the punishment of mendacity under the existing system. Now suppose a system substituted, having for its ends in view the ends of justice. Great beyond present possibility of conception would be the security which, against fraud and deception would be given, by attaching punishment to mendacity. In whatever instance mendacity had been uttered, either on a judicial occasion or for a judicial purpose, punishment would stand attached to it of course. Against fraud and maleficent deception, to whatsoever purpose endeavoured to be applied, great not only beyond example but beyond conception would be the security thus afforded. Oaths and perjuries abolished, punishment for mendacity would be at liberty to bend itself, and would of course bend itself to the form of every offence, to every modification of which the evil of an offence is susceptible. Judicial is the *occasion*, in so far as it is in the course of a suit actually commenced, that the assertion is elicited : judicial the *purpose*, that is to say, the eventual purpose, where the assertion is uttered for the purpose of being eventually employed as evidence, should ever a suit have place, on the occasion of which it might serve as evidence.

Take, for instance, a false *recital* in a conveyance, in an engagement meant to be obligatory; false vouchers in accounts.

Thus in the case of a voucher. Receptor in account with creditor, produces from Venditor or from Faber a *voucher*, acknowledging the receipt of a sum of money for goods furnished to Receptor, to be employed in the service of Creditor. In fact, he has received no more than half the sum : the other half being undue profit divided between them. Under the existing system, on evidence in no better shape, are accounts audited : evidence received as conclusive, the mere production of a receipt. To creditor in this case what difference does it make whether it be by a forged receipt that he is defrauded of this money, or by a falsely asserting, though genuine receipt, as above? Yes, for no such false assertion is there any punishment appointed under the name of punishment: under the name of satisfaction, refunding of the undue profit, yes. But for this a suit in Equity is necessary; a suit in which, for the recovery of five shillings, at the end of five years, or in case of appeal ten years, creditors may have to advance 500*l*. or 1000*l*., losing in case of success a fourth part of the money in unallowed costs. On no better security against fraud than this have public accountants received discharges for hundreds of millions of pounds.

On the ground of any such *voucher*, any such *Venditor* or *Faber* might be made examinable at any time, and in case of original fraud, as above, or false asseveration in the course of the examination, punishable according to the quality and quantity of the wrong.

Fraudulently or otherwise mendaciously false recital in conveyances, in engagements meant to be obligatory, (including contracts)—falsehood in the recitals of instruments, in which registration of obligatory dealings of either of those two classes is performed, newspaper or other paper under false denominations, printed and circulated for the purpose of influencing the prices of public securities—all these vehicles of falsehood would thus receive a mode and degree of repression at present unexampled and until now unconceived.

Thus intimate is the connection between legalized swearing and fraud : in a word, as has been seen, between this compulsorily and irresistibly legalized vice, and crime and immorality in every imaginable shape : with lawyer's profit from every imaginable source.

Swear not at all! Cease to take the name of the Lord in vain—by these commandments, repeated every day at table, with or without the grace before meat in every house,—more would be done towards the extinction of crime and immorality, than would ever be done by preaching, though every house were to have a pulpit in it.

How long will men continue to seek to cause God to apply a punishment he had no intention of applying? To cause him, say rather to *force* him, leaving only the time and the quantum to his choice? For, on the ceremony performed the everlasting punishment is assumed to follow as a thing of course.

When will legislators and judges cease to be suborners of perjury? Of perjury on an all-comprehensive scale?

The passion for these universal oaths, and (which is the same thing) for perjuries, can there be no means of administering to its gratification without the boundless expenditure of crime, immorality, and consequent misery? If without the special and specific mischief produced in so many shapes as above, simple oaths, with correspondent perjuries will content them, perjuries of both sorts, assertory and promissory, they may have their fill of. Each man may perform them for himself, and he may have strings of beads to tell them on: each man may thus perform them for himself; or, in proportion to his opulence, he may, for adequate remuneration, cause them, in any desirable quantity, to be performed by others. By means of pre-established signs, he might even for this same purpose press into the service the powers of machinery and steam. He might perform them in the Chinese style: and for every oath taken, have a saucer broken: and thus at no greater expense than the sacrifice of religion, morality, and happiness, confer a benefit on that branch of trade. For the loss by *assertory* perjuries, *amateurs* might indemnify themselves by increase given to the stock of promissory ones.

If this be not agreeable, let all hitherto published editions of the Bible be called in, and appropriately amended editions substituted. Out of, " Thou shalt not take the name of the Lord thy God in vain," let be omitted the word *not*. For " Swear not at all," after the word *swear*, let be inserted the words *swear and cause swear, whatever you will,* whenever by you or yours anything

is to be got by it. Thus would be wiped clean
the irreligiousness of the practice; and nothing
would be left in it worse than the immorality
of it.

Not inconsiderable is the service so recently
rendered by the extending to cases styled criminal,
the admission so long ago given to Quakers' and
Moravians' evidence. Yet how inadequate, and
thence how inconsistent the remedy, if it stops
there?

Finally, in whatsoever is now deemed and taken
to be perjury, guilt, over and above that which
consists in the mendacity, either has or has not
place: if guilt there is none, then, by the supposition, the ceremony by which the mendacity is
constituted perjury, is of no use: if guilt there is,
we humbly pray that whatsoever by the Honourable House can be done may be done towards ex-
onerating us and the rest of his Majesty's subjects
from the burthen of it: and in particular, such of
us, whose destiny on any occasion it may be to
serve as jurymen: for if in perjury there may be
guilt, we see not how, by men's sitting in a jury-
box, it is converted into innocence.

Accordingly, that which, in relation to this subject we pray for, in conclusion, is—that by the
substitution of the words *affirm* and *affirmation*, or
asseverate and *asseveration*, to the words *swear* and
oath, all persons at whose hands, on a judicial
occasion, any declaration in relation to a matter
of fact is elicited or received, may be put upon
the same footing, as, in and by the statute of the
9th of his present majesty, chapter 30, Quakers.
and Moravians are, in respect of matters therein
mentioned: and that, on no occasion, on which,
in the course of a trial, a person is called upon to

deliver evidence, any question be put to him, having for its object the causing him to make declaration of any opinion entertained. by him on the subject of religion.

Now for the petty juryman's oath. Assertory or promissory? to which class shall it be aggregated? As the interval between promise and performance lessens, the promissory approaches to, till at last it coincides with, the assertory. Assertory, beyond doubt, is the *witness's* oath: as clearly would be the *juryman's*, if the verdict followed upon the hearing of each witness's testimony, as promptly as the delivery of that same testimony follows upon the performance of the swearing ceremony.

Of this instrument the inefficiency as to the production of the professedly desired effect—that is to say, the exclusion of mendacity,—its efficiency, on the contrary, as to the production of the opposite effect, with the perjury in addition to it,—these are the only results, the exhibition of which belongs, in strictness, to the present purpose. But, another point, too closely connected with this, and too important to be passed over, is its *mischievousness.* Another distinguishable point is the absurdity of this part of the institution : and without bringing this likewise into view, neither the inefficiency, nor the whole of the misefficiency, can be brought to view.

Indeed to show the absurdity of the notion, is to show its mischievousness: at any rate, if intellectual imbecility in the public mind be a mischief, and adherence to gross absurdity a proof of it.

Mark well the state of the case. Men acting together in a body, *twelve:* business of the body, declaration of an opinion on two matters aken in conjunction—matter of fact and matter of law.

First, as to the matter of fact. Subject-matter of the declaration, a question between A and B. A being either an individual, or a functionary acting in behalf of the public. On a certain occasion, at the time and place in question, did an individual fact, belonging to a certain species of facts, take place or not? This species of fact—is it of the number of those in relation to which provision has been and continues to be made by such or such a portion of the law?

Of this sort in every case are two points, in relation to which, each man of the twelve is called upon to deliver his opinion, as expressed in one or other of two propositions, one or the other of which, they being mutually contradictory propositions, cannot fail of being true: laying out of the question for simplicity's sake the rare case of a sort of verdict called *special*.

Yes; on the question of law: for, the comparatively rare case of a special verdict excepted, in the subject matter of the opinion declared is the matter of law included, as often as a verdict is delivered. Say, in cases called *civil*, but implicitly: but in cases called *penal*, as often as the verdict is against the defendant, most explicitly. For, in the legal sense of the word *guilty*, (which is the only sense here in question,) be the act what it may, doing it is not being *guilty*, unless that act stands prohibited by some law: really existing law in the case of written statute law: feigned to exist in the case of *common law*, in this one of the four or five different meanings of the word.

Be the subject matter of opinion what it may—

be the class of men what it may—be the number of
them what it may—to cause them to be all of
one mind, all you have to do is to put into their
heads the opinion it is your wish to see adopted,
and having stowed them in a jury chamber, keep
them till they are tired of being there.

In what abundance might not time, labour, and
argument—all these valuable commodities—thus
be saved? Take the uncertainty of the law: this,
if not a proper subject for redress, is at any rate,
in no inconsiderable degree, an actual subject-
matter of complaint. Make but the full use of
the jury boxes, or though it were but of one of
them, this uncertainty may at command be changed
into unanimity; and this unanimity, if not the same
thing as the certainty, will at any rate be the best
evidence of it; or, at any rate, the best consola-
tion for the want of it.

Having taken them up from these several
courts—taken them up from the seat of aggregate
wisdom, which they occupy altogether,—pass
through this machine the twelve judges, you save
arguments before these sages; pass through it the
members of the House of Lords, you save arguments on appeals, and writs of error before the
House of Lords.

To return to the unlearned twelve. To each
one of them, application is at the same time made
of two distinguishable, two widely different, instruments.

One is the *oath*. Of the application made of
this instrument, what in this case is the object?
To secure, in this instance, verity to that declaration of his which is about to be made.

2. The other instrument is a certain quantity of
pain: pain, according as he and the others com-

port themselves ; increasing, in a quantity proportioned to the duration of it, from the slightest imaginable uneasiness, to a torment such as, if endured would extinguish life : but which no man in the situation in question was ever known, or so much as supposed, to have endured.

A compound of several pains is this same pain : principal ingredients, the pains of hunger and thirst : slighted and first commencing ingredient, the pain of privation, consisting in the non-exercise of whatsoever other occupations would have been more agreeable.

Under these circumstances, if so it be, that, as soon as the evidence with the judge's observations on it, if any, are at a close, either of the two mutually opposite opinions is really entertained by all of them, on the part of no one of them does any breach of his oath take place ; as little, on the part of any one of them, does pain in any degree take place : the verdict is pronounced by the foreman, without their going out of the box.

But, as often as, instead of their delivering their verdict, they withdraw into the room prepared for them, then it is that a difference of opinion has place ; and then it is that, on the part of all twelve of them together, the appropriate operations begin to be performed. Then it is that, to an indefinite amount, all twelve are made to suffer, that that same number of them, from one to eleven, may be made, and until they have been made, to utter a wilful falsehood, and thus break the oath which they have just been made to take, under the notion of its preventing them from uttering this same falsehood.

True it is, that if any one of them there be, in whose instance pain has had the effect of causing

him no longer to entertain the opinion first entertained by him, but to entertain, instead of it, the
opposite opinion declared by the verdict, no such
falsehood will in his instance have been uttered.
But exists there that person who can really believe
that, in the case in question, pain can have any
such effect?

And even supposing the effect produced, where
is the benefit to justice? Of the two opposite
verdicts, to which is it that the pain will produce
the transition? for it presses upon the whole number of them. Upon the adoption of the verdict
eventually delivered, as well as upon the opposers
of it; and whichever of the verdicts it be that is
thus adopted, what reason can there be for regarding this as being more likely than its opposite
is to be the proper one?

But though to produce a change in the opinion
really entertained is a thing which pain cannot
do in the instance of any one, yet to produce a
change in the opinion declared to be entertained,
is a thing which pain, and this very pain, not only
can do in the instance of some one of them, but is
even known not unfrequently to have done in the
instance of all but one.

Of this so triumphantly trumpeted, so anxiously
preserved, and so zealously propagated unanimity,
what then as often as the jury quits the box is the
result? Answer—two doses: one composed of
pains, the other of wilful falsehood and perjury.
The dose of falsehood, some number, from one
to eleven, are made to swallow; the dose of pains,
all twelve: all this without the least imaginable
benefit to justice.

The verdict, with the opinion expressed by it,
being given, comes now the question—in what

way is it, that, on that side, and not on the other, the victory terminated? Answer—In this: the foreman, having been the object of the general choice, the person the most likely to prepare for acceptance one of the two verdicts, is this one. If then by any one or more of them the opposite opinion is entertained, declaration will of course be made of it by all those who entertain it, and the number on each side will thus be seen at once.

Whereupon it is, that if to any one of them a reason occurs, which, as appears to him, has not been brought to view by advocate or judge, naturally and generally, every one who has in his own mind any such reason, will out with it. What in this case does doubtless now and then happen is, that after all the observations delivered by the experienced advocates and judge together, have failed to produce the impression in question, an observation produced by one of the comparatively inexperienced jury has succeeded. But this case, though sometimes exemplified, cannot be stated as the common one.

The oath to make a man speak true; the torture to make him speak false. Such is the contrivance. A two-horse cart; the horses set back to back, with the cart between them: in this behold its parallel.

A contest (and such a contest!) between will and will; and by whom set on foot? By the creator of the unanimity part of the institution. And by whom kept up? By the supporters of it.

In the declaration of the opposing will, others, in any proportion to the whole number, may have joined; thereupon has the pain continued to be endured by all, till those on one side, unable any longer to endure it, have gone over to the other side. :

Exists there that man, in whose opinion, by the power of pain, any such change of the judgment from one side to the other ever had place?

Exists there that man, in whose opinion, on any future occasion, any such effect from such a cause is probable?

So much for opinion : now for experience. Experience says, that, while in this assembly, in which there is torture to produce it, unanimity thus constantly takes place,—in another, in which there is no torture to produce it, instances in abundance are continually happening in which it does not take place.

It is by the institution of another sort of jury— the grand jury—that the experience is furnished. Every day, where this institution has place, before these same petty jurymen, in number exactly-twelve, had pronounced their pretended unanimous opinion on that same question, under the name of grand jurymen, in number from thirteen to twenty-four inclusive, with dissentient voices, in any number, from one to eleven inclusive, had been pronouncing theirs.

Yet, only on one side does a grand jury hear evidence; on the two opposite sides the petty jury. In the opposition and conflict, which in the petty jury case has place, is there anything that is of a nature to render coincidence of opinion the more assured?—more assured than when the evidence is all on one side?

Now, if in either of these cases, there could be the shadow of a reason for the compulsory unanimity, in which case would it be? In the case of the grand jury assuredly, rather than in that of the petty jury. Why? Because, in the grand jury, as above, only on one side is evidence ever heard : in the petty jury constantly on both sides. Is it by conflict in evidence that agreement in opinion is more apt to be produced than by agreement in evidence?

Such being the absurdity of the device, such its inefficiency to every good purpose, behold now the bad purpose in relation to which it is *efficient*. One case alone excepted, of which presently.

1. First as to justice. Assured possessor of the irresistible evil, the fabled wishing-cap is yours : enter in triumph into any jury box you please : on your will depends the verdict.

Compared with this power of yours, what is the influence of the most skilful judge? He can but cajole : you necessitate. Behold how sure your success, how small the cost of it. Every time the jury have staid out of court so much as an hour, not to say every time they have gone out of court at all—there has been a difference of opinion, and next to a certainty, perjury. In no one instance endurance of the uneasiness for so long a term as forty-eight hours has ever been known. Yours being the verdict, behold in this sufferance the limits to the utmost price you can have to pay for it.

Man of desperate fortunes! would you retrieve them? In civil cases, as often as it happens to you to be on a jury, and the value at stake is such as makes it worth your while, if on the wrong side there is consciousness of wrong, and the case next to a desperate one, the more depraved the character of the wrong-doer, the more assured you

F

will be that an offer to share it with you will not be refused.

In penal cases, keep on the look-out for the richest criminals.

Defendant, with another man's money in your hands, look well over the jury list: observe whether there be not this or that one of them, whose surely effectual service may be gained by appropriate liberality.

Murderer, incendiary, go through the whole list: if one experiment fails, pass on to another: you have nothing to lose by it: you have everything to gain by it.

II. Now as to religion.   Behold the effect here.

Lowering the efficiency of the religious sanction in its natural and genuine state, clear of this spurious pretended additament, is or is not this an evil? In no known instance has the force of the oath had the effect of causing the torture to be endured for so long a time as eight-and-forty hours. Thus weak being the religious sanction, even with the benefit of this reinforcement, what would be the amount of its influence, if operating alone? Next to nothing would decidedly be the answer, were it not for the torture. But, by the torture, this argument in proof of the inefficiency is, at any rate, weakened if not repelled altogether. For, from the insufficiency of the religious sanction to prevail over pain when screwed up to such a pitch as to extinguish life, it follows not that any such insufficiency has place where no such pain has place.   Oath or no oath, perjury or no perjury, scarcely will any man apprehend for himself, at the hands of the Almighty, punishment

for non-fulfilment, of an obligation, for performance of which the physical capacity will, in his
eyes, be altogether wanting: at any rate, scarcely
will it to any man appear probable, that, to any
considerable extent, the obligation will, in quality
of a cause of such endurance, have been capable
of producing any considerable effect: or accordingly, that it is consistent with Almighty wisdom
to employ it to such a purpose. And, as to the
cessation of the endurance after a duration comparatively so short, why make an attempt, the
success of which is plainly impossible?

That in these considerations there is more or
less of reason will hardly be disputed. But, from
this it follows not, that they will present themselves to everybody: and, in every eye, to which
this, or something to this effect, does not present
itself, the efficiency of the religious sanction in its
natural state will, to say the least, be by this supposed reinforcement, greatly weakened, not to say
reduced to nothing.

By these considerations is moreover suggested
a course of experiment, by which, on the degree
of efficiency, if any, on the part of this ceremony,
no small light would, it should seem, be cast.
Continuing to apply the torture as at present in
all instances, apply the ceremony in some, omitting
it in others: then, let observation be made of the
proportionable number of instances, in which the
jurors betake themselves to the retiring room, and
of those in which they do *not:* and in regard to
those instances in which they do give this proof
of the efficiency of the religious (not forgetting
the moral) sanction, minute down the length of the
endurance.

Of those right reverend persons, who, as above,

had sworn, each of them, to set up, and endow
schools,—the majority are known to have actually
forborne to commit the correspondent perjury.
But, as to jurors, on the part of all those who have
ever sworn to forbear to express an opinion opposite to their own, notwithstanding all torture—
in other words, to forbear from perjuring themselves, what instance was ever known of such
forbearance? Conclusion, this. Supposed, a pretended effect of this spurious additament strength-
ening the instrument it is added to: real effect,
weakening it.

Mark now the sort of charity which the unanimity part of the institution, and the use of such
an instrument as the oath for the production of the
effect, proves and inculcates: proves to have existence on the part of the creators and preservers of
it: inculcates into those minds to whom the force
of it is applied. Numbers (suppose) eleven on
one side, one alone on the other. Says the one
of them now to himself—do what the others may,
never will I perjure myself. Saying this, does
he not at the same time say this also: Yes—these
my brethren, eleven in number—all these I will
make perjure themselves: damned I will not be
myself: but damned shall be these my brethren.
If the word damned be *not* the proper one, substitute, ye who object to it, substitute that which *is*.

Ye—if after this exposure any such there be—
Ye, who persisting in the application made of the
ceremony: in the application made of it, in any
case, and in the case of jurymen's oaths in particular,—do really believe, that, for every instance
of perjury, a punishment over and above that for
simple mendacity, will in the life to come be suffered by the delinquent,—think of the magnitude

of the evil, which you are endeavouring to perpetuate! take balance in hand and say—whether, by the application thus made of the ceremony, it is in the nature of the case, that good, in any such quantity as to outweigh the evil, should be produced.

Take any man by whom, in any instance, this perjury has been committed: either he believes that punishment in the life to come will attach upon him, or he does not: if not, then is the oath in its professed character, in the instance in question, compleatly ineffective: if he does, think then of the suffering which it produces. Inefficient or mischievous, (and who can say to what a degree mischievous?) such is the alternative.

Now for the benefit from this unanimity: meaning now the benefit—if not to the creators, to the preservers and promoters.

To entertain any such opinion, as that by pain, unaniniity of real opinion, on the part of every or any twelve men is actually produced, may be or not be in the power of human folly. But to produce the desire and the endeavour to *cause* this same opinion to be entertained, is but too much in the power, and too abundantly in the practice of human knavery. To the existing system of English-bred jury law in general, and to this part of it in particular, continues to be ascribed this miracle. Then comes the practical use. A system by which such miracles are at all times wrought, and these miracles such delightful ones, —how impossible is it to change it for the better! how dangerous to meddle with it.

In so conspicuous a part as this, no change in the English-bred judiciary procedure system could be so made or attempted, without drawing the

public eye upon the whole of it: but, let but the
public eye pervade the whole of it, behold it falls
to pièces.

Such of Judge and Co. was the end in view, and
such to Judge and Co. has been the use. Such
moreover it will continue to be, so long as jurors
shall continue to be made of clay, and judges the
potters working it. But under their hands, thanks
to their carelessness, it has grown and continues
to grow stiffer and stiffer. While teaching these
their pupils thus to contemn the law, these sages
have themselves fallen to such a degree into contempt, that the scholars themselves have at length
begun to contemn their own teachers. Every day
is this contempt increasing: and if so it be, that
contempt of a bad system is necessary to the substitution of a good one, a more beneficial result
than these two conjoined, cannot be wished for.

Thanks to this carelessness? Yes: for it is by
arbitrary power above, that the arbitrary power
below, superior on many occasions to that of its
creator, has or hath been seen created. By arbitrary power in one quarter or the other, thus it is
that everything is done: in both, the law is trampled upon. Of the mixture of oaths, perjury and
torture, this is one effect: so far therefore of the
oaths.

Blind and speechless acquiescence, under an
absurd tyranny, being the result, by what process
of reasoning were the inventors led to expect it?
Answer—by the following. On each occasion,
the portion of law, to which the jury are called
upon to join in giving execution and effect, being
supposed beneficial,—as, for the purpose of the
argument it cannot but be, one thing desirable is,
of course, that, in the instance in question, and by

means of the verdict pronounced, execution and effect should be accordingly given to it. But, at the same time, another thing alike desirable, is that, *that* same desirable effect being produced, it shall by the people at large be believed to be so.

This desirable belief, if produced, in what way then will it be produced? In this way. In the body of men thus selected, the people at large behold their own representatives, and moreover their own reporters. Better ground for their persuasion than the report made by these their reporters, they cannot have. On the occasion in question, they, (the people,) have not themselves had the means of informing themselves: these their representatives and reporters, *have.*

Now then, how to make the people believe that, on every occasion on which a petty jury is employed, everything is thus as it should be? Such was the problem. The solution, this: On this, as on any other occasion, take any considerable number of unobjectionable persons for judges,—the larger the portion of those who agree in the same opinion, the greater is found by experience the probability of their being in the right: thence it is, that, on every occasion, in the majority of such men, the confidence is greater than in the minority. Still, however, remains this same minority by which, in proportion to its number, this so desirable confidence is diminished, and prevented from being entire. Now then, let but this troublesome obstacle be entirely done away, entire is thereby rendered this so desirable confidence. Well then —apply the torture, the minority vanishes.

Another feature belonging to jury trial is the secresy of which the retiring chamber is the scene.

But, not belonging to the subject of oaths, this feature belongs not to the present purpose.

Would but the mendacity content them, this they might have without the oath: without the oath, the torture would give it them at least as surely as with. But, for such important purposes as above this same instrument of imposition was needed: and on the same occasion in particular, to make men by the terrific appearance shut their eyes, and prevent them from seeing into the absurdity of the contrivance.

In the shape of an exception, allusion has been made to one good effect of the power of conquest thus given to the strongest of the twelve wills. The good effect is this. A law (suppose) has place, by which, were execution and effect given to it, maleficence would be infused into the whole frame of government: absolutism for example, with all its attendant miseries. Individuals at the same time are not altogether wanting, each of whom, if, in his capacity of juryman, the law in question were brought before him for execution, would oppose to it this irresistible will, would in a word apply his *veto* to it. By the King and the Lords this veto is applicable to the laws in the first stage of their progress—the stage of legislation: by juries, in the last stage—the stage of judicature.

In the case of offences stiled *political*, and in these perhaps alone, is its usefulness indispensable, as it is concentrative: meaning, by political offences, those by which the effective power, of the functionaries exercising in chief the powers of government, is struck at: treason, for example, sedition, and political defamation: meaning, in this last case, acts striking at the reputation of men in official situations, considered as such, in which class of cases, constituting as it does the main, not to say sole security against absolutism, rather than part with it, better it were to endure much more than the evil of it in all other cases.

That by the fear of punishment at the hands of the Almighty, no such endurance to the amount of two days, has ever been produced, is indeed matter of demonstration: since, as above observed, to that amount, in no instance whatsoever has the effect been produced at any time.

But that in instances relatively not unfrequent, by sympathy for the happiness of the community at large, corroborated by antipathy towards men regarded as acting in hostility to it, instances of endurance such as have actually been productive of this good effect, there seems reason sufficient to believe to have had place.

To this generous self-devotion does the country appear to be altogether indebted for such portion of actual though unsanctioned and ever precarious liberty; sole security for all other salutary liberties the press is in possession of.

That but to too great an extent the abovementioned disastrous supposition stands verified, is but too undeniable. Under the existing system, take away this irregular power of the jury, neither are laws wanting, nor power conjoined with will to give execution and effect to them, sufficient to convert the form of government, such as it is, into as perfect an absolutism as anybody could desire.

Determined instruments of absolutism,—and, as such, with scarce an exception, determined and inexorable enemies of the press, have at all times been—all English judges: accordingly, on every occasion of a prosecution for a so-called libel, in which censure in any shape has been applied to the conduct of any public functionary, in that same proportion has been the constancy of the directions given by them to juries, to pronounce for their verdict the word *guilty*. Yet every now and then has an English jury refused to render itself in another sense *guilty*, by the utterance of that same momentous word.

Now then, admitting the effect to be good, in what way—by what *means*, has this same determined will been productive of it? By contributing to give execution and effect to the body of the law? No; but by successful obstruction and frustration applied to it.

Accordingly, in this instance is it any part of our prayer that the torture, thus applied, should be taken off? No; but that so long as the form of government continues what it is, it should be continued.

One set of cases there is, in which the real, or what comes to the same thing, the supposed interest of the ruling few, is in a state of but too decided opposition to that of the subject many ; and to the whole extent of these cases, our prayer is, that this same state of things, anarchical as it is, may continue unimpaired.

Thus much for elucidation : to make out any catalogue of these cases belongs not to this place.

Will it be said, that in some of these cases it is to the direction of the judge, and not to the evidence, that the verdict has been in opposition? Perhaps so. But, at any rate, neither are cases wanting, in which, with the salutary view in question, verdicts have been given by jurors in the very teeth of evidence. Upon their continuing prepared upon occasion so to do, depends, so to us it appears, all possibility of escape from the jaws of absolutism.

Not that we are not fully sensible that, in various particulars, the power of the jury is, in the nature of the institution, of essential, not to say indispensable service to justice; in particular, in respect of the obligation it lays the judge under, of giving reasons for his conduct, and bestowing on the question the degree of attention necessary for that purpose; as also, the furnishing to him such information respecting various grounds for it, as he could not otherwise be in possession of. But, as an ultimate test of truth, that the least should possess a better chance than the most exercised and instructed judgment, of being the most apt, is a notion which we do not feel it in our power to embrace. But on the subject of juries, more will be to be said under another head.

VI. *Device the sixth. Delay, in groundless and boundless lengths, established.*

Delay (need it be said) is denial, while it lasts. One third of the year, justice, pretended, as above, to be administered: the two other thirds not so much as pretended. Such was the state of things determined upon, and produced accordingly.

A calculation was made: one third of the year was found to suffice for getting into the law granary all the grist that the country could supply it with; that was the time for the mill to go: remained the two other thirds on which the miller was free to amuse himself. One third of the year, said he, will suffice for getting in all the money that the whole people can muster for laying out in our shops: work for one third of the year, amusement for the two other thirds. Sittings out of term time belonged not to those days. At the present day, while some judges, as far as gout will let them, sit at ease, other judges overwork and overfatten themselves. But so managed is the work, that the delay, with its profits and its miseries, continues undiminished. Moreover, by the delay was left a correspondent interval for incidents capable of being made productive of fresh fees.

What is the day on which justice ought to sleep?—what the hour? That on which injustice does so too.

Look now to other departments; see how things would go on if like delay were there: what if during one part of the year, taxes being collected, during the other two thirds they were left uncollected?

What if, during one third of the year, the naval force being on duty, during the other two thirds the seas were left open to enemies and pirates?

What if, during one third of the year, the army being on duty, the other two thirds the country were left undefended, while enemies were at the work of plunderage and devastation?

From internal enemies, for want of justice, the sufferings of the people would not be so great as from external enemies for want of defence. True; but a suffering's not being the greatest possible, was no reason why men should be subjected to it. How came it that, in those days, while men were guarded in some sort against sufferings at the hands of external, they were subjected to it at the hands of internal evil-doers? Answer: By

the suffering produced by the foreign adversaries
these judges would themselves have been sufferers.　By the sufferings produced by the domestic adversaries they were gainers.

Look now to professions.

What if, on being called in by a man with a
stone in his bladder, a surgeon were to say to
him, "Lie there and suffer while I am amusing
myself: four months hence I may perhaps come
and cut you." By surgeons this is not said. No
surgeon has a monopoly of surgery. Judges do
say this. Judges, in small numbers, have among
them the monopoly of the commodity sold under
the name of *justice*. .

In the eyes of Blackstone, all this evil is so much
good. First, because it was done so early in the
good old times. But, above all, because it was
done by lawyers. To a husbandman, during harvest time, attendance in a court (he observed)
would have been attended with inconvenience.
True: and this was one reason why, instead of
two or three hundred miles, he should have had
but ten or twelve miles to travel ere he reached it.
Attendance to get back a farming stock unjustly
taken, would have been inconvenient. True: but
leaving it in the hands of the depredator, and thus
leaving the harvest to rot in the ground, was still
more inconvenient. So much for harvest time.
But all the year is not harvest time, and the whole
remainder of the year had its judges' sabbaths as
well as harvest time: sabbaths, not of days, but
of months continuance.

What the people *now* suffer from the system of
delay thus organized,—what the judges now get
by it, belongs not in strictness to the present head.
But neither is it without claim to notice.

Chiefly to the cases called *civil* applies what is above. Now for cases called *penal*. Behold here the interest of judges changing, and with it of course the provision made by them.

In penal cases, and in particular in those most highly penal, not a day in the year but courts are open to receive complaint: and complaint made, men complained against, guilty and innocent together, are put into jail. How so? because, as above observed, judges have bodies, judges have gouts, judges have lives: so also, as well as other men, have all those who, in point of interest, are in any particular way connected with them: bodies, goods, and lives, which, but for some such protection, might be wounded, carried off, or destroyed.

When in jail, there they are, guilty and innocent together, from 2 days to 182, as chance pleases. How so? Because, to judges and those who are in league with judges, whether, in this case a man is innocent or guilty—stays in jail 2 days or 182 days, makes no difference: not to speak of counties and cases in which the 182 days may be doubled.

Oh yes: to Judge and Co. the time does make a difference: for, from the difference between the 2 days and the 182 days, come fees. Jail produces bailing and bailing produces fees. Innocent or guilty, those who can find bail and fees, are let out: those who are too poor to find either, stay in. How can it be otherwise? Under English judge-made law, the only unpardonable crime is poverty.

Contamination! contamination! Between uncompleted examination and definitive trial, whole days, weeks and months are rolling on: contamination thickening all the while. Complaints of

this evil not sparing: not least abundant by this
or that one, of those by whom it is caused. He,
who can remove the evil and does not, causes, if
not the commencement, at any rate the continuance of it. Of such contaminators, the most
insensible, the most obdurate, the most inexorable,
the most inexcusable, are they not legislators?

All contamination in prisons—all unintended
sufferings in prisons—all possibility of escape from
prisons, they might prevent and they will not.
Why will they not? One word, *Panopticon*, ex-
plains the mystery. Pitt gave acceptance to it
while he lived, gave support to it, such as he was
able. Royal vengeance stopt it. Interest, sinister and all-powerful interest, opposed to every
thing good in proportion as it is good, keeps it still
out of existence. A little while, and the inventors
will, both of them, have the merit of being dead:
when their eyes cannot be rejoiced at the sight of
it, then will it rise from under the oppression
which has thus long kept it down: then will the
public eye open itself: then will public indignation kindle; then will the public voice break out
afresh, and resistance no longer be deemed com-
patible with prudence. To conclude—Delay gave
ease: delay bred incidents: incidents were made
to breed fees: so it must have been in those early
times: so it is in these present times. Ease and
fees—fruits so sweet, both together from one plant:
how felicitous!

Two causes there are, by either of which, without blame in any shape to anything or anybody—
to a judge, or to the system of procedure:—delay,
to any amount, may be necessitated.

Of these causes, those whose interest is served
by the delay and by the system in which it is an

inseparable ingredient, take of course their advan-, tage and do what depends upon them towards making the people believe that the existing delay is alike necessary in the cases to which these causes do not apply, as in those in which they do.

1. One is, non-forthcomingness of evidence : of this cause, the influence, it is manifest, extends itself to every case, to every species of suit.

2. The other is *complication :* complicatedness of the subject-matter or other circumstances belonging to the suit. This applies not beyond a particular class of suits : but, in the nature of things this is unavoidably but too extensive.— Subject-matter, suppose, a mass of property : in the course of the suit, operations to be performed on it, collection and distribution of the component parts of that same mass : as in the case of the disposal made of the effects of a person lately deceased, or of a person in a state of insolvency. Over what parts of the globe may it not happen to the subject-matter on the one hand, to both debtors and sharers in the balance, if any, to be dispersed. So likewise where without death on suspicion of insolvency, demand is made of an account, by a party to transactions to which it may happen to have been not less complicated than the above.

In a country cause, by this or that accident— absence for example of a material witness, trial, without loss of cause to the party in the right is at that moment rendered impossible. What is the consequence ? The cause goes off for six months : expense of witnesses, counsel, attornies, all disbursed in waste : and at the end of the six months, if it happens to it to be on the *remanet* list, for another six months—unless the party is ruined by the preparation for the first trial, profit to Judge and Co. upon the second, and perhaps upon a third. Necessary or not, motion for a new trial, with additional profit thereupon, according to circumstances.

Suppose now the court sitting all the year round : the accident of one day may now be repaired the next.

Of further particulars as to the evil and causes of delay, mention will require to be made under the head of *Jurisdiction Split.*

VII. *Device the Seventh.—Precipitation Necessitated.*

Under the fee-gathering system, states of things the most opposite—delay and precipitation—concur in giving existence to the desired effect.

Of delay, the mode of establishment and the relative usefulness have just been seen. The precipitation grew by degrees out of the delay. At the early period in question, scarcely could it have been contemplated : not but that from the first, precipitation, with its evils, were among the natural effects of the opposite abuse. But at present it flourishes, and on each occasion produces its fruits : and only for the purpose of the present time is the state of the system at that early period here brought to view.

Be the business what it may, if, of the time that might and should have been allotted to it, a portion is kept unemployed, proportioned to the increase given to the quantity of the business will be whatever hurry takes place in the course of the time which the business is allowed to occupy.

Suits at common law, and as such brought for trial, or pretended so to be brought before a jury, may be divided into two classes : those of which it is known that, by possibility, they may be tried by a jury, and those of which it is known that they can not.

Cause of incapacity of being brought under the cognizance of a jury, complexity. Of modes of complexity capable of producing this effect, examples are the following.

1. Multitude of facts which, by one and the same demand or defence are undertaken to be proved or disproved on one or both sides: for example, in an account.

2. Multitude of witnesses liable to be examined in relation to each alleged fact: especially if *alibi* evidence, or evidence as to character, is received.

These sources, however, are but two of a multitude of distinguishable sources, out of which complexity is in use to arise.

Suit called on, jury in box, the impossibility of trial is universally recognized. What follows? Off the suit goes to arbitration. Aptly learned and well-wigged gentlemen in plenty, there they sit, all known as such by the judge. Choice is made of one for each side, or the same for both. Now again comes the time for delay. Five guineas a day, or less, secures and maximizes it: exemplary are then the care and deliberation. For securing the whole of the mass of evidence which the case affords, the powers are not now altogether adequate. But neither would they have been found so, had the trial gone on: for, under the existing system, no assemblage of powers, adequate to the purpose, has place anywhere.

Setting aside this deficiency and premium for delay, here may be seen the natural mode of procedure. Supposing the judge but one, with an audience sufficient in quality and quantity to compose a bridle for his discretion, and he salaried instead of feed, here would everything be as it should be. But the misfortune is—that, instead of being substituted to the elsewhere established technical mode of procedure, the natural mode is here added to it, leaving the burthen una'leviated.

So much for all jury causes taken together. Enter now the topographical distinction—*country* causes and *town* causes. The country outweighing the town causes in the scientific *mixture* of delay and precipitation.

Country causes are dispatched post haste: the whole machinery running round in a circuit. At each assize,—upon the blind fixation principle, (of which presently,)—allotment made of a certain number of days :—two, three, or four, as the case may be : business, for which two or three hours might have been more than sufficient, or two or three months less than sufficient, crammed into the compass of those same two or three days. By leaving evidence unheard, arguments undelivered or unattended to,—one part, of the whole number of suits set down for trial, is now made to undergo that process : the other part remain unheard, and are called *remanets* or *remanents*. Six months is the shortest interval before they come upon the carpet a second time : that is to say, if come they do : for, various are the causes, by any of which they may be extinguished : deperition of evidence, drainage of purse, death : death, in a certain case, whether natural or no, not the less violent because lingering : offence, manslaughter (to say no worse): manslaughter by Judge and Co. with their delay, expense, and vexation : substitutes — how safe convenient and profitable !—to poison, sword and dagger.

Remanets increase and multiply.   Begotten by the remanets of Spring, are the remanets of Michaelmas.

Eminently instructive would be a regularly published list of all of them.

Now as to *town* causes.   Here the scene changes. Of delay, considerably less: thence, so of precipitation.   For trials, in the whole of England, with the exception of the metropolis, assizes in the year no more than two ; in some counties, no more than one.   In the metropolis, *Terms* four : with Sittings before, in, and after each : total, 12 : and in each of the 12, upon an average, more days than in an assize.   Under these circumstances, in the metropolis, may be seen a choice made : not made by one Hercules, but by two of them.   The one who has fewest causes gets most ease : the one who has most causes gets most fees.   Health suffers : and martyrdom to duty is the name given to canine appetite for fees.   Velocity in horsemanship sees itself rivalled by velocity in judicature.

Mark now how admirably well adapted is this compound of delay and precipitation to the ends of judicature.   Carried on to the last link through the chain of useless proceedings, has been the corresponding chain of fees : so much for *fees*. Pending, the suit may have been for years, not a syllable all the while suffered to present itself to the mind of a judge, such is the fruit of the *mechanical* mode of judicature, (of which presently,) substituted to the *rational* : so much for ease.   Then comes the agreeable circumstance of making recommendation of the man or men, by whom, though without the name, the functions of the judge are then to be performed : so much for *patronage*.

The boots that fitted all legs—the *seven-leagued* boots—may be seen in fable. The judicial establishment which, should parliament so please, would fit itself to all quantities of business, may be seen, as below, in sober truth. *Deputation* is the name of the instrument, by which this quality would be given to it. *Powers of deputation* is the name given to the so highly elastic and self-accommodating boots.

VIII. *Device the Eighth.—Blind Fixation of times for judicial operations.*

Where flexibility is necessary, fixation made. Example—most prominent, effective, and instructive—that which is afforded by the appointment of days for attendance, at the judgment seat: attendance of parties, or witnesses, or both.

Commencement (suppose) given to the suit,—as, in every case, it might and should be—by application, made by some person in quality of suitor, or, in case of necessity, by some substitute of his, at the sitting of the judge. Where a suit is intended, (simple information without suit being out of the question,) the applicant demanding, that he himself, or some person mentioned by him, be admitted as pursuer against some person as proposed defendant. If on this first occasion, the suit for the commencement of which the application is thus made, is not dismissed, some day for the continuance of it will of course be to be appointed: some day thereafter, say for example, in ordinary cases, the second, third, or fourth day, as it may happen, distance in place taken into account, reckoning from the day on which the originating application is made. So much as to what should be the practice: now as to what it is. In pursuance of the device here in question—say upon the *blind fixation principle*, the existing system appoints for all cases without distinction some one day by general rule : for each subsequent operation, 15 days suppose, reckoning from the one last preceding. Blind fixation, say without difficulty : for, blind, when made by a universally and indiscriminately applying rule, such fixation cannot but be.

As to the originating application,—in neither case can in the nature of things any fixt day for it have place. Such application imports actual appearance of a suitor in the presence of the judge. But, applied to the existing system, how erroneous is this conception ! For, such is the established etiquette, to no suitor, till the day on which conclusion is to be given to the suit, is his lordship at home. What then is the mode which commencement is given to it ? Answer, this : By a person acting as an attorney for the plaintiff, the appropriate instrument, *the writ* (as the phrase is,) is *taken out :* in plain English, bought at the justice shop, of a clerk, employed by the judge, in serving out the commodity, to every one who will pay for it, no question asked. The writ itself is a mass of unintelligible absurdity : but the result is, that if the proposed defendant does not constitute himself such by appointing an attorney to act for him in the correspondent manner, the judge will, at his charge, cause the plaintiff to have whatever it is that he demands.

In regard to defendants, setting aside for the present the question as to witnesses, co-pursuers, and co-defendants, what is clear is, that, sooner or later, to each proposed defendant the faculty ought to be afforded of acting, if so disposed, in contestation of the demand made at his charge, by the individual admitted as pursuer. But to his so acting, a necessary condition is, that he should have received notice of his being called upon so to act. To his being so, another condition necessary is, that a mandate for the purpose should have been delivered at some individual spot which, at that same moment, is the place of his abode.

Now then, as to this same abode, it may be within a stone's throw of the justice-chamber, or without, being out of the local jurisdiction of the court, at about three hundred miles distance, more or less. In the first case, supposing the defendant at home, and the judge at home, and disposed to hear him, two or three minutes would suffice for the production of the necessary intercourse, i. e. the interview between this suitor and the judge in the chamber of justice; in the other case, twice as many *days* would not suffice. What on an occasion of this sort does judicial practice? It appoints one and the same day for every individual defendant; no regard paid to distance in place, or quantity of time necessary to be expended in passing from the one place to the other.

So much for the *operation,*—the operation of attending, or, as the word is, *appearing.* Now for instruments. Where all that is to be done at the appointed day is appearance in a chamber mentioned, short in comparison is the interval that may suffice for adequate notice: and such and no other was the state of things at the primeval period all along in view. But where, within the appointed interval, an ulterior operation comes to be performed, that operation consisting in the drawing up and exhibition of a written instrument of a certain sort; in a word, say one of the sort of *written* instruments above spoken of by the name of *written pleadings;* widely different now is the

aspect of the case: the time requisite may, upon
a scale of indefinite length, be varied by the
quantity of writing necessary, not to speak of an
unconjecturable variety of other circumstances.
And thus it is, that, in this case, so it may be
that by the next day may be afforded notice long
enough, or by the next day two months, notice
not long enough. Against the notice's being
neither too long nor not long enough, the chances,
it is evident, are, so to speak, an infinity to one.

Of the individual in whose instance attendance
is requisite to be paid, or some other operation
performed, some instrument already in existence
established, or some written instrument, not already in existence, to be framed, and thereupon
exhibited, the residence is, as above, *supposed* to
be within the jurisdiction of the court. But, on
the other had, it may, in fact, be in another
hemisphere; and so it frequently is. No matter,
the day is fixt,—fixt by the general rule: fifteen
days, suppose, are given for a proposed witness,
with his evidence, to make his appearance from
British India, or Australia, or Peru.

Such, then, under the direction of this blind
fixation principle, is the practice throughout the
whole of the existing system of the technical
judicature. It was the natural, and, in a manner,
the necessary result of the virtual and effective
exclusion which, at the primeval period all along
in question, by the exclusive use of a language
foreign to them, was put upon the parties.

Of this same blindness, behold now the consequences; for in these consequences may be seen
the *motive*,—the motive, by the operation of which
the eyes were at that time shut, and to this day
continue to be shut. In each of the two opposite

'events, disservice is rendered to the interest of justice, correspondent service to the interests of judicature.

The time allowed, is it too long? If yes, then by the overlength is created so much needless delay; and of evil in that shape, the consequences have been already brought to view. Is it too short? Then comes a demand for the enlargement of it; and with this demand comes down a shower of *fees*.

A *motion* requires to be made : a motion having, in a common law court, commonly for its support, some alleged fact, or set of facts, with an affidavit, or set of affidavits, by which allegation of their existence is made; and of this motion, the ground made is here, by the supposition, in point of reason, uncontestible. But it follows not that, in point of fact, it will not be contested. From the motion have, at any rate, come some fees; and from the contestation, if any, will come many more fees.

Every motion made is, in fact, a suit within a suit; and of the thus needlessly interpolated suit, the expense is abundantly greater than under a system having for its ends the ends of justice would, in the vast majority of cases, be the whole of the needful expense.

By *motion* understand here a motion which is *not* of course. For motions are divided into *motions of course*, and *motions at large*, or say *not* of course. Of the mention thus made of the distinction, the object is, that notice may thereby be received by the Honorable House, that every sum obtained for making a motion of course, is money obtained from the suitors by extortion, practised on false pretences, no motion being really made :

sharers in the produce of the extortion, the attorney, the advocate, the subordinate judicial officers, and the judge.

Of this contrivance for the manufacture of motions,—mark well the absurdity, in any other character than that of the manufacture of fees. If in judicature this is right, let it now be applied to legislature, and observe the consequences. Except where the appropriate facts are deemed of themselves sufficiently notorious, no operation is ever performed by the Honorable House, no proceeding carried for which a determinate ground has not been made by special evidence. By your Honorable House, either in the whole House, or in and by its committees, according to the occasion and the purpose, evidence is convened from every part of the island, and upon occasion from every part of the globe. Now then, for argument sake, suppose (what in reality is not possible) suppose an Honorable Member to stand up and make a motion, that, on every occasion on which any person is ordered to be in attendance at the House, for the purpose of being examined, the day of attendance shall be on a day certain, and in every instance one and the same: say, for example, the fifteenth day, reckoning from that on which the motion shall have been made. A motion made to any such effect,—would it not be regarded as evidence of mental derangement, and that but too conclusive? Yet in judicature this is no more than what has all along been the practice; and till this moment without objection by all judges, professing at the same time to be directing their practice to the ends of justice.

But justification will perhaps be attempted: and if it be, imagination will be set to work for the creation of it : process, fallacy: result, in so far as successful, illusion and deception: Principal instruments of the fallacy, the words *irregularity* and *regularity*.

The mode in which they have acquired this recommendatory property seems to be this. With the word *irregularity*, sentiments of disapprobation have from the earliest time of life stood associated : at school, irregularity has betrayed itself by straying out of bounds : at a later period, by purchase of present pleasure at the expence of greater good in future contingency. Irregularity is therefore a bad thing ; and as such, attended with bad consequences. But bad consequences ought to be prevented ; and to this end whatever operation is chargeable with irregularity, ought to be set aside, and to this purpose considered as not having been performed ; whence the motion for " setting aside proceedings " (as the phrase is), for irregularity.

But of irregularity, regularity is the opposite : irregularity being a bad thing, regularity is in a proportionable degree a good thing, and whatsoever is good, ought to have place everywhere. Apply it accordingly to judicial procedure : whatever operation requires to be performed, a day *certain* ought to be fixed for the performance of it : and intimate is the connection between regularity and certainty : and as fixation is the mother or daughter, no matter which, of regularity, so is she of certainty.

In proportion as the interval is too short, and thence the existence of motions for enlargement more certain, the rule receives the praise of *strictness :* for strictness is regularity, in a transcendant degree, or say in perfection. Accordingly, equity practice teems with rules of this kind—(say *time-fixation rules*)—compliance with which is notoriously and confessedly impossible.

Rule—is it a good thing? Yes: in so far as directed, and with success to a right object: no; if directed to a wrong object: no; even if laid down without an object: for, on the field of law, all rule imports *coercion:* and, taken by itself, coercion is evil, and that evil pure. Now then, the rules in question—what are they? To outward appearance, nothing worse than rules without an object: but in inward nature and design, rules with a bad object: rules laid down for a bad purpose; for the purpose of producing by extension, under colour of justice, the object of the all-ruling passion—fees.

IX. *Device the ninth. Mechanical substituted to mental judicature.*

Of the arrangement by which the parties, and in particular the first applying party, the plaintiff, was excluded from the presence of the judge, this was an immediate result, as well as an intended fruit. Already, in the blind fixation device, may be seen part and parcel of it: a peg or a nail driven into a board, is the prototype of a day fixt.

How to cause the suit to be carried on down to the last stage without the judge's knowing anything of the matter, this was the problem to be solved, and solved it was: fruit of the contrivance, profit gained: all trouble, all time, all labour, all responsibility, saved.

By the parties in conjunction, that is to say, not the parties, but their respective agents, with the judge's subordinates, all impregnated with interests. repugnant to the interests of parties, everything requisite to be done was to be done: agent fighting against agent, with arms respectively bought by them at the shop kept by the judge for the purpose.

Mechanical this mode may truly be stiled, in opposition to mental: of no such faculty as those the aggregate of which is termed *mind*, any application being at any part of the time made by him: irrational and non-rational are terms that fall short of the monstrosity of it.

A cider-press, worked by steam, is the emblem of a judicatory, acting in pursuance of this device. By the press, with its moving power, the juice is squeezed out of apples: by judges, and by means of the machinery of which their predecessors were the inventors, and themselves the preservers and improvers, the money, in the shape of fees, is squeezed out of suitors. By the piston, no thought is applied either to the apples or to the sweets extracted from them. By the judge as little, to the operation performed and instruments exhibited under the authority of his name, or to the effects of them on the suitors: not so as to the *sweets:* little are they in danger of being out of mind.

An attorney, along with a fee, puts a written paper into a box, the judge knowing nothing about the matter. This done, into the same or another box, another fee is dropped, with another written paper, of which the judge has the same knowledge.

By each fee, the agent on one side purchases of the judge the faculty and benefit of plundering, impoverishing, and vexing at the same time his own client, and the suitor on the other side;

whereupon, the agent of the party on the other side does the like: and thus the compliment, as the phrase is, is returned.

For elucidation follows an example: that of *signing judgment*: by this one, all others may be rendered needless. " I have signed judgment," (says somebody), who, would it be supposed, is this somebody? A judge? no: but an attorney: the attorney of one of the parties. What? Is not then the judge the person by whom the act of signature is performed? Not he indeed: but the attorney, is he, by whom alone any thought is applied to the subject, any *judgment* exercised; the judge signs nothing: a clerk under the judge signs what is given him to sign as above. Under the fixation system, as above, a day has been fixed for the attorney of the party, say the defendant, to do something: say, to send in some written instrument, on pain of loss of cause. The day passed, the attorney takes to the proper officer the instrument stiled *the judgment*, and so, as above, a clerk of the judge puts his signature to it.

The problem has been already mentioned. The result aimed at in the first instance is judicature without thought. In so far as this is effected, the solution is complete; in so far as this is unattainable, next comes judicature with the minimum of thought: in this case, an approximation is all that lies within the power of art and science.

Of the case in which the solution is complete, that in which a clerk's is the hand by which the judgment is signed, is an example: the judge whose name has been written by him on a piece of paper or parchment knows no more about the matter than his learned brother who is sitting at the same time upon the Calcutta bench.

At all times, of the whole number of actions commenced, a great majority would probably be found thus disposed of. For such will be the case, where the so stiled defendant, being by indigence disabled from becoming so in reality, sits helpless while the suit is taking the course which the mechanism has pre-established.

As to his property, instead of going, in proportionable shares among his creditors, it is in the first instance, by Judge and Co. divided, if not the whole of it, always a large part of it, among themselves.

Creditors are made to abate from their demands : Judge and Co. know not what it is to make abatement.

One little improvement remains to be made : substitution of an automaton to the judge. Written by a penman of this sort have been seen lines more beautiful than were ever written by a judge. Of the essential characteristic of English judicature, the grand instrument of delusion—the masquerade dress—this deputy would not be left destitute. Bowels, if given to him, would be but surplusage : if his principal had had any, he would not have been where he is.

Suppose now a system of procedure under which everything was done by the appearance of the parties in the presence of each other, before an unfee-fed judge. Creditors more than one— *equitable adjustment*, as the phrase is, would have place : equitable adjustment, without that injustice for which this phrase has too often been made a mask : for the reducing, on both sides taken together, the burthen to its minimum, the arrangements requisite would be made. To the debtor respite might be granted, where, to both interests taken together, the grant were deemed more beneficial than the denial of it. Respite to the debtor is, indeed, so much delay to the creditor; but delay to the one may be a less evil than ruin to the other.

Where, besides the creditor by whom the demand has been made, other creditors remained unsatisfied, all of them being called in, a *composition* would be made among them, they appearing in person, as far as needful, under the direction of the judge: the effects would be divided among those to whom the shares were due, instead of a fellowship, consisting of attorneys, counsel, bankruptcy commissioners, judiciary functionaries of various sorts, and their universal patron, by whom the seals are put to the universal system of plunderage.

X. *Device the Tenth.—Mischievous transference and bandying of suits.*

When justice is the object, cases of necessity excepted, in whatsoever judicatory a suit is begun, in that same is it continued and ended.

Where fees are the object, it is without any such necessity or use, transferred of course, from one judicatory to another: where, after transference, it does *not* return to the judicatory from whence it went, say *transference;* where it *does* return, say *bandying.*

Appeal is not here in question. In case of appeal, a suit is not, without special cause, sent off from one judicatory to another: in the case here in question, it is without any cause.

Instances of cases in which justice is the object,

are afforded by one of the two classes of the cases in which jurisdiction is given to justices of the peace, acting singly.

Preparatory and *definitive*, by these two appellatives let them be distinguished : *preparatory*, where, from the judicatory in which it originated, a suit, to receive its termination, must be transferred to some other : *definitive*, when it is in the originating judicatory that the suit is not only begun, but continued and ended. To the class of cases in which the jurisdiction is definitive belong those in which justice is the object.

In the preservation of the practice, not in the invention and creation of it, consists, in this case, the device.

First, as to the simple transference. In the case in which the jurisdiction of a justice of the peace is of the preparatory kind,—from his judicatory, according to the place in which the suit originates, the nature of the case, and the gravity of the punishment, it is transferred to one of four others.

1. If in London and Middlesex, in the grave cases to the Old Bailey.

2. If in the country, in these same cases, as also in the lighter ones, to the assizes.

3. In the metropolis, as above, in some cases to the assizes, in others to the general sessions of the justices of the peace.

4. In the metropolis, in the lightest cases, to the sittings before, in and after, term in the King's Bench.

In its way to each of these ultimate or penultimate judicatories, if it has arrived at its destination, it has been strained through that seat and instrument of secresy, partiality, and irresponsible despotism, the grand jury.

H

Evidence, time, and money: of all these valuable articles, loss, in vast and incalculable abundance, is the consequence.

In all these instances, the case is, in one degree or other, a penal one.

For a faint conception of all these losses, and of the useless and mischievous complication by which they are effected, take now that state of things which, in respect of the evidence, is most simple, and which, at the same time, is not unfrequently exemplified.

Percipient witness to the transaction but one: circumstantial evidence, none. Suppose the originating judicatory aptly constituted, and appeal allowed; what, in this case, should hinder the suit from being ended where it began?

A duty that might be imposed on the judge as upon the justice of peace it is imposed,—is that of causing to be set down every syllable of the evidence. This done, why should it not be made thereupon his duty to pronounce judgment, and in case of conviction, give execution and effect to it? What, (says somebody) if death were the consequence? Answer—O yes: though death were the consequence: provided always, that, in every case, appeal were allowed: appeal to a judge with jury, in cases to which the powers of a jury were deemed applicable.

Is this the course? No. From the justice of the peace it must go to a grand jury: from the grand jury, if not sunk in that dark pit, it must go to one or other of the four judicatories above-mentioned.

Three times over must the tale of this percipient and narrating witness be told. Here then, in every case, is the labour, expense, and complication of two appeals, without the benefit of one. Were appeal instituted, it would no otherwise be allowed than upon grounds deemed sufficient, and in so far as it was deemed subservient to justice, say, in one word, of *use*.   On the other hand, under the existing system, there is the complication of appeal organized and established in all cases, including those in which the operation is without ground, and without use.

Were the matter of the first narrative preserved, it might serve as a check and a security for the correctness of the second : and so the first and a second for the correctness of the third.   No : neither of the second nor of the first is such use, or any use, made.

Moreover, for deperition of the evidence by design or accident—by purchase, emigration, sickness, or death, all this time, all these chances, are allowed.

I. Here then is loss the first : loss of. *evidence.*

II. Now for loss of *time.*

i. Old Bailey.   In the year, sessions 8.   Average duration of each session, days 10 : time lost, days, from 1 to   .

ii. King's Bench.   Terms 4 : sittings, before, in, and after term, as many.   Times of trial, these same sittings.   Time thereby lost—days, from 1 to   .

iii. Assizes.   In the year, days of sitting in most counties, 2 : in some, but one : in each town, from 1 to 3 : days lost, from 1 to 182 : in some cases, no less than 364.

iv. General sessions of the justices of the peace. In the year, sittings 4.   Times of trial, these same sittings,   days of sitting, upon an average,

: Time lost, days from 1 to   .

III. Now for loss in *money*. Only for remembrance sake can this item be set down: to determination it bids defiance.

So as to the loss in the two other abovementioned shapes: from anything that could be done towards filling up the above blanks, the benefit would not pay for the burthen. According to his opportunities, every person, whose regard for human suffering suffices for the motive, will perform the operation for himself.

So much for simple transference: now for *vibration*, or say *bandying*: that is to say—after sending the suit from the originating judicatory to another, regularly bringing it back to the first. Neither was this branch of the device part and parcel of the original system. In process of time, two causes concurred in the production of the effect.

Cause the first.—As opulence, and with it the possibility of finding the purchase money for the chance for justice received increase, the local judicatories being killed, business kept flowing in to greater amount than King's Bench and Common Pleas together knew what to do with, in the compass of that portion of the year, which, under the name of *term-time*, had originally been allotted to it. Cause the second.—At the same time, the burthen attached to jury service, borne as it was twice in the year by men in dozens from each county, travelling for King's Bench suits in the train of the King during his rambles, or though it were only to a fixt place, such as London, from Cumberland or Cornwall, was such as, in the aggregate, became intolerable.

Hence came the *circuit* system: that system, by which part of the time, originally under the name of *vacation*, consecrated to idleness, was given up to business, and, to a correspondent amount, *ease* exchanged for *fees*: judges being detached from the Westminster-hall courts, to save to jurymen a more or less considerable proportion, of the time and money, necessary to be expended on journies and demurrage.

As to the local judicatories thus extinguished, they sat every day of the 365: at least, nothing was there to hinder these days. Was the equivalent allowed for the 365, by the circuit-system principle, the allotment of a finite and minute quantity of time for an infinite quantity of business? When it is conducive to public health that, by medical men, wounds shall be dressed, teeth drawn, and limbs amputated at full gallop,—the circuit mode of trying causes, at like speed, will be conducive to justice.

Under the technical system, if ever in a case such as this, evil receives alleviation, it is from some other evil. It is from the device by which mechanical operation is substituted to mental: it is from this, that the evil produced by the bandying device, by which a suit is dealt with as if it were a shuttlecock, may be seen to receive such palliative as it is susceptible of.

That the series of the proceedings of which a suit is constituted, should be divided between judicatories more than one, is a source of mis-decision, for which, in some cases indeed, necessity affords even a justification, but for which nothing short of necessity can afford so much as an excuse. Why? because in this case, the judge, on whose judgment the fate of the suit depends, has had before him no more than a part of the matter of which the ground of that judgment ought to be composed.

In the case of circuit business, this source of misdecision is purposely established and universalised. In every one of the three common law courts, in the metropolis it is that the suit takes its commencement, and with it the history of it, called the *record*: When, on the circuit, the detachment of judges, sent from Westminster-hall in couples, make their progress through the counties, with them travel these same records, and so again on their return: whereupon, they are reconveyed to the offices, from whence they issue: of this practice of dealing with a record as with a shuttlecock, what is the use? None whatever: always excepted, the univeral use: serving as a pretence for fees: a shuttlecock is lighter than a record, and would, in these cases, be an advantageous substitute to it.

Of the whole proceedings, in each suit the essential part (need it be said?) is the evidence. Well then; of each record this same evidence constituted, (one might have supposed) the principal part. Well then; does it compose the principal part? No: nor so much as any part, whatever: a mixture of immaterial truth and absurd lies : such is the matter of which the principal part is composed.

As to the evidence, instead of a compleat written designation of everything relevant that has been said, traced by a responsible hand, the judge takes or does not take what he calls his notes; which notes are of course in quality as well as quantity whatever it pleased him to make them: on a motion for a new trial, but not otherwise, they are read. Now then for the *palliative*. It consists in this: setting aside occurrences, which are purely accidental, and which happily do not take place,—perhaps in one suit out of twenty,--no more than one judge is there in truth, whose mind is, in any part of the proceedings applied to the matter of the suit. This is the judge, under whose direction has been performed the elicitation of the evidence.

Auspices were what a Roman emperor contributed and received admiration and praise for, when a victory was gained a thousand miles off: auspices are what the judges of a Westminster-hall judicatory contribute to a suit begun and ended in their courts.

When from the circuit the record is brought back by the judge, under whose direction the evidence has been elicited to the Westminster-hall court in the office of which the suit and the record took the commencement, the form by which judgment is pronounced receives the hand-writing of the chief justice, as in his sleep a plate of glass would his breath, without his knowing it; and thereupon, if the judgment be in favour of the plaintiff's side, and money is to be raised in satisfaction of a debt pronounced by the judgment to be due, is sent down ordinarily to the county, to which the record's useless journey had been made, an order called a writ of *fieri facias*, by which a functionary stiled the *sheriff* of the county, is required to raise the money by sale of the defendant's goods, and remit it to the office of the court, in which the suit was commenced.

When it was at Westminster, and thence in the very justice chamber in which the suit took its commencement, that the elicitation of the evidence belonging to it had to be performed, here was no journey for the record to perform : next to none when in the city of London, at less than two

miles distance.   A trial performed at a county
town in the course of a circuit was said to be performed at the assizes : a trial performed in Westminster in London, as above, was said to be performed at nisi prius : *nisi prius*, when interpreted,
is *unless before :* and with that interpretation your
petitioners choose to leave the matter, rather than
attempt to lead the Honorable House through the
labyrinth, through which, often, beginning at
nonsense, the mind must make its way, ere it
arrives at common sense.

But the county at which the elicitation of the
evidence is to be performed—what shall that
county be?   Under the natural system, there
would be variety, but without difficulty : without
difficulty, because without decision : without decision, because by the judges, unfee-fed as they
would be, nothing would be to be got by it.

Under the existing technical system chicane is
busy : difficulty proportionably abundant.   Hereupon, comes a sort of a thing called a *venue :*
question, shall it be changed or remain unchanged?
in plain English, the county in which the trial is
performed—shall it be that which, by means of
the appropriate gibberish, the plaintiff's attorney
had fixt upon for this purpose.

Such is the stuff, out of which, under the technical system, what is called *science* is composed.
If a suit were sent to be tried at the *venue*, and
the motion were for change of *unless before*, the
profundity of the science would be rendered still
more profound.

One thing is throughout intelligible : at the
bottom of everything are fees : at the bottom of
the *unless before*, are fees : at the bottom of the
changeable *venue* are fees : the greater the quan-

tity of parchment in the shape of a record, the greater the quantity of gold in the shape of fees, the greater the patience of us his Majesty's subjects, the more cruelly will every one of us be trod upon by every dishonest man who is richer than he, and by the men to whom, under the name of judges, we are delivered over to be tormented, the more insatiably squeezed for fees.

Particular case just alluded to that of a motion for a new trial. Judges of the three Westminster-hall common law courts, 12 : before one alone it is that the trial has been performed. Two to one, therefore, is the chance that the abovementioned palliative, such as it is, will not have had place : for, upon the notes taken by the one judge, at the assizes in the county, or *nisi prius* at the metropolis, is grounded the decision of the four judges in Westminster-hall, on the question whether the new trial shall or shall not have place.

Under natural procedure, supposing a new trial, it might, instead of the next quarter or half year, take place the next day; and thus before the witnesses were dispersed.

Let not mistake be made. Absolutely considered, neither on simple transference nor yet on bandying can condemnation be passed, consistently with justice. Suppose two hundred local judicatories, having each of them in its territory a witness or a party, whose testimony was needful in one and the same suit. On such case, transference to some one, or bandying the suit to and back from each, might perhaps be productive of less delay and expense, than the fetching of them all to the originating judicatory.

The grievance consists in the performance of both operations, conjointly, and as a matter of

course, where there is neither need nor use. Sending, for example, on the strength of the word *venue*,
suit, parties, witnesses, and record to Cornwall or
Cumberland, when all are within a stone's throw
of the seat of ultimate judicature.

XI.—*Device the eleventh. Decision on grounds
avowedly foreign to the merits;* or say, decision
otherwise than on the merits; or, more shortly,
decision not on the merits.

Under all the devices, as yet brought to view,
the sinister design has shrunk from observation,
and with but too much success sought something
of a veil for the concealment of it. But by him,
by whom for the designation of the decision, pronounced or sought by him, this phrase was employed, all veils were cast aside, and the principle
acted upon, avowed and exposed to all eyes, in all
its deformity and foul nakedness. To all eyes?
yes : but these eyes—whose were they? Under
one or other of two descriptions they all come : eyes
of the sharers in the guilt, with its profit, or eyes—
which, by the devices that have been brought to
view, they had succeeded in blinding, concealing
from them, the cause, and the authors, of the suffering they were experiencing all the while. But
for this blindness, insurrection would have been
universal, the yoke of lawyer-craft shaken off, all
the other devices rendered useless, and universal
abhorrence, not to speak of condign punishment,
the only ultimate fruit reaped from so much ill-
spent labour by the authors.

" To decide, sometimes according, sometimes
not according to the merit—such has been my
habit, such continues my determination." What
a profession this for a judge! In what other class
of men could any instance of such openly avowed

depravity ever have been found? In what other part of the official establishment any such avowal of accomplished inaptitude? Look to the military. My design is sometimes to obey my commanding officer, sometimes to disobey him. Look to the financial. My design is sometimes to hand over to the Treasury the money I have collected; sometimes to put it into my own pocket. Look to the medical profession. My design is sometimes to cure my patients, sometimes to kill them. In the soldier, the tax-collector, and the surgeon, if such there could be, by whom respectively such language could be held, would be seen the exact parallel of the judge, who avowedly and purposely decides otherwise than according to the merits.

In painting the deformity of this practice, can any power of exaggeration go beyond the plain exposition of the simple truth?

In what instance, on what occasion, did the Honorable House ever profess to make a decision, not in accordance with the merits? On the occasion of any dispute between child and child, between servant and servant, did ever any member of a family, non-lawyer, or even lawyer, ever declare himself thus to decide? The essential word *merits*, being a word over the import of which something of a cloud may on this occasion appear to hang, whatsoever may be necessary we humbly hope will not be regarded as misemployed, while employed in dissipating it.

To have a clear view of the sort of operation meant by a deciding *not according* to the merits, a man must first have a correspondently clear view of the sort of operation meant by a deciding *according* to the merits.

Taken in its all-embracing description, a decision *according* to the merits, is in every case a decision by which, on the occasion in question, execution and effect is given to the law: to the really declared will of the legislature in the case of statute law: to the imagined will of the imagined legislature in the case of *common law*, in that sense in which it is synonymous to judge-made law.

In the sort of case called a *civil* case, that which is done by a decision according to the merits, is giving to the plaintiff the benefit claimed by his demand, if so it be that his individual case is contained in the species of case in which it has been declared by the law that, by every individual, whose case is included in that same species of case, a benefit of the sort so designated shall, on his demand, be put in possession by the appropriate judge: thus giving to the plaintiff the benefit in question, if his case is within that same species of case, and thereby of necessity subjecting the defendant to the correspondent burthen: refusing the benefit to the plaintiff if his case, as above, is *not* within the species of case, and thereby keeping the defendant clear and exempt from the correspondent burthen.

In the sort of case called a *penal* case, a decision, according to the merits, is a decision by which the defendant, if guilty, is pronounced guilty: if not guilty, not guilty.

On each occasion, two questions, essentially different, how intimately soever connected, come necessarily under consideration: the question of *law* and the question of *fact*. But of this distinction, for the present purpose, nothing further will

require to be said. Only that it may be seen not
to have been overlooked, is this short mention
made of it.

Such being the description of a decision according to the merits, now, in exact contrast to it, comes
the description of a decision not according to the
merits.

In its general description, as above, a decision
according to the merits being a decision by which,
on the occasion in question, execution and effect
is given to the law: in the case of a decision
not 'according to the merits, on the occasion in
question, execution and effect is *not* given to the
law.

In a civil case, a decision according to the merits
was a decision, by which the plaintiff was put in
possession of the benefit in question, as above: a
decision not according to the merits, is accordingly
a decision, by which, in that same case, the refusal,
express or virtual, is made so to put him in possession, as above.

In a penal case, a decision according to the merits, was a decision by which, if the defendant was
guilty, he was pronounced guilty: if not guilty,
not guilty: a decision not according to the merits,
is accordingly a decision by which, if the defendant
was guilty, he is pronounced not guilty: if not
guilty, guilty.

Here then are four distinguishable forms of injustice: and by every decision not according to
the merits in some one or more of these forms, is
injustice committed.

Moreover, in no other than in one or other of .
these same four forms, by a judge acting as such,
can injustice be committed: into one or more of

them will be found resolvable every decision to which, with propriety, injustice, or say contrariety to justice, can be imputed.

Of the injustice committed by means of this device, the prime instrument is the word *nullification*, with the other words, nouns substantive, nouns adjective and verbs connected with it, and the phrases in the composition of which they have place: null, void, null and void, bad, error, irregularity, flaw, vacate, avoid, avoidance, quash, set aside, annul, nullify, fatal, quirk, quibble.

Compared with this of nullification all other modes put together, in which injustice is capable of being committed by decisions not according to the merits, the importance would be found inconsiderable: the burthen of research and examination would not, on this occasion, be paid for by the benefit of the acquisition.

In the group, composed of these four great aggregates, are united four elementary ingredients, by universal consent acknowledged in the character of so many modifications of injustice; these are punishment *ex-post-facto*, or as some stile it, *retro-active*—disappointment of established expectations, compleat arbitrariness, mis-seated punishment. Of retro-active punishment the so flagrant and incontestable injustice is an established and frequently drawn-upon source of condemnation: and this even under statute law, under which it is so rarely inflicted, even by the worst constituted and worst exercised governments.

In the case of judge-made law, this retro-activity is of the very essence of this species of law, as contradistinguished from statute law: and this even when the decision is on the merits.

⠀But, when *not* on the merits, it stands upon
ground very different from what it does when on
the merits : ground widely different and much
worse.

When *on the merits*, there is always some analogy
between the state of the case on the occasion of
the decision in question, and the state of the
case on some anterior decision or decisions, to
which reference is made : and those to which the
analogy it bears is looked upon as being the closest,
are uniformly those which are looked out for in
preference. How constantly opposite in this respect is the case where the only grounds on which
the decision is formed, are such as avowedly have
nothing to do with the merits !—bear no analogy
whatsoever to the merits !

As to punishment, the name is on this occasion
employed, because whether or no the suffering
produced is produced under the name of punishment, such upon the individual who suffers is the
effect.

Now as to disappointment. Of an occurrence from which expectation of benefit in any
shape experiences disappointment, pain, in some
degree or other, is a constantly attached consequence : in the exclusion put upon this pain may
be seen the sole but perfectly sufficient immediate
reason for giving to every man whatsoever is
deemed his own, instead of suffering another to
get or keep possession of it. No otherwise than
by statute law, and in proportion to the extent of
it, can this so desirable exclusion be effected : by
statute law pre-established, fore-known and fore-
notified. Of judge-made law, the general incapacity
of conveying this same so desirable information is
the essential and distinctive characteristic. But, on

every occasion, as above, even under judge-made law, it is more or less extensively an object of endeavour to confine this sort of uneasy sensation within as narrow bounds as may be; to exclude it altogether, if possible; and at any rate, on each occasion, to render the probability of its having place as small as possible. On the contrary, in the case of a decision not on the merits, the probability of the existence of evil in this shape is at its maximum: in a word, it coincides with certainty. For, unless where, in the individual case in question, corruption, or some uncommon distortion of the intellectual frame, on the part of the judge, is supposed or suspected to have place, by whom is it that the existence of any such phenomenon can naturally be apprehended, as that of a judge so lost to all sense of shame, as to stand forth a self-declared perpetrator of injustice?

Now then by the practice of deciding on grounds palpably foreign to the merits, has power to this degree arbitrary been actually established in themselves by English judges. In general, they are expected to tread in one another's steps: and in the degree, in which this so indispensable habit is conformed to, depends altogether such feeble and even vacillating degree of security, as it is in the power of judge-made law to afford. But when at length the eyes of the public have to a certain degree opened, the evil which has been the result of their thus treading in one another's steps in some cases of quibble, has become so palpable and grossly mischievous—giving impunity, for example, to murderers, because some word has been miswritten or left unwritten by somebody,—when things have come to this pass, not only allowance but applause has been bestowed on a departure.

Then it is that the judge finds himself at perfect liberty to give, or to refuse impunity to the mur-·derer, at pleasure: if he refuses it, liberality is his word: if he gives it, *stare decisis.*

3. Now as to the complete arbitrariness. Arbi-trary to a degree of perfection, if in any case, is the power of a judge in a case in which, without danger either of punishment at the hands of the law, or so much as censure at the hands of public opi-nion, he can give success to plaintiff or to defend-ant, according as he happens to feel inclined. Such is the case where, within his reach, he sees two opposite sources of decision, from either of which he can draw at pleasure: one which will give success to the plaintiff's, the other to the de-fendant's. A sort of vase has been seen, from which, at command, wine, either of one colour or another, has been made to flow. From this em-blem, the name of the *double fountain* principle has been given; to the principle on which, by this means, and in this shape, a power, which to the extent of it is so completely arbitrary, has been established.

To such a pitch of perfection has the exercise of power in this shape been carried, that of late days a judge has been seen scouting the quibble one day, giving effect to it the next: to what cause such inconsistency should be ascribed, whether to corruption, or to that wrong-headedness which, to so great an extent, judge-made law cannot fail to propagate, it is not possible to determine: to-day it is probably wrong-headedness: to-morrow it may be the other cause.

While decision on any other ground than the merits is allowed of, in any case, thus the matter must continue: and for the extirpation of this

I

enormity, nothing short of an entire system of procedure can suffice,

4. Lastly, as to *mis-seated punishment*. Delinquency, such as it is, being imputed to one person, not on him, but on some other—and that other one to whom no delinquency in any shape is imputed, is the burthen of suffering imposed. The attorney (say of the plaintiff) is supposed to have written some word wrong: for this impropriety, real or pretended, if real, intended or unintended, his client, the plaintiff, is made to lose his cause. If the case be of the number of those in which, in conjunction with the individual, the condition of the public at large is considered as suffering, as in the case of robbery and murder, of those in which the evil diffuses itself through the public at large, without infringing on any one individual more than another, as in the case of an offence affecting the revenue: in either of these cases, it is the public that thus, for the act of the individual, is made to suffer: to the guilty individual impunity is thus dealt out: to the not guilty individual, or public, groundless sufferings.

In the expression by which, upon any operation or instrument, *nullification* is pronounced, employment given to a sort of fiction is involved: one operation which has been performed is spoken of as if it had not been performed: the instrument which has been brought into existence is spoken of as not having had existence: at any rate, things are put, and professed to be put, into the state in which they would have been, had no such operation, no such instrument, had place. Amidst instances of mendacity so much more flagrant, scarcely would such a one as this have been worth noticing: but for exemplification and explanation

of the effects, this mention of it may be not without its use. An offender for example, has been
brought to trial, and conviction has ensued : in the
instrument of accusation, (say the *indictment*) one
of those *flaws*, manufactured perhaps for the purpose, has been discovered : in consequence of the
observation, arrest of judgment as the phrase is,
has been pronounced. What is the consequence ?
Whatever *has* been done is to be considered as if it
had *not* been done : information which has been
elicited, is to be considered as not having been
elicited : evidence, by which the fact of the delinquency has been put completely out of doubt, has
been elicited, and with perfect accuracy been committed to writing : it is to be considered as never
having had existence.

In civil cases, the effect is the same—the same
convenient extinction of evidence has place, when
a new trial has been granted and brought on :
though, in this case not being needed, no such
word as *nullification*, or any of its synonyms, as
above, is employed.

Peremptory and *dilatory :* by these two words
are designated the two so widely different effects
produced, in different cases by nullification. Case
in which the triumph of injustice is most compleat,
that in which the effect is peremptory, or say definitive, because a word has been mis-spelt by a
copying clerk, a convicted murderer, for example,
walks out of court, under the eyes of his deliverer
and accessary after the fact—the quibble-sanction-
ing judge, to commit ulterior murders. Throughout the whole field of penal law, of nullification
pronounced on the proceedings on grounds foreign
to the merits, this, according to the general rule,
and expressed in the language of Roman law by

the words *non bis in idem,* is the effect. Needlessly promotive of guilt as this rule would be in any case, it would not be near so amply so as it is, were it not for the blind fixation principle, applied to days, as above. Endless is the variety of accidents—endless the variety of cnntrivances, by any one of which a necessary witness may be kept from being forthcoming at the day and within the hour prescribed; while on a circuit, the judges, with their et ceteras, are circumgirating, as if by steam, on a wheel without a drag.

Humanity, that humanity which has penny wisdom for its counsellor, that humanity which can see the one object under its nose, but not the hundred of the like objècts at a few rods distance, applauds the impunity given in this case: consistency would, if listened to, extend the impunity to all other cases: then would society fall to pieces: and in Blackstone's phrase, everything would be as it should be.

All this supposes the case to be of the number of those called *criminal* or *penal:* for, to these words substitute the word *civil,* the eyes of humanity are closed. In every case called *civil,* a new trial may be granted: in cases called *penal,* not: in the case called *civil,* the loss a defendant stands exposed to, may amount to pounds, by tens of thousands a year: in the case called *penal,* it may not amount to ten shillings; but cases called civil may, on revision, be found pregnant with fees to any amount: cases called penal are comparatively barren.

When the immediate effect is no more than dilatory, the evil is not so *complete,* nor in every part *certain.* But, to a more or less considerable extent, evil has place in every such case—evil by delay; and delay of justice is, so long as it lasts, denial of justice: add to this, evil by expense of the repetition :—that evil, out of which cometh forth that same relative good—Judge and Co.'s profit—the contemplation of which constituted the motive and efficient cause by which the arrangement was produced.

Add now the effect of the instruments of regularly organised delay called *terms* and *circuits*, combined with that of the *blind fixation* principle, applied to *days*. Now, in the case of a new trial, comes an interval, in some cases, of half a year, in others of a whole year, interposed between the original series of proceedings, and the repetitional proceedings, if granted. In this state of things, to a prodigious extent, the dilatory operation of the virtual nullification put upon the original set of proceedings becomes in effect peremptory and conclusive. A necessary witness dies, goes off of himself to the antipodes, or is bought off: of the suitors, at whose charge, in case of nullification, the quibble has been made to operate, or without need of nullification the necessary piece of evidence has been kept out of the way, the purse or the spirits have become exhausted. As often as this has place, the dilatory effect, though in name and outward appearance less pernicious than the peremptory, is in reality much more so: the expected remedy is extinguished : and to the expense and vexation attached to the pursuit of it, a fresh quantity is added.

Such is the advantage which, by the so elaborately and successfully organized system, is given to dishonesty when conjoined with opulence, that, in many instances, to the purpose of the preponderantly opulent depredator or oppressor by whom

the depth of his destined victim's purse has been
sounded, so far as regards ultimate success, the
difference between the peremptory and the dilatory
effect of nullification may be made to vanish.

XII.—*Device the Twelfth.*—*Juries subdued and subjugated.*

Not at the period here in question was this ex-
ploit hatched : juries, it seems probable, were not
at that time in existence. But it was at that period
that the foundation was laid, of the power by which
this subjugation was accomplished : and the only
use of the inquiry being how the yoke imposed on
the people by Judge and Co. may be shaken off—
a yoke of which this forms no inconsiderable a
portion, a topic so important could not be left un-
touched.

The origin of the jury institution is lost in the
clouds of primæval barbarism : inference must
here be called in to do the work of narrative. That
which inference suggests is this. Of some greater
number, twelve or any other determinate number
could not but have been a sort of committee. To
the eyes of the historian not uniformly distinguishable was the entire body and the committee. When
the one supreme criminal judicatory—the sometimes metropolitan, sometimes travelling judicatory
—was instituted, then, all over the country, were
extinguished the small territorial and adequately
numerous local judicatories, in which the inhabi-
tants in general took that part, which, scarcely in
those rude ages, could be well defined, and if ever
so well then defined, could not now be determined
and stated. What was to be done? Even under
the then existing thraldom, subversion, completed
at one explosion, might have been too shocking to

be endurable. "Come to me, wherever I am, and sit under me, as you do now under your several judges. Come to me: I do not say all of you, for in that case all production would be at a stand—but a part of the number selected from the whole: in a word, a committee; and let the number of it be twelve." When from one of these small judicatories, a suit was first called up to the one high and great one, something to this effect must, it should seem, have been said. The shorter the journey, the less burthensome the duty. Whether this be more or less burthensome, the more important the occasion, the more plausible the excuse for the imposition of that same duty. Thus it was, that practice might make its way by degrees. As to the number, why twelve? Answer—Twelve was the number of the apostles: in favour of no other number could so cogent, unanswerable a reason be assigned.

. Be this as it may, in the very nature of the case, never could juries have been altogether acceptable associates to judges. How should they, any more than independent Houses of Commons to Kings? Whatsoever was the disposition of the judge, partial or impartial, crooked or upright, proportioned to the share they took in the business, most frequently by intellectual inaptitude, but sometimes by intellectual aptitude, sometimes by moral aptitude, they would be troublesome. Act they could not without being so. By their mere existence a troublesome duty was imposed upon the judge: the duty of giving something in the shape of a reason for the course prescribed by him.

. Here then, on each occasion, on the neck of the judge was a yoke, which, if it could not be shaken off, was to be rendered as light as possible. In case of non-compliance, it might by nullification, as hath been seen, be got rid of. But nullification, as hath also been seen, did but half the business. True it is, that when applied to cases called *civil;* it could always prevent a well-grounded demand from taking effect; but it could not so constantly give effect to an ungrounded one. Applied to *penal* cases, it could at pleasure give impunity to crime; but especially in capital and other highly penal cases, scarcely of itself could it be made to subject innocence to punishment.

What remained applicable was a compound of intimidation and delusion: intimidation, applied to the will; delusion, to the understanding.

Of the intimidation employed, the one word *attaint*, will serve to bring to view a specimen. Persons, all twelve, imprisoned; moveables, all forfeited; dwellings, all laid low; habitations, lands, completely devastated; with et ceteras upon et ceteras. Maleficence must have been drunk when it came out with this Pandora's box: actual cautery applied, as often as a flea-bite was to be cured. Down to the present hour, this is law: continued such by judge-made law. In the course of a few centuries, statute law added a few trifles, that these serious things might remain unaffected. Statute law is repealable: common law unrepealable. Parliaments are allowed to correct their own errors: judges, under the name of the tyrant phantom, remain irresistible, uncontrolable, and incorrigible. No otherwise, it is true, than by compliance on the part of twice the number, could vengeance be taken for the non-compliance of the twelve. But the instances first chosen for this infliction would naturally be those in which, on the part of the sufferers, the delinquency had been least questionable. At any rate, upon Judge and Co. would infliction in such sort depend, that, of non-compliance, *attaint* could scarcely fail to present itself as a more or less probable consequence.

Of an infliction thus atrocious, the frequency, as it presents itself in the books, is perfectly astounding to a reflecting mind. No otherwise than by attaint, could the effect produced in these days by new trial, be produced in those. As often as a new trial is granted now, conceive the Pandora's box opened there.

Note well the efficiency of the instrument. Like the fabled razors, it performs the work of itself, without need of a hand to guide it. As it is with corruption, so is it with intimidation. To produce the effect, neither discourse nor expression of will in any other shape, is necessary : for the production of the effect, relative situation is perfectly sufficient. Where the intimidation was inapplicable, afterwards when at length the stream of civilization had washed it away altogether,—remained, as the only instruments applicable, arrogance and cajolery. Of the two instruments, arrogance was, of course, to the operator, the more acceptable. The use of it presented no great difficulty. " The law (quoth the judge) is so and so." So far the judge, but what law? No law was there in the case. Who made it? The law—meaning that portion of it to which he gave the force of law—it was he who made it; made it out of his own head, made it for his own purpose, whatsoever that purpose happened to be.

Take for example libel law. A libel? What is it? Answer—If I am a judge, any piece of printed paper, it would be agreeable to me to punish the man for. Is he a man I choose to punish? I make it a libel : is he a man I choose not to punish? I make it a non-libel. But is it possible that, to a man in power, it should be agreeable to leave unpunished any individual audacious enough to say anything otherwise than agreeable to a man in power? O yes; it is just possible. Witness Morning Chronicle in the days of *Perry*, and Lord Chief Justice Ellenborough.

Now suppose a *code* in existence. Juries are now emancipated. Judges in effect now : no longer dupes ; no longer tools ; and, by the shackles imposed on the mind, made slaves. Judges in effect now, because ennobled and qualified so to be. The law (say they) is so and so : how should it be otherwise? Not be what they thus say it is? The book is opened : there the passage is—they see it. More effectually learned would be the least learned juryman in such a state of things, than, under the existing system, the most learned judge.

To the *existing* system apply (be it remembered) these remarks : not to an improved system, under which judges would be made responsible, and appeals to a superior judicator, effectual, as well as the appeal to public opinion, strengthened by extension given to publication : under such a system, greater might be the power reposed in the experienced, less in the unexperienced hands.

" Thus stands the law !". Under the existing system, when a declaration to this effect is made by a judge, from what set of men, in the situation of jurymen, can non-compliance, how necessary soever to justice, be ordinarily expected? In this case, that being assumed as true, which, in every common law case, is so opposite to true—that is to say, the existence of the law in question—to the judge must this same law be known, if to any body; as to these his unlearned pupils, to them it is completely unknown: so the inward consciousness of each man of them testifies. With the law, which thus, at the very moment of its being made, is revealed to them, begins and ends their knowledge. In such a state of things, so effectually, by the consciousness of their own ignorance, were they and are they blinded, their appointed guides may, to any degree be blind, without being seen by them to be so. Under these circumstances, what but blind compliance could, then be—aye, or can now be—the general practice? What exceptions there are, are such as are formed by here and there a rare occurrence, operating upon a rarely exemplified set of dispositions.

Of the acquitted decapitator, mention has been made above. If, by a union of past absurdity and present arrogance, a jury can be brought to this, to what is it they can not be brought? But, in that case, how much is to be ascribed to judge's influence, how much to jurymen's abhorrence of death in the character of a punishment, can not be affirmed with certainty: and so long as the punishment is death, impunity will, every day, be approaching nearer and nearer to the being every day's practice.

XIII.—*Device the Thirteenth.—Jurisdiction where it should be entire, split and spliced.*

Jurisdiction has two fields—the *local* and the *logical*: the *local*, or say. *territorial*, divided into *tracts* of *territory*; the logical, divided into *sorts of cases*. In the local field, that which the interests of justice require is, as hath been seen, *multiplicity*; in the logical field, as will be seen, *unity*. So much for reason: now for practice. Where, by

the interests of justice, multiplicity was required,
the interest of Judge and Co. established, as has
been seen, the *unity:* where, by the interests of
justice, unity was and is required, the opposite
interest of judicature, that is to say, that same
sinister interest will now be seen establishing *multiplicity.*

From the expression *jurisdiction split,* let it not
be conceived, as if at the initial point of time in
question, the field of legislation was, in its whole
extent, covered as it were by one large block; and
that, at different times thereafter, by the introduction of wedges or otherwise, the block was broken
into the existing splinters, connected together, as
they may be seen to be, by the conjunct sinister
interest. The case is, that it is by degrees, as
will be seen, that the aggregate composed of the
splinters has been brought into its present so commodious state : namely, in some instances by fissure, in other instances by the gradual addition
of portions. of new matter *spliced* to the older.
Splitting and *splicing*—by the union of these two
operations has the actual aggregate result been
brought into existence.

Matter of the aggregate this. Of the substantive branch of law different masses, three or four :
and, for giving execution and effect to them, more
than twice as many of the matter of the adjective
or say procedure branch of law; constituted every
one of them, chiefly of the fictitious, or say judge-
made sort; with only here and there a patch of
real law—of legislature-made law—stuck in.

In the *keeping* of these portions of matter in the
hands of different sets of judges, not in the *originally placing* them in these or any other separate
hands, consists, at present, the sinister practice—

the *device :* in the union of them, in each territory, in one and the same hand, the sole remedy.

As to the *splitting,* in some instances, the operation, by which it was effected, was performed at one stroke; that is to say by one statute : call the mode, in this case, the *all-at-once* or *declared* mode; in other instances, silently, gradually, and imperceptibly: call it, in this case, the *undeclared* or *gradual* mode.

So likewise, as to the *splicing.*

Short description of the modes of operation in the two processes this.

Original stock or block, the grand judicial authority, instituted by William the Conqueror, and stiled the *Aula Regis :* Anglicé, the *King's-hall* or *court.* .

1. Splinter the first, court *Christian,* alias *Spiritual,* alias *Ecclesiastical :* species of operation, difficult to say whether the splitting or the splicing. Mode of operation, at any rate, the *gradual.* By the terror of punishment in the future life, it acquired as will be seen, powers of legislation and judicature in the present.

2. Splinter the second, courts of *Exchequer,* stock or block, as above. the *Aula Regis* jurisdiction. Out of the *administrative* authority, now called *the Receipt of the Exchequer,* instituted for the collection of the revenue, grew the *judicative,* called the court of Exchequer. Where contestation has place, if and in so far as professional assistants are called in, *administration* becomes *judicature.* Mode of operation, gradual; members of the court, a portion of those of the *Aula Regis.*

3. Splinter the third, chancellor's jurisdiction. Stock or block, the Aula Regis jurisdiction. This functionary, decidedly a member of the Aula Regis,

officiated therein as Secretary of State: and, at the same time, his being the office from which issued the instruments, still stiled *original writs*—instruments, by which commencement was given to so many sorts of suits, exercised thereby, in subordination to the legislative authority of the monarch, a sort of unperceived, but not the less real authority of the same kind. Species of operation, the splitting: mode, the gradual.

4. Splinter the fourth, jurisdiction of the court of Common Pleas. Stock or block, the jurisdiction of the Grand Justiciary. Species of operation, the *splitting*. Mode, the *all-at-once* mode. Splitting instrument, *Magna Charta:* remnant of the original stock or block, the court of King's Bench. Business now stiled *civil*, allotted to the Common Pleas; business now stiled *criminal* or *penal*, reserved to the King's Bench: also, either reserved by original institution, or acquired by encroachment, the appellate's superiority over the Common Pleas.

5. Splinter the fifth, equity jurisdiction of the Chancellor's court. Stock or block, the aggregate of this same functionary's authority. Species of operation, splicing: mode silent, unperceived, gradual. Remnants, the common law business now stiled the *Petty-bag* jurisdiction: petty in name, petty in bulk and nature.

6. Splinter the sixth, equity jurisdiction of the court of Exchequer. Stock or block, the common law business of that same court. Species of operation, splicing. Mode unperceived, gradual: performed in imitation of the Chancellor's equity jurisdiction.

7. Splinter the seventh, Bankrupt Petition court. Stock or block, the chancery jurisdiction.

Species of operation, splicing. Mode, the all-at-once mode. Splicing instrument, the statute 34 and 35 Henry VIII. ch. 4.

8. Splinter the eighth, Insolvency court, Stock or block, again the chancery jurisdiction. Species of operation, splicing. Mode, the all-at-once mode. Splicing instrument, 53 Geo. III. ch. 102: Subsequentially applied instruments, 54 Geo. III. ch. 28, and 3 Geo. IV. ch. 123.

9. Splinter the ninth, jurisdiction of the justices of the peace acting collectively in general sessions. Stock or block, the King's Bench jurisdiction. Species of operation, splicing: mode, the *all-at-once* mode: splicing instrument, statute 1st, Edw. III. st. 2, ch. 16.

10. Splinter the tenth, jurisdiction of justices of the peace, acting collectively in not fewer than two at a time in petty sessions. Stock or block—original, the King's Bench jurisdiction, as above: immediate, the above-mentioned general sessions jurisdiction. Species of operation, splicing: splicing instruments, various consecutive statutes. On the part of each, mode of operation, the all-at-once mode: on the part of the aggregate, the most thoughtful, silent, or unperceived and gradual.

11. Splinter the eleventh, jurisdiction of justices of the peace, acting severally throughout the suit. Stock or block—original, the King's Bench jurisdiction: immediate, the general sessions jurisdiction, as above. Species of operation, mode of operation, and instrument, as above.

12. Splinter the twelfth, jurisdiction allotted to justices of the peace, acting severally, and exercising, at the outset of a suit, a fragment of

jurisdiction: the suit being, for its completion, transferred to some one of four other judicatories: as to which, see above, Device XI, *Needless transference and bandying:* stock or block—the King's Bench jurisdiction. Species of operation, splicing. Mode, the all-at-once mode. Splicing instrument, statute 1 and 2 Phil. and Mary, ch. 13.

13. Splinter the thirteenth, jurisdiction of small debt courts. Original stock or block, the *court of Requests*, in Westminster-hall, long since abolished. Species of operation, splicing: mode, in the instance of each, the all-at-once mode: splicing instruments, a multitude of statutes, each confining its operations to some narrow portion of territory.

Note, that in almost every one of these cases, the course taken for the ascertainment of the truth, in relation to the matter of fact, is different: as to this presently.

Ecclesiastical judicatories for maintenance of discipline among ecclesiastical functionaries:—military judicatories for maintenance of discipline among land-service military functionaries:—the like in relation to sea-service military functionaries. Admiralty prize courts: on the subject of these judicatories, the demand for explanation not being cogent, and room being deficient, the sole purpose of the mention here made of them is the apprehension lest, otherwise, they should be supposed to have been overlooked.

Mark here the chaos! Different branches, or say masses, of substantive law, spun out in this dark way by judge-made law, thus lamentably numerous! and for giving execution and effect to them, to each a different mass of procedure, or say adjective law: masses framed in so many different modes, and upon different principles! ·

Single-justice courts, petty sessions courts, and small debt courts, the more entitled to remark, as affording, perhaps, the only instances in which judicial procedure has had for its main ends the ends of justice. ·

Essentially repugnant to the ends of justice (need it be said?) essentially repugnant, if anything can be—this system of disunion: proportionably subservient to the actual ends of judicature: hence the arrangement so recently employed in keeping it up: in particular, as between equity courts and common law courts.

Conducive to the ends of justice will this splitting and splicing work be said to be? Well then: here follow a few improvements, on the same principle. To the *bankruptcy* court, add a *stock-breaking* court: to the *insolvency* court, a *non-solvency* court, a *non-payment* court, a *non-liquidation* court, and a *non-discharge* court: each, with a different mode of procedure. Taking for the twelfth-cake the jurisdiction of the *aula regis*, let lots be drawn by all these courts, for these their respective stiles and titles. · Allot to each of these courts one commissioner to begin with; then three commissioners (the number in the *insolvency* court in its improved state), then the square of three, 9; then the cube of three, 27; then the fourth power of three, 81; by which last the number of the commissioners of *bankrupts*, or *bankruptcy*, will be surpassed by eight, and proportionally improved upon. To secure what is called *qualification*, meaning thereby *appropriate aptitude*, impose as a task and test the having par-

K

taken of a certain number of *dinners*, in some one of four great halls. Of situations of different sorts, in, under, or about these courts, number capable of being occupied by the same person at the same time, ten.; by which the number occupied by a son of the ex-chancellor, the Earl of Eldon, will be outstript by *one*. To complete the improvement, conclude with pensions of retreat, after ten years' service, and pensions for widows, orphans, and upon occasion, sisters.

At the end of a certain length of time, the existing incumbents will be found, each of them, at the same time insufficiently and more than sufficiently apt, as was the case with the metropolitan police magistrates : then will be the time for adding one-third to their salaries : with or without the like addition to the other just mentioned so equitable and comfortable appendage.

We proceed now to present to the view of the Honourable House the evils, of which this system of disunion is, and so long as it continues in existence cannot but be, so abundantly productive : we shall point out the cause by which it has been produced : namely, the mixture composed of primæval inexperience and sinister interest.

In particular, in regard to imprisonment for debt, on its present footing, to wit, at the commencement of the suit—a period at which it is so frequently groundless, and so constantly ungrounded, it will be seen that it had no better origin and efficient cause, than sinister interest, in its foulest shape : special original cause, as will be seen, of this abuse, the splitting of the Common Pleas jurisdiction from that of the King's Bench ; thereafter immediate cause, the grand battle between the two courts, in the reign of Charles the Second.

The use of confusion has already been brought to view: behold now one pre-eminently useful mode or efficient cause of, it. In the practice of a large proportion of all these courts, both branches of law spun out together, the substantive branch out of the adjective, in the shape of *twist*, by the judge in the course of the operations of procedure, the twist afterwards woven into piece goods by the firm of report-maker, report-maker's bookseller, abridgment-maker, and his abridgment's bookseller: and in this way it is, that, on pretence of judicature, even the whole field of law, power of legislation continues to be exercised: exercised by the combination of such essentially and flagrantly incompetent hands!

Are you a chief justice? Have you a law to make? to make on your old established mode? The following is your *recipe*. Take any word or number of words the occasion requires: choosing, as far as they go, such as are already in the language: but if more are wanted, you either take them from another language. old French or Latin, or make them out of your own head. To these words you attach what sense you please. To enable you to do, by this means, whatever you please, one thing only is now wanting. This is, that, in the accustomed form, by some person other than yourself (for you cannot yourself, as in some countries, give *commencement* to a suit), the persons and things to be operated upon must be brought before you by the king's attorney-general, or an individual in the character of plaintiff. This done, you go to work, according to the nature of the case. Is it a civil one? To the plaintiff you give or refuse as much of defendant's property as is brought before you. Is it a criminal or

say penal one? you apply, or refuse to apply, to
the defendant, the whole, or more, or less, of the
punishment demanded for him at your hands.
This you do in the first instance before and without any law to authorise you : for no such autho-
rising law have you any need of : after which, in
the way just mentioned, what you have done receives, in print, authority, extension and perma-
nence, from the abovementioned hands, being by
them manufactured into a sort of fictitious law
doing the office of, and upon occasion overruling,
an act of parliament.

From the process pursued in the principal of
these manufactories, a conception, it is hoped,
tolerably clear and correct, may be formed, of the
manner in which this species of manufacture has
been, and continues to be, carried on.   These
are—1. Equity courts.   2. Common law courts.
3. Courts christian, alias spiritual, alias ecclesiastical courts.

I. Turn first to the self-stiled *equity courts*. Words
comprising the raw materials, *trust, fraud, accident,
injunction, account*, with the word equity at their
head—here we have the whole stock of them or
thereabouts : stock in *words* small : but in *matter*
as abundant as heart can desire.   One of them,
the master-word *equity*—so rich is it, that out of
it, and by the strength of it, anything could yet,
and to this day can be done, that lust of power or
money can covet.   What can it not do? It can
take any wards, every infant, out of the arms of
any and every father, and at the father's expense,
keep cramming it with the pap of imposture and
corruption, till the father is reduced to beggary,
and the entire mass of the child's, rendered as foul
as that of the crammer's mind.

Equity?, what means it? A bettermost, yes, and *that* the very best, sort of justice. But, justice being, the whole together, so good a thing, what must not this very best sort be? Be it what it may, that which, on each occasion, is done by the judge of an equity court, is it not equity? Well then, by the charm attached to this fascinating word, to whatsoever he does, not only compliance and acquiescence, but admiration and laud, in the accustomed and requisite quantity, are secured.

II. Next as to the *common* law courts; and in particular the great criminal law court—the *King's Bench.*

Conspiracy, blasphemy, libel, malice, breach of peace, bonos mores, with their et cæteras, of these raw materials is composed the stock of the common law manufactory. That which equity does for chancellor, that or thereabouts, the single word, *conspiracy,* would of itself be sufficient to do for chief justice of King's Bench. With this word in his mouth, what is it a chief justice can not do? who is there he can not punish? what is there he can not punish for?

Persons *conspire,* things *conspire*—to produce effects of all kinds, good as well as *bad.* In the very import of the word conspiracy is therefore included the conspiracy to do a bad thing: now then so as proof has been but given of a conspiracy, that is to say, of the agreeing to do a something, or the talking about the agreeing to do it, the badness of this same something, and the quality and quantity of the badness, follow of course: they follow from the *vis termini,* the very meaning of the word, and may therefore without special proof be assumed.

So far, so good, where you have two or more

to punish. But how if there be but one? In this case a companion must be found for him. But this companion it is not necessary he should have a name : he may *be a person unknown* : for, because one of two criminals is unknown, is it right that the other should escape from justice?

So much for the King's Bench manufactory taken singly. Now for ditto and Common Pleas *united*, cases and suits called *civil: verbal stock* here—*case, trover, assumpsit*, with their et cæteras.

Conspiracy, blasphemy, peace and malice— these words were found already in the language, and, whatsoever was the occasion or the purpose, required only a little twisting and wresting to make them fit it. *Bonos mores, trover*, and *assumpsit* had to be imported ; *bonos mores* and *assumpsit*, from Italy ; *trover*, from France : all of them had to undergo, in the machinery, more or less of im- provement, ere they were fit for use. *Face* would would have been as intelligible as *case*, and served as well, had fortune been pleased to present it ; *clover*, as *trover: mumpsit* as *assumpsit:* but *case, trover*, and *assumpsit*, had fortune on their side.

III. Now as to *Court Christian*. No *fissure*, violent or gradual, requisite here. Nothing requi- site to be done otherwise than in the quiet way, by *splicing :* by splicing performed imperceptibly, and in the dark ; in the pitchy darkness of the very earliest ages : no need of custom, of snatching, in the manner that will be seen presently, from any other branch of the Judge and Co. firm : simple addition was the only change needed.

Mode of proceeding, or say *recipe* this. Take any act of any person at pleasure, call it a *sin :* add to it a punishment, call the punishment a *penance.* Observe that the agent has a *soul :* say, that the soul wants to have good done to it : say that the penance will do this good to it. If, frightened at the word *sin*, the people endure to be thus dealt with, any body is employed to accuse any body of any one of these sins : if then he fails to make answer in proper form, you make him do this *penance* : so, of course, in case of conviction.

Now as to *fees*. Fees you receive for calling for the answer : fees for allowing it to be made : fees for making it ; and so on successively for every link in the chain. But, suppose no such answer made ? Oh, then comes *excommunication* : an operation, by which, whether he does or does not think that he will be made miserable in the *other* world, he will at any rate be made sufficiently so in *this*.

A circumstance particularly convenient in this case, was and is, that, besides the fees received in the course of the prosecution, the penance and the excommunication themselves have been made liquifiable into fees.

Sin, in this case, it was necessary should be the word : not *crime* or *civil injury*. But the same obnoxious act might, and may still, be made to receive all these different appellations ; and, on account of it, the agent dealt with in so many different ways ; made, to wit, after the truth of it has, by the three different authorities, in and by their several different and mutually inconsistent processes, been ascertained.

The act supposes a blow, and the sufferer, a clergyman. Common Pleas gives to this same sufferer money for remedy to the civil injury : King's Bench takes money from the man of violence, for the king : Court Christian takes money from the same for the good of his soul, distributing

the bonus among the reverend divine's spiritually
learned brethren.

True it is, that, upon proper application made,
—one of these same judicatories, (the King's
Bench to wit,) may stop proceedings in one of the
others—the Court Christian to wit. But defendant
—what gets he by this? One certain suit, for the
chance of ridding himself of another. And note,
that in this fourth suit, the mode of establishing
the fact which is the ground of the application is
different from every one of the modes respectively
pursued in the other three.

Such is this species of manufacture : spinning,
out of words, the sort of piece-goods called *law*,
and *that* of the goodness that cloth would be of, if
spun out of cobwebs. Now then, even from early
time—time so early as the year 1285—time not
posterior by more than two centuries to the original period all along in question—what need or
pretence has there been for it? Not any. So
early as the year 1285, Parliament gave birth to
an idea, by which, had it been pursued, appropri-
ately-made law might in no small proportion have
been made in such sort as to occupy the place
usurped by the spurious sort thus spun out blind-
fold, in the *ex-post-facto* way, in the course of judicature. At the tail of a paragraph, having for
its subject-matter an odd corner of the field of law,
the scribe of that day, as if by a sudden inspira-
tion, soars aloft, and as if from an air-balloon,
casting his eyes over the entire field, goes on and
says, " And whensoever from henceforth it shall
fortune in the Chancery, that in one case a writ is
found, and a like case, falling under the law, and
requiring like remedy, is found, the clerks of the

Chancery shall agree in making the writ:" after which, for appropriate confirmation, follows reference duly made to the superordinate authority, the next Parliament.

Behold here provision made for codification. Here was seed sown, but the soil not yet in a state to admit of the growth of it. In the barbarous mode of *ex-post-facto* judge-made law, were therefore of necessity fumbled out such indispensable arrangements, without which society could not have been kept together.

For ages, by common law alone, equity not being grown up to sufficient maturity, were these arrangements made. But, after all that had been thus done, and amidst all that was afterward doing by common law, abundant and urgent remained the need of such arrangements, in addition to those the topics legislated upon, in this same blind and spurious mode, by chancellors, with the word *equity* in their mouths, may serve to show.

1. *Trust*, 2. *fraud*, 3. *accident;* these three have been already mentioned. Add to them—4. *injunction*, (meaning *prohibition*,) as to use made of property in unmoveables : 5. *injunction* as to pursuit of remedy at common law : 6. *account;* expressions all these so handy and commodious, because single-worded. Add to them moreover, 7. obligations to deliver *in kind things* due : 8. obligation to perform *in kind services* due ; these, with the exception of *injunction* as applied to common law *suits*, belonging to substantive law. Add, to all, the following, which belong to adjective law, or say judicial procedure : 9. elicitation of evidence, from the parties on both sides,—oral from their testimony, real and written from their possession : 10. At the time allotted to elicitation of orally elicited

evidence, the quantum rendered always adequate to the demand : 14. elicitation and recordation made, for eventual use, without actual suit.

All these objects had and still has common law, as we shall show, left in a manner to shift for themselves : left either without any provision at all made for them, or without any other than such by which the purpose can not, in any tolerably adequate degree, be answered.

Think now, of the enormity of the deficiency left, and inaptitude exhibited, by the assemblage of all these gaps.

1. First as to *trust*. Think of a system of law, under which, in relation to this head, nothing or next to nothing was done. Over the whole field of law, particularly over the *civil*, extends the demand, for the matter which belongs to the head of *trust*. Power exercisable for the benefit of the possessor, it is called *power* : power, in so far as not exercisible but for the benefit of some *other* person or persons, is called *trust*. In particular, in the hands of all public functionaries, considered as such, what power soever has place, is so much trust.

2. Secondly, as to *fraud*. Over the whole expanse of the field of law, more particularly the penal branch, extends the need of provision in relation to *fraud :* in whatever shape *maleficence* operates, *fraud* shares with *violence* the privilege of officiating as its instrument.

3. Thirdly, as to *accident*. Of the import of this term, the vagueness immediately strikes the eye. But, for bringing to view some conception of the application on this occasion made of it,—the two words—*conveyance* and *obligatory-engagement*, may here serve. Of the provisions requisite to be

made under this head, the principal beneficial purpose is the *prevention of disappointment :* the grand and all-comprehensive purpose, by which the purport of the portion of law occupied in the giving security for property, requires to be determined.

4. Fourthly, as to *injunction,* applied to the purpose of restraining mischief to immoveable property: *injunction,* meaning interdiction, or say inhibition or prohibition : for, in ordinary language, we speak of *enjoining* a man to *do* a thing, as well as to *forbear* doing it. As to the operation, performed under this name by a Court of Equity, it has for its correspondent and opposite operation that which, under the name of a *mandamus,* is performed in the courts of common law. In the case of the *mandamus,* the act commanded is a *positive* act; in the case of the *injunction,* a *negative* act.

Note here, by the bye, that to the provision made by both these remedies together belongs the property of inadequateness.. For, to the evil, whatsoever may have been the amount of it, which, antecedently to the attempt made by them respectively to stop it, has already taken place—no remedy do they attempt or so much as profess, to make application of: no compensative remedy, no satisfaction in any other shape, no punitive : and at the charge of an honest, what is the profit which a dishonest man will not be ready to make, if assured that the worst that can happen to him for it, is the being stopt from making more ? To himself no punishment; to the party wronged no satisfaction ? But, as to any such ideas as those of all-comprehensiveness and *adequacy,* nearer would they be to a bed of Colchester oysters, than they are to a bench of English judges! A bench—what-

soever be the number of seats on it, whether one,
four, or twelve.

5. Fifthly, *Injunction*, as applied to the pursuit
of remedy at common law. Now for a riddle.
To itself by itself this operation would not naturally
be expected to be seen applied: it would be to
the same operation performed by equity, what
suicide is to the species generally understood by
the name of *homicide*. As little would it, under
the same judicial establishment, have been applied
to the operations of any judicatory, by another
calling itself a *Court of Equity*, if, to common
sense, in union with common honesty, it were
possible to obtain admission into such a theatre.
Setting up one judicatory, to put a stop, at the
command of any man that will pay for it, to the
operations of another, and frustrate what in profession were its designs, and thus, without so much
as a supposition of error on the part of the judicatory so dealt with, in an arrangement such as
this, may be seen a flower of ingenuity that
assuredly would in vain be looked for in any other
field than that of English judicature. But, though
no common law court, as such, nor therefore any
common law court which is merely a common law
court, has as yet, it is believed, been in the practice of thus dealing by itself, yet an English judicatory there is, which, being, like the Marine
Corps, of an amphibious, and moreover of an am-
bodextrous nature, has been, and as often as called
upon continues to be, in the practice of robbing the
chancery shop of this part of its custom, by employing one of its hands in tying up the other, and
one portion of its own thinking part, such as it is,
in frustating what had in profession been the

designs of the other. This riddle is the *Court of Exchequer*. For a parallel, suppose this : Enactment that no public building shall ever be erected —no church, no palace, no prison, no posthouse— without employment successively given to two architects, the first to erect a building in one style —say the Gothic—the second to pull it down, and erect upon the site of it another in a different style — say the Grecian. Taken in both its parts, matched thus in absurdity would the Equity injunction system be : exceeded it would not be : were the mental cause of the evil mere folly without knavery, Gotham itself would find itself here out-Gothamised.

6. Sixthly, as to *Account*. Think of a judiciary establishment, with three superior courts in it, professing, each of them, to settle mutual accounts to any amount, and on that ground receiving fees before any thing is done, and, at the hands of all applicants : these professed auditors two out of the three all the while unprovided with the machinery, without which that which they undertake to do, cannot be done.

The case is—the process of account is—not, as in other cases a simple and transitory, but a compound and a continuous process, the subject-matter being an aggregate, composed of two sets of demands ; made one on each side, each of them, in case of contestation, capable of affording the matter of a separate suit. The process, continuous as it is, the Common Pleas the only one of the three courts which, in a case between subject and subject, took cognizance of it by right, gave itself no means of performing, otherwise than within the relatively short and determinate space of time, into which the business, if performed at all, could be

injected and condensed, like the business of a *play*,
under the dominion of the unities.   This business
the only judicatory capable of going through in all
cases, is the Equity Court.   This has, it is true,
machinery enough, and takes time enough.   But,
the machinery of it, having for its object and effect,
the multiplication of fees, and thence the prolong-
ation of time, the only sure result is the division
of a large proportion, if not the whole, of the property of the accountant parties, among the tribe of
auditors : and it is like a prize in a lottery, if any
portion of the net balance finds its way into the
pocket of him to whom it is due.

7. Seventhly, *as to delivery of things to the right
owner:* the case of *restitution* included.   Think of
a system of law, by which no one moveable thing
whatsoever *was*, or to this day *is*, so much as
undertaken to be secured to the rightful owner!
No: not so much as *undertaken*.   For, if a man,
not even imagining himself to have right on his
side has possessed himself (as, without exposing
himself to punishment he may do) of whatever
moveable thing of yours, you most value—(a horse,
a picture, an unpublished manuscript, for example)
—what remedy have you? An *action*. Behold
now how much better off, in this case, your dishonest adversary, the wrong-doer, is, than you, the
party wronged!   Only in case of its not being
worth so much as it is valued at, does he give you
back what he has thus robbed you of.

And by this action, what, even in case of success, is the utmost you can get? Not (unless the
man, who has thus injured you, so pleases) the
thing itself, but; instead of it, what is called the
value of it: this value being what has been set
upon it at full gallop, by twelve men brought

together by chance: twelve men, not one of them, unless by accident, understands anything about the matter. The estimate having been thus made, this same wrong-doer it is, who, after the days or months he has had for consideration, takes his choice and determines whether to let you have your property back again, or to convert it to his own use. And this money, when the jury have awarded it to you, will you have it clear? Not you, indeed: not this money will you have, but the difference between this and what you will have to pay your attorney, after he has *received* what, in the name of *costs*, has been awarded to you at the expense of the wrong-doer. And the amount of that same *money received*—what will it be? Something or nothing, or less than nothing, as it may happen: provided always that the said wrong-doer has the money, and *that* money capable of being reached by the so precariously effective process of the law: estates in land, money in the funds, shares in joint-stock companies, with property in an indetermediate number of other shapes, being of the number of things not thus reachable.

8. Eighthly, as to *fulfilment of obligatory engagements*. Think of a system of law, which gives not effect to any one sort of engagement, which men, living in society, have need to enter into, unless the intended violator of the engagement pleases.

In this case, behold the same favour to the wrong-doer as in the just mentioned case: instead of fulfilment, money received from the dishonest man, if he has it, and choose to give it, fulfilment effected; unless he choose to give it, none. Agree, for example, for the purchase of an estate. Common law does not so much as profess to give it you. Natural procedure would give it you in a few days. Equity will give it you or not give it you, but when? At the end of several times the number of years.

The case is, that, bating the obtainment of a lot of land in entirety, or a portion of it by partition among co-proprietors, or a portion by a writ called an *elegit*, in lieu of a debt,—a process too complicated and rarely exemplified to be worth describing here,—such is the lameness of the law, that, for administering to a party wronged, satisfaction for the wrong, the only species of remedy, which the common law partners in the firm of Judge and Co. are (saving the narrow exception afforded by the case of a *mandamus*,) to this hour provided with, is *that* which consists in money: money of the defendant's, if, after paying charges, by good fortune any such money is left, and can moreover be come at: for which purpose, the sheriff of the county, that is to say, under his name, and by his appointment, a nobody knows who seizes and causes to be sold whatever is comeatable and saleable: the remedial system being in such a state, that a man may have to the amount of any number of millions in the shape of government annuities, and each one of a variety of other shapes, without the sheriff's being able, were he ever so well disposed, to come at a penny of it: one consequence of which is, that a dishonest man, with other men's money in his hands, may consume it in luxuries, or do anything else with it he pleases, if he had rather continue in a comfortable apartment in a prison, than part with it.

So much as to substantive law: now as to adjective law, and therein as to evidence.

9. Ninthly, *as to elicitation of evidence from the*

testimony and the possession of parties. Think of a
set of judges, with whom it was and still is a
principle, to keep justice inexorably destitute of
evidence from this its most natural, most instructive, and oftentimes sole and thence indispensably
needful, source!

A defendant (suppose) is in court. Is this or is
it not your hand-writing? My lord chief justice—
will he put any such question to him? Not he,
indeed. Will he suffer it to be put to him? As
little. Good reason why. Infinite is the crop of
fees, that would be nipt in the bud by any such
impertinence: and if a question of this sort were
to be allowed to be put, what reason could be
given for refusing to give allowance to any other?

Considering how unpleasant it would be to a
dishonest man, with an honest man's money in his
hands, to part with it; still more so to a malefac-
tor to do anything that could contribute to his
punishment—considering all this, and in all sin-
cerity sympathizing with these their partners and
best friends—conscience, in these tender hearts,
revolts at the idea of any such cruelty. Thus it is
with the common law branch of the firm.

Somewhat less sensitive are the nerves of the
equity branch. Evidence it *has* brought itself to
draw from this so surely reluctant source. But it
is on one condition: and that is—that years be
employed in doing that which might be so much
better done in a few minutes, and pounds by hundreds or thousands in doing that which might be
so much better done at no expense.

10. Tenthly, *as to the time allotted to the elicitation of really elicited evidence; and the adjustment of
the quantity of it to the demand.* Very little to the
taste of the common law branch is any apt adjust-

L

ment of this sort. In what manner .it..reconciles
opposite mischiefs—*delay* and *precipitation*—turning them both to account, has been shewn under
these same heads. General rule—the less the
quantity of such evidence, and the less the time
consumed in the elicitation of it, the better : for
nothing is there to be got by it. As to elicitation
in the *epistolary* mode, nothing, even at this time
of day, does common law know of any such thing.
For this employment of the pen, neither at the
primæval period in question, nor for many centuries thereafter, were hands sufficient to be found.
That sort for which alone there was, in all that
time, *clerk power* in sufficiency, was that which,
being essentially false, was distinguished, as abovementioned, by the name of *pleadings* — written
pleadings : and by which, as much money thus
employable as the pecuniary means of the country
could furnish, was to be got. So much for common law. For equity it was that fortune reserved
this the richest mine in the field of procedure.
Observing how much was to be got by penman-
ship, it sets its inventive genius to work, and
having invented this new mode of elicitation, stept
in, proffered its services, and got to itself this new
branch of the evidence-eliciting business : terms
and conditions as usual : time, by years : pounds,
by hundreds or thousands, as above.

　　Under the head of the *mendacity device* reference is made to the present one, for a hot-
bed, and mode of culture, in and by which this
fruit, so delicious to learned palates, is forced.
Now for a sketch of it. Frequently, not to say
generally, a part more or less considerable, of the
evidence necessary to substantiate the plaintiff's
cause, has for its source the recollection of the

defendant. Of course, not always without more
or less of hurt to his feelings can this sort of information be furnished by this same defendant. In
tender consideration thereof, common law judges,
as above, refuse so much as to call upon him, or
even to suffer him, to furnish it. The keeper of
the great seal and of the king's conscience, is not
quite so difficult. He has his terms however to
make with the plaintiff, and they are these.
" Whatever the defendant knows that will help
your case, you will, of course," says his lordship
to the plaintiff, " be for asking him for, and putting questions to him accordingly. Good: and
the answers he shall give. But, it is upon this
condition. Before you ask him how the matter
stands, you must yourself begin and tell him how
it stands: otherwise, no answers shall you have.
This is what you must do, as to every fact you
stand in need of. Now then, to do this, you must,
of course, for each such fact, have a story framed,
such as will suit your purpose: but *that* story it is
your counsel's business to do for you. He, and
he alone knows what is proper for the occasion.
What it consists of is a parcel of lies, to be sure.
But that's his concern, not yours: you have not to
swear to them. As to the story's being a lie, that's
no concern of yours. I and mine get money by
all this: so there is no harm in it: and, as you
do not swear to it, you can't be punished for it.

" As to another world, *that* to be sure there is,
and with a God's court in it. But there, it is your
counsel that will have to answer for it, not you:
you can't help it: no, 'nor' he neither, without
losing his fees. I, for my part, have some thousands of these lies upon my back, or I should not

be where I am : look at me : what am I the worse
for it ?"

11. Eleventhly, as to *elicitation and recordation,
made, for eventual use, without suit.* Be the occasion what it may, be the source what it may, evidence obtainable to day may cease to be obtainable tomorrow. Here then may be seen a deficiency : but, as to the want of supply for it, at the
early age in question, no wonder it should have
had place. In the field of justice much insight
into future contingency was not to be expected
from men who, to so vast an extent, were blind to
what was, in this same field, passing under their
own noses.

For this deficiency, *equity* had no objection to
afford a supply : but of course upon her own
terms,—those terms, which have so often been
brought to view. Those terms required *a suit* on
purpose : for, a suit was necessary to *equity*, how
little so ever necessary to *justice*.

As to recordation,—at the early period abovementioned, clerk power enough there was for the
pleadings—the mixture of *lies* and absurdities above
described ; none was there for the evidence, the
only sort of matter which presented a chance of
being chiefly composed of relevant and material
truths. Accordingly, in the mass of matter called
the *record*, no sort of matter can there be so sure of
not being found, as that which stands distinguished by the name of evidence.

Not but that, to prove its own existence, the
entire hodge-podge may, on a particular occasion
(fees being first received), be admitted under the
name of evidence : to prove, for example, that a
man was convicted of murder : but by what it

was that the murder was produced, whether, for example, by an endeavour to kill the man, or by an endeavour to kill a fowl (for, for this has a man been convicted of murder), if this be what at present you want to know, in the newspaper you may be sure to find it, in the record you will be sure *not* to find it.

Such, for exigencies of all sorts, being the provision made by common law before the birth of equity,—made in the common law courts, before the formation of the equity courts,—behold now the account given of it by *Blackstone*.

Speaking of an old book in Latin, called the *Registrum Brevium*,—composed chiefly of forms of orders called *writs*, given in the name of the king to the sheriffs,—in it, (says he, III, 184), " *Every man who is injured* will be sure to find *a* method of relief *exactly* adapted to his own case, described in the compass of a few lines, and yet *without the omission of any material circumstance.*" So much for Blackstone. To the dream of this reporter, would you substitute the sad reality? For *a* put *no:* for *omission insertion:* make these corrections, the picture will be nearer the truth. Dates none, arrangement none, other than the alphabetical, either in the collection itself, or in judge Fitzherbert's commentary on it, and in the additions made to that commentary in any subsequent editions made of it. So much for the universal oracle. Such is the source from whence the notions of the universal unlearned as to what the law is, have down to this time been derived !

To return to equity court. In the provision made by common law, gaps requiring to be filled up, sure enough sufficient: sufficient in number, sufficient in magnitude: necessity of filling up sufficiently urgent. But, for the filling them up, was any additional court, either a necessary or so much as a proper instrument? An additional court thus kept destined and separate from the court to which it was added? More particularly, a court invested with such powers as, in relation to the court it was added to, were assumed by this same so called *court of equity*? a court superior to it in effective power, and yet without being, either in name or nature, a court of appeal from it? Taking up the matter at the pleasure of any man, who, without any ground whatsoever, would pay the price set upon the injustice at any stage of the suit, riding over the competent authority, and rendering useless everything that had been done, and thrown away every penny that had been expended in that same judicatory? The thus maltreated judicatory all the while not the less abundantly lauded, for being regarded as requiring to be dealt with?

A sort of severance this, mischievous enough, —and, as such, worthy enough of remark at any time. But, *at present*, a circumstance which gives to it, in the particular case in question, a particular degree of importance,—gives, to the particular case of severance here in question, and produces accordingly the need for thus dwelling on it, is—the care, which, on the occasion of the *recently instituted improvements*, has been taken, to keep it up (this same severance), and, of course along with it, the uncertainty, delay, vexation, expense, and lawyer's profit, engendered by it.

Lastly, as to the aggregate composed of the four courts thus instituted,—the several separate denominations of necessity attached to them, the jurisdiction formed by the several splinters thus

put side by side, and one mischievous consequence flowing of course from the very nature of
the operation—splitting and splicing operation.

Of the application thus made of so many different names the consequence is, the implied
information and assurance of the existence, and
thence of the necessity of so many different natures,
and modes of proceeding on the part of the several
courts thus differently denominated.

In the case of these denominations what serves
to fix and thicken the cloud composed of them is,
their being derived from different sources : in
some cases, the source is the name of the *species*,
or rather, as will be seen, the *sub-species* of suit ; in
other cases, the *initiatory process*—that is to say, the
written instrument by the delivery of which, on
the *operation* by the performance of which, the
suit takes its own commencement.   Behold them,
here they are.

I. Under the species of suit termed *civil*, name
of the initiatory process, if in the Common Pleas,
action: if in the King's Bench, in one sort of case,
action likewise ; in another sort of case, comes the
name of the instrument *mandamus;* name of an
operation by which it is preceded, *motion for a
mandamus;* in another sort of case, name of the
instrument, *quo warranto;* name of the antecedent
operation, *motion for a quo warranto :* in an equity
court, including the equity side of the amphibious court—the exchequer—*bill;* in the common law side thereof, *action;* in another sort of
case, in a Christian court, name of the instrument,
libel.

II. Under the species of suit termed *criminal*
or *penal*—common to all these courts in one sort of
case, is one sub-species, *attachment :* to which de-

nomination is in some cases substituted the cir-
cumlocutory and milder denomination, constituted
by the antecedent operation—*motion that the defendant may answer the matter of the affidavit* (this
being the initiatory instrument): in another sort of
case, in the King's Bench, name of one sort of instrument *indictment;* in the same sort of case, in
that same court, name of another sort of *instrument,
information:* name of the *antecedent operation, motion for leave to file an* INFORMATION: in the same
sort of case, still in that same court, name of the
instrument again, *information :* name of the antecedent operation, *filing an information,* to wit by the
attorney-general, without *motion ;* in another sort
of case, in the Exchequer, name of the instrument
qui tam information ; in another sort of case, in the
Christian court, name of the instrument, *libel*
again : note here, by-the-bye, in the case of this
word *libel,* the confusion further thickened, by the
giving to one and the same appellative the commission of officiating as the sign of two opposite
things signified : namely, an alleged *disorder,* and
a professed *remedy.*

Sufficient, it is hoped, this exhibition, without
the addition of the rarer sorts of suits, such as the
scire facias and its *et cæteras.*

Such is the enrichment which the vocabulary of
English jurisprudence has actually received, from
the principle pursued by this practice : the employing different operations with different instruments, for the attainment of the same end. What
bounds are there to the ulterior enrichment, which,
from the same principle, it might, with as good
reason, be made to receive ? Take a few examples.

First, as to *courts :* by multiplication given to

the names, and with them to the species, of these judicatories. One example may here serve. Take for a model the *court* of *equity*, with this its sentimental name: additional courts with like imitative names, court of *probity*, court of *integrity*, court of *common honesty*, court of *honour*, court of *righteousness:* another such winning name, court of conscience, in point of propriety, forming a striking contrast with the court of equity, has already been brought into employment by statute law.

Take secondly and lastly, for the instrument of multiplication and confusion, the name of the instrument, by which commencement is given to the *process.* Model, in this case, the word *libel;*—a word meaning, in the original Latin, a *little book:* proposed imitative names of instruments—*leaf*, *sheet*, *roll*, *scroll*, *volume.* Yes, *volume:* for, in some cases, in equity more especially, scarcely to the existing sort of instrument—the *bill* to wit— would even this appellative, notwithstanding the seeming exaggeration, be altogether misapplied.

Now as to the degree of *appositeness*, with which the signs are here coupled with the things signified. For an emblem of it, take two hats: into one put the *things;* into the other the *signs;* which done then, having drawn out of the one a *thing*, draw out of the other a sign for it: as, on a Twelfthday, styles and titles are coupled with slices of cake and names of cake-eaters.

In the aggregate of all this surplusage, may moreover be seen, one out of the host of visible examples, of the way, in which, by the English lawyer, as by the astrologer,—and for the same purpose,—has been created, out of nothing, a sort of sham science.

Correspondent to this science, with the art be-

longing to it, is the list of official functionaries, employed, on this occasion, in the exercise of the art.
Note well the multiplicity and ingenious variety of
their denominations. By one single one alone of
the four Westminster-hall courts, the King's Bench,
is furnished the list which follows. But, for a
standard of comparison, note first the sorts of
functionaries which, under the official establishment hereinafter proposed ‚for giving execution
and effect to the here proposed natural system
of procedure, would be requisite and necessary
under the command of the judge. Here it follows: 1. *Registrar.* 2. *Prehensor*, or say *Arrestor*.
3. *Summoner*. 4. *Doorkeeper*. 5. *Jailor*. Now then
follows the list of those actually in existence as
above under the King's Bench.*   " 1. Chief
clerk. 2. Master. 3. Marshal of King's Bench
prison. 4. Clerk of the rules. 5. Clerk of the
papers. 6. Clerk of the dockets, judgments, satis-
factions, ‚commitments, &c. 7. Clerk of the declaration. 8. Clerk of the common bails, posteas, and
estreats. 9. Signer of the writs. 10. Signer of the
bills of Middlesex. 11. Custos brevium. 12. Clerk
of the upper treasury. 13. Clerk of the outer treasury. 14. Marshal and associate. 15. Sealer of the
writs. 16. Judge's clerks. 17. Sheriffs of London
and sheriff of Middlesex. 18. Secondaries. 19.
Under-sheriff. 20. Ushers, tipstaffs, &c." Here at
length ends the list of the swarm of locusts which
buzzes about this one of the four courts—the
King's Bench : ·places of feeding, no fewer than
ten : some of them not less than three miles from

---

* Taken from an instructive little treatise intituled, a Complete History of an Action at Law, &c. by Thomas Mayhew,
Student of Lincoln's Inn, 1828 : pages, no more·than 82.

one other. Calculate who can the quantity of time consumed with expence correspondent, by attornies, in the journies necessary to be made all over this labyrinth.

XIV. *Result of the fissure—groundless arrest for debt.*

Comes now the battle royal :—battle of the courts: battle for the fees. Result, groundless arrest. As at present, on pretence of debt : effect, imposed on innocence an aggregate of suffering, vying in severity with that inflicted on the aggregate of crime.

Let it not here be supposed, though it were but for a moment, that, on imprisonment for debt, condemnation without reserve is meant to be pronounced. Condemn in the lump, condemn without exception, imprisonment, and even imprisonment for debt, for debt you would condemn all satisfaction, and as well might you, for all crime, condemn all punishment.

Look for the proper time, you will find it in that of the *second* of the operations requisite to be performed in the course of the suit : at the time of, and by, the first, the existence of an adequate demand for this same second operation having been ascertained : improper time, that of the first operation : this same first operation being the arrest itself, performed without any such ascertainment: performed by the judge, without enquiry, and at the pleasure of any one who will purchase of him this service, at the price he has set upon it:—upon so simple a distinction turns, in this case, the difference between the perfection of good, and the perfection of evil.

Ascertained, (asks somebody), the existence of

this same adequate demand? by what means?
Answer. By this means—To give commence-
ment to the suit, attends in court the plaintiff, and
stating his demand, states at the same time the
need there is of the arrestation: subject matter of
it, either the body of the proposed defendant, or
some property of his, or both: this operation in
the first instance: otherwise on hearing of the
demand, off go person, or property, or both, and
therewith all hope of recovery for the debt—all
hope of effectual justice.

Mark now the security afforded by the here
proposed course, against the oppression now so
completely established, and so abundantly exercised—the oppression exercisible at pleasure by
any man in the character of plaintiff, on almost
any man in the character of defendant: at the
same time, the superior efficiency of the means
afforded for the recovery of the debt.

Being thus in the *presence*, the applicant is completely in the *power*, of the judge: unlimited is
the amount of the punishment, to which, in case
of purposed and mischievous misrepresentation,
he may be subjected. In this state of things,
two opposite dangers present themselves to the
judge's choice: in case of the non-exercise of this
power of precautionary seisure,—danger of injustice to the detriment of the plaintiff, by loss of the
debt; in case of the exercise of this same power,
danger of injustice, to an indefinite amount, to the
detriment of the proposed defendant thus dealt
with.

Between these two opposite mischiefs, who does
not see, that no otherwise than by a scrutiny into
the circumstances of each individual case, can any
tolerably well grounded choice be made? and, for

this scrutiny, no source of information has place as yet, other than the evidence of the applicant, extracted by his examination: an information, without which, or any other, under the existing system, arrestation is performed without scruple: that is to say, on the *body;* and with as little might it be, though at this stage of the proceedings it never is, on *property.*

This power then, either it is exercised, or it is not: if yes, security will need to be taken for two things: 1. for the applicant's effectual responsibility, to the purpose of compensation or that of punishment, or both, as the case may require: 2. for his being eventually reached by a mandate, or, in case of need, by a functionary armed with a warrant for arrestation, wheresoever it may happen to him to be, during the continuance of the suit: a security this last, the demand for which (it may be seen) has place, in the instance of every person, to whom, for whatever purpose, in whatever character, it happens to have presented himself to a judge: a security with which, for reasons that will be seen, Judge and Co. know better than to have provided themselves with.

Why say *attendance,* not *appearance?* Because, by lying lips and pens, the word *appearance* has been to such a degree poisoned, as to be rendered unfit for use. When, in the record, entry is made of what is called the defendant's appearance in court, what is the real fact? Never that he, the defendant, has made his appearance in court; always that an attorney employed by him has made *his* appearance: nor even this in the court, but in another place: to wit, in one of the offices, of the nature of those contained in the above-mentioned list.

To return to the applicant's here proposed actual attendance: in most instances it will be possible and with advantage practicable. But in some instances it will be either impossible or not with advantage practicable. Of these last cases, for the purpose of the here proposed system, a list has been made out: so likewise of all the *shapes*, of which the just-mentioned security is susceptible: which list may be seen below: so likewise of all the several diversifications, of which the mode of securing *intercourse*, or say *communication*, with an applicant, or any other person who has made his appearance during the continuance of the suit, is susceptible.

For the institution of this little cluster of arrangements, a combination of common sense, and common ingenuity, with common honesty, was indeed necessary, but at the same time sufficient. In the provision made by the existing system, where is there to be seen any symptom of the union of these same requisites? How should there be?— Without the existence of the applicant in the presence of the judge at the outset of the suit, nothing of all this can be done: and, as there is such continual occasion to observe, scarcely can the presence of a *dun* be more appalling to a spendthrift, than, in a *civil* case, to an English supreme-court judge, the presence of an individual, whose property (and under the system of mechanical judicature, as hath been seen, in most cases without knowing anything about the matter,) he is disposing of.

Now, for want of some such as these proposed arrangements, under the existing system behold the state of things. General rule this. At the pleasure of any man, without grounds existing or so much as pretended to exist, any man may be arrested and consigned to a jail, with no other alternative than that of being, if able and willing to pay for the accommodation, consigned to an arresting-house, called a *lock-up-house*, or a *spunging-house*.

Exceptions are—1. where the debt does not amount to so much as 20*l.*: 2. when it does amount to that sum, the plaintiff omits to make an affidavit, whereby he avows upon oath, that the sum demanded by the suit is justly and truly due. And this, without adding *upon the balance:* so that a man to whom another owes 20,000*l,* may be arrested by him, on a particular account specified, for 20*l.* Originally the sum mentioned on the occasion and for the purpose of the limitation thus applied, was no more than 10*l.*: it is by a recent Act, that it has been raised to this same 20*l.* 1826: original act, that of the 12 Geo. I. ch. 20; year of our Lord 1728. Date of the act under which, for the benefit of the Court of Common Pleas the practice of arrest for debt was established, year of our Lord 1661: thus had the abomination been reigning four-and-sixty years before so much as this alleviation was applied to it. Yet, such as it is, keen in Judge and Co. was the sense of the injury thus done to the whole partnership. Faces, lengthened by the recollection and report of it, were witnessed by persons yet alive.

Oh, precious security! Mark now a set of incidents, any one of which would suffice for rendering it ineffectual.

1. In case of *mutual* accounts, a man who is a debtor on the balance, and moreover in a state of insolvency, in such sort as to be incapable of making compensation for the wrong, is free to

make use of it in such sort, as to inflict vexation and perhaps ruin on the creditor thus dealt with.

2. No limit is there to the multitude of knowingly false demands, which, to the wrong of one man may thus be made by any other, and this without his being at the expense of a perjury; by which, however, if committed, he would not, in more than the trifling degree which, under the head of *oaths*, be exposed to hazard.

3. To a man who is about to leave England, having therein no property, or none but what he is taking with him, or none which, by such inadequate means as the law affords, can be come at, this apparent check is, it will be seen, no real one.

4. On so easy a condition as the finding another man, who, being a man of desperate fortunes, will, for hire, perform his part in this so extensively contemned ceremony,—any man may cause his intended victim to be arrested for sums to any amount, and thereby for a sum for which it will not be possible for the victim to find bail.

5. The assertion is admitted, without being, in any case, subjected to cross-examination. Hence the invitation to mendacity and perjury.

6. To those alone whose connections on the spot, in addition to the opulence of their circumstances, admit of their finding bail, is the privilege of being conveyed to a spunging-house instead of a jail, extended.

So much for inadequacy: now for incongruity. To the above-mentioned efficient causes of inadequacy, may be added the following features of incongruity, relation had to the existing system.

1. Swearing to the existence of the debts, the affidavit-man is forced to swear to his knowledge

of the state of the law: that same law which, with such successful care, it has been rendered and kept impossible for any man to know.

2. The testimony thus delivered, is testimony delivered by a man in his own favour, in contradiction to a rule and principle of common law. Note, that *inconsistency*, not *inaptitude*, is the ground of condemnation here.

General result—with the exception of the privileged few, every man exposed to ruin at the pleasure of every other, who is wicked enough, and at the same time rich enough, to accept of the invitation which the judges and their associates in the iniquity, never cease thus to hold out to him.

So much for the *evil* done by the battle, and the *good* which so obviously should have occupied the place of that same evil. Now for the battle itself. Origin of the war—power, thence custom, surreptitiously obtained from Parliament, by the judges of the Common Pleas, a little after the Restoration, at the expense of the judges of the King's Bench. The power thus obtained was, that of employing, in an action for *debt*, this same operation of arrest, in giving commencement to the suit. By the known acquisition of this power, was made, to all who would become customers, the virtual offer of the advantage that will be seen. In the case of the honest plaintiff, it consisted in the obtaining his right in a manner more prompt and sure than before: in the case of the dishonest plaintiff, to this same advantage was added, as has been seen, the power of ruining other persons, in a number proportioned to the compound of cupidity, malevolence and opulence belonging to him, at pleasure.

This plan succeeded to admiration. Common Pleas overflowed with customers. King's Bench

M

became a desart. Roger North, brother and bio-
grapher of Lord Keeper *Guildford*, at that time
Chief Justice of the Common Pleas, depictures,
in glowing colours, the value of the conquest
thus made. At this time, *Hale*—the witch-hang-
ing *Hale*—prime object of Judge and Co.'s ido-
latry—was Chief Justice of the King's Bench.
Chagrined, to the degree that may be imagined,
by the falling off of his trade, he put on, of course,
his considering cap.—What was to be done? After
the gravest consideration, he at length invented an
instrument, (as a manuscript of his, published in
Hargrave's Law Tracts, informs us,) an instrument,
with the help of which he himself, with his own
hands, succeeded in stealing that same power which
the legislature had given to the court of Common
Pleas. Yes: so he himself informs us: so blind to
the wickedness of telling lies, and getting money
by it—so dead to the sense of shame, had been
made, by evil communication, this so eminently
pious, as well as best-intentioned judge, that ever
sat upon a Westminster Hall bench.—Name of
the instrument, the *ac etiam :* description of it not
quite so short. To give it, we must go back a
little.

At the primæval period so often mentioned, the
great all-competent judicatory had received, of
course at the hands of the Conqueror, this same
power of arrestation, applicable at discretion. At
the time when, by the original *fissure*, the allotment of jurisdiction was given to the Common
Pleas—to that judicatory, to enable it to give
execution and effect to its decrees, was given the
power of operating, to this purpose, on property,
in certain of its shapes : the power of operating on
person not being given to this court; except that,

at the end of a long-protracted course of plunderage, of which presently, came the process of *outlawry:* outlawry—a rich compost, in which, in a
truly admirable manner, barbarity and impotence,
to the proper and professed purpose, were combined.

On this same occasion, the cases remaining to
the King's Bench branch of the all-comprehending
jurisdiction, after the fissure, were those in which,
under the name of *punishment,* suffering was purposely inflicted: sometimes called *penal,* sometimes *criminal,* was the class composed of these
cases. By the words *treason, felony,* and *misdemeanour,* were originally marked out so many
degrees, (treason the highest,) in the scale of
punishment: with like effect, between felony and
misdemeanour, was afterwards inserted the word
premunire. In process of time, a little below *misdemeanour,* King's Bench contrived to slip in the
word *trespass:* and thus armed, as opportunity
served, it began its encroachments on the jurisdiction and fees of the helpless Common Pleas.

Misdemeanour meant and means *misconduct,* or
say *misbehaviour: trespass,* meant *transgression:
transgression,* in the original Latin, *transgressio,* is
the going beyond a something: the something, on
this occasion understood, was of course a law.
Not that any such thing was in existence: no
matter. On this, as on every other part of the
field of common law, it was feigned.

When, for anything or for nothing, it was the
pleasure of the king, or for any man whom it
pleased him to allow, thus to act in his name,
that a person should be dealt with in this manner,
plaintiff's attorney went to the shop, and the foreman, on hearing it, sold him an order directed to
the sheriff, in the body of which instrument that

functionary was informed that defendant had committed a trespass, and from the sheriff the information would, in course, pass on to the defendant, when the time came for his finding himself in Lob's pound.

In process of time came a distinction : a distinction between *trespass* simply, and trespass *upon the case*. Much the wiser the defendant was not for the information, in either instance, how much soever the poorer : trespass meant nothing except that the man was in the way to be punished, and trespass upon the case meant just as much.

Here then were two instruments : now for another such : this was the word *force*. Whatever was done, by *force* not warranted by legal authority, was (it was seen) in everybody's eyes a *crime* : out of this word was accordingly made this other power-snatching instrument. One vast acquisition thus made with it, and it was a vast one, was the cognizance of suits having for their subject-matter title to landed property. To every man who claimed a portion of land, intimation was given—that, if he would say he had been turned out of it, instead of *turned out* using the word *ejected*, relief should be given to him by King's Bench : relief, by exemption from no small portion of the delay, expense and vexation, attached to the preliminary, and, as will be seen, so ingeniously wire-drawn, process of the Common Pleas. *Ejected* means turned out by *tossing :* and how could anybody be tossed out of anything without force.

Emboldened by success thus brilliant, they went on—these pre-eminently learned and ingenious combatants—to the case of *adultery*. Here, court *Temporal* had to fight with court *Christian*, alias *Spiritual*. Court *Spiritual* had seen in this practice a *sin*, and dealt with it accordingly. With this sin Common Pleas had found no pretence for intermeddling. More fortunate, more bold, and more sharp-sighted, was his lordship of the King's Bench. He saw in it (so he assured, and continues to assure the sheriff) a species of *rape:* a crime of some sort it was necessary he should see in it, and the nearest sort of crime was this of *rape.* It was committed, he said, *vi et. armis*—by *force and arms.* This invention was quite the thing: that *arms* had, in every case, more or less to do in it, was undeniable: and seeing that, on the occasion in question, motion could not but have place, and considering that motion can scarcely be made without a correspondent degree of force, thus was this part of the charge made good: and in return for their custom, injured parties received from the learned shopkeeper, at the charge of the adulterers, money under the name of *damages.*

Inconsistency was here in all its glory, *crime* had *punishment alone,* not *damages,* for its fruit: this was a principle: yet adultery was thus made into a crime, and at the same time made to yield damages: it was thus a *rape* and *not rape:* rape, that it might be made into a crime: yet not *rape,* because, if it were rape, adulterers would be all of them to be hanged: to which there were some objections.

Of the weapon employed on this occasion, the form was the same, as that of the weapon employed, as above, in the war with the court of Common Pleas; and here follows a further explanation, for which, it must be confessed, *that* former place was the more proper one: but, in discourse, clouds are not quite so easily dissipated as formed. Speaking to the sheriff after commanding him to take up the defendant on the ground of an accusation of *trespass,*—trespass not giving intimation of anything, except the eventual design of punishing as for a crime,—his lordship went on to add, *as also* to a demand on the score of debt, to an individual (naming him).   Here then, by his learned lordship, were two real crimes committed in the same breath, for the purpose of pretending to inflict punishment for, and really reaping profit from, this one imaginary crime : one at the charge of the Common Pleas judges, to whom alone, by *Magna Charta* as above, belonged the cognizance of cases of debt : the other, at the charge of every member of the community, thus subjected to the power of groundless arrest and imprisonment, as above. On this occasion, in dumb show—dumb indeed, but not the less intelligible—was this his language. " All ye who believe yourselves to be in the right, and all ye who know yourselves to be in the wrong, but, at the same time, wanting the accommodation for the purpose of ruining some person you have fixt upon, come to my shop : there is my prison, and to it he or she shall go."

Thus much to wished-for customers. Now to the sheriff.   "Take up *Thomas Stiles,* and put him into your jail : when there, he *will be* in our power, we will make him pay a sum of money which *John Noaks* says he owes him."   Such, in the address of the chief justice to the sheriff, was, and is the language of the appropriate document— the only source, from which any conception could be formed, of the calamity into which the proposed defendant was, and is thus destined to be plunged. It was a *writ,* addressed to the sheriff of the courts in which the defendant was, or was assumed to be, resident,   "Will be in our power?" Be it so:

but, suppose him actually in their power :—his being so, did it give them, in relation to their younger brethren of the Common Pleas, any right which they did not possess before ?

As to his being already in their power, neither was this the case, nor was it so much as supposed to be. But, should it so happen that the sheriff had taken the man up and brought him to his lordship, whose clerk's signature is to the writ, then the destined victim would be in his said lordship's power, and then he would make him comply with the demand, or defend himself against it, or abide the consequences.

As yet here is no lie. But, if the supposed residence of the destined defendant were any where but in Middlesex, then came the demand for lies, and with it the supply. *Lie the first*, averment that defendant's residence is in Middlesex : and by this was constituted the warrant, such as it was, for *writ* the first, with its fees.

Lie the second—said defendant is lurking and running about (*latittat et discurrit*) in this county of : the blank being filled up with the name of the county in which it suits the purpose of the plaintiff, or his attorney, to suppose him to be. This is what he was and is told, in the text of another writ, addressed to the sheriff of county the second, for whose information the writ, addressed to his brother of Middlesex, is thus recited, and the difference between the cost of the one writ and that of the two writs, is a tax or penalty, which all persons who omit to live in Middlesex pay for such their default.

Such was the plan of the counter-invasion. Serious and sensibly felt it cannot but have

been, to the potentate whose domain was thus invaded.

How to get back the advantage was now the
question. Under English practice, *deception* (need
it now be said), is, on each occasion the readiest,
most efficient and favourite instrument. A man
had forged a hand, "don't trouble yourself about
proving the forgery," said his learned adviser,
"forge a release." A similar instrument was accordingly fabricated by the Common Pleas, and
succeeded. Not but the re-conquest had some
difficulties to contend with: for, (as honest Roger
informs us), king's tax and chancellor's fees were
affected by it: but these difficulties being the only
ones, and these removed, King's Bench's mouth
was thus closed.

No hypocrisy here. For a cloak of any sort,
no demand so much as suspected. Two sharpers
playing off their tricks against one another—such
is the character, in which, even with his approbation, the two lord chief justices are held up to
view, by this confidential brother of one of them.
"*Outwitting*," one of the words employed: *device*,
another. Encrease of business the avowed object: of business such as has been seen: proportioned to the success, the exultation produced by
it: proportioned to the amount of the booty, the
triumph of the irresistible robbers.

Sole interests so much as pretended to be con-
sulted, the interests of Judge and Co.; of this
firm, his majesty was, as above, declared, one of
the partners: the swinish multitude, with their
interest, thought no more of, or professed to be
thought of, than so many swine.

The King's Bench was not the only place at the

hands of which the helpless offspring of Magna Charta lay exposed to invasion. Another inroad was that made by the Court of Exchequer. In the pretence made in this case, no such downright and all-involving lie was, however, included. In this case, the king was indeed stated as delivering the commandment; and, forasmuch as his majesty knew not, on any occasion, any more of the matter than the pope of Rome—in this shape and thus far was a lie told. But that which his majesty was represented as insinuating, though but insinuating, had commonly more or less of truth in it. It was, that the plaintiff was in his majesty's debt: a state of things which would, of course, have place, in the instance of any man, who had tax to pay, or service to render.

But this same court of Exchequer, to which no such power had been given, what business had it to meddle or make, while there sat the Common Pleas, to which the power *had* been and continued to be given? Had there even been no such judicatory as the Common Pleas, the only persons, in whose instance anything done by the Exchequer could contribute to the proposed effect, would have been such as were in a state of insolvency: nor yet all of these: for, till all demands on the account of the king were satisfied, never was so much as a penny allowed to be touched by any other creditor than his said majesty. Yes, as above observed, *insinuating* and nothing more. For, all that his majesty is represented as saying is, that *the plaintiff says*, he owes a debt to his said majesty, not that such is really the case.

So much for this enormity. Out of it grew another, to which the word *bail* gives name. *Finding bail*, as the phrase is, is the name of one species of those *securities*, allusion to which has been made, as above. In this case, after having been arrested by an emissary of the sheriff's, and consigned to the appropriate gaol, or, on paying for the indulgence, kept in the house of this same emissary, or some person connected with him (name of the house, a *lock-up house* or *spunging house*) he is, if certain persons render themselves responsible to the sheriff, or without this security, if the under-sheriff so pleases, liberated. These persons are stiled the bails: number of them, one, two, or more, commonly two. As to what they undertake for, it is, in different cases, different: but, for the most part, it is the consigning the defendant to the gaol, or else satisfying the plaintiff's demand.

As to the remedy which this same security affords—nothing could be more completely of a piece, with the so industriously and inhumanly fabricated disease. To the comparatively opulent, an alleviation—to the comparatively indigent, an aggravation. Compleat, in an admirable degree of perfection, is the machinery employed in the application of it: to such a degree, that lengthy treatises are occupied in the description of it: enormous the complication, proportionable, of course, the delay, vexation and expence, produced by it.

As to all this suffering, what do Judge and Co. care about it? Just as much as they care for the rest of the mass of suffering which the system, in its other parts, organizes. What a steam-engine would care for the condition of a human body pressed or pounded by it.

Directed to its proper end, the process of *judicia. security-finding*, is an operation, having for its object *alleviation* to the hardship inseparable from the process of subjecting a patient to the sorts of operations performed upon him by the judge: in each individual case, applying the maximum of the alleviation of which that particular case is susceptible. To all the several modifications, of which this hardship is susceptible, to apply one and the same modification of this process—is about as reasonable as it would be to apply, to every species of disease, one and the same medicine.

Of the modifications of which this process is susceptible, we shall presently have occasion to present a view to the Honourable House.

On each occasion, to the circumstances of the individuals in the individual case, does the nature of things render the adaptation of it necessary: and on no one occasion, under the existing system, can it be thus adapted.

In some cases, of which the present case is one, on the *defendant ;* but in other cases, and on the occasion of every suit in the *first* instance, that is to say at the *outset* of the suit, on the *plaintiff*, does the obligation require to be imposed. In each such instance, to the elicitation of the same individualizing circumstances, the examination of the individual by the judge himself, is necessary: and to this process, (one exception excepted, of which presently,) not more unquestionable can be the abhorrence of the most profitable *malâ fide* suitor, than, under the existing practice, that of an English judge.

On each occasion, the subserviency of the operation to the purposes of justice will depend, upon the proportion of the hardship of being subjected to the particular obligation in question, and the hardship which, were it *not* imposed, might have place : *probability* being, in both cases, taken into account.

As to incarceration and confinement, the more extentious and vexatious the modes of them respectively are, the more urgent is the motive, by which the sufferer is impelled, to make choice of this *bail-finding*, or any other, mode of escape from them: escape, perpetual or temporary only, as the case may be : choice, that between the fire and the frying-pan. Whichever it be that is embraced, the exigencies of the lord chief justice were of course effectually and abundantly provided for : from the bailing process, fees upon fees : from the incarceration, a vast mass at once in the shape of patronage. Forty thousand pounds has been stated as having been refused : on the occasion of the recently alleged mutiny, from 8,000*l.* to 10,000*l.* a year stated as being the profit of the jailor. To ascertain in each case the quantum of the enjoyment extracted by these two associates from the misery of the many—the quantum and thence the proportion—is among the operations, the performance of which we beg leave, with all humble submission, to propose to the Honorable House.

Required at the hands of *plaintiffs*, the security would have kept out *dishonest plaintiffs*—Judge and Co's. best friends and customers. Of course it was not to be thought of. Hypocrisy required that the profession should be made : and so, in the language of some of the courts, it was made :— *si fecerit te securum :* sinister interest required that it should be no better than a pretence.

Performed or exacted of defendants, directly opposite is the effect of this same security : thus placed, the obligation renders the abovementioned ample service.

As to this matter—the jakes, of late so notorious by the name of the *Secondary's Office* in the city of London—this abomination, with the immense mass of filthy lucre at the bottom of it, and the forty years' patience of the constituted authorities under the stench of it, speaks volumes.

To the case in which the process of taking examinations was, and is, an object of abhorrence to the judge, an objection has just been alluded to as having place. It is this. To the sight of mere *parties*, and in particular in the situation of plaintiffs, at the outset of the suit, at which stage the examination might nip it in the bud, abhorrence unassuageable:—to persons coming in, at a stage at which the suit is established, and the examination can have no such injurious effect, open arms and welcome. Why this difference? Answer: At the first stage, the examination would exclude fees: at this subsequent stage, it necessitates fees.

To the performing or hearing the examination of a party in relation to the matter of his suit, the horror of an English judge is, as above, insuperable. To the hearing and conducting the examination of the same man under the name of a *Bail*, in relation to a matter foreign to the matter of the suit,—repugnance none. Cause of difference, the so oftened assigned universal cause. Examination of the party, the time being that of the outset of the suit, would, as above, nip the fee-harvest in the bud: examination of bail, gives increase to it.

After all, it depends upon incidents—incidents too intricate to be here developed—whether it is by the four sages—or now of late day, one of them—that the opposition and eventual justification—so the examination is called of the bail—shall be per-

formed, or by some attorney, without the benefit
of that same scrutinizing process.

The attorney is an under-sheriff;—the under-
sheriff of the county in which, as above, the
species of egg called the *venue*, has been *laid*, or
into which it has been *removed*.

The under-sheriff is, on every occasion, the
deputy of the sheriff. The sheriff is a great land-
owner who, (every year a fresh one,) is appointed
by the king: a servant who, in the teeth of reason
and scripture, is appointed to serve not two only,
but twice two masters: that is to say, at the three
Westminster-hall common law courts, with the
addition of the court of general sessions of the
peace.

To this same business, as well as to all business but that of parade, the sheriff contributes—
what a Roman emperor used to contribute to a
victory gained at a thousand miles distance—
auspices: the sheriff, auspices: the attorney,
mind and legal learning: legal learning an accomplishment in which, authorised by their sanction,
the *one*, in so inferior a degree learned thinks it
not *robbery* to be equal to the *four* sages.

If, with the requisite amendments, necessitated by change of times, the system of local
judicatories were restored,—each judge would,
for all purposes, be provided with his own ministerial subordinates: and for all of them he would
be responsible.

In the city of London, the acting functionary
under the sheriffs is stiled *the secondary*. Forty
years of depredation, production of so many unheeded mountains, heaped up one upon another,
of correspondent misery, have at length attracted
to the subject the attention of the local authori-

ties. But, while eyes are shut against causes, eloquence may abound, effects all the while continue undiminished.

Moreover, in the same bailing process there is a gradation : witness the phrases *bail below*, and *bail above*. Bail *below*, are bail whose aptitude is established by the attorney. Bail *above*, are bail whose aptitude, after or without opposition, is established by the four sages. Bail *above* are, in some cases, the bail *below*, thus promoted : in other cases, a fresh couple.

Above and *below* together, bail generate *bail-bond* : bail-bond, *assignment* thereof, with eventual suit : bond, assignment, and suit—fees. To justice, use for bail and assignment the same as for an old almanack.

From these particulars, imperfect as they are, some conception, how inadequate soever, may be formed, of the proportion in which the aggregate property, of all the unfortunates so arrested, is transferred from the ordinary and undignified destination of operating in satisfaction of debts, to the dignified function of contributing to the fund provided for the remuneration of legal science.

Note here, that he who makes a prudent use of the offer so liberally held out by the judges to every man—the offer thus made to ruin for him, on joint account, as many men as he wishes, will take care that the debt sworn to shall be greater than the utmost sum, for which, for love or money, bail can, by the destined victim, be procured.

Here ends our exposition, and we humbly hope the sufficient exposure, of the devices, by the too successful practice of which, the attainment of the ends of radically corrupt judicature have been substituted to that of the ends of justice.

Praying thus for justice, and *that* justice accessible, we proceed to pray for the means necessary to the rendering it so: rendering it so, to all of us without exception. In particular,—of the arrangements, which, in our eyes are calculated to produce that so desirable effect, and for the establishment of which we accordingly pray,—a brief intimation is presented by the propositions following:—

I. First, as to the JUDICIARY ESTABLISHMENT.

1. That, for suits of all sorts, criminal as well as civil, there be two *instances*, or say *stages*, or *degrees* of jurisdiction: stile and title of the judges, before whom the suit is brought in the first instance, *judge immediate*, of those before whom it is brought in the second instance, or say in the way of *appeal, judges appellate*.

2. That with two exceptions, and these as limited as the nature of the service will permit, to each judicatory, cognizance be taken of all sorts of causes: those included, cognizance of which are at present taken by the aggregate of the several authorities by which judicature is exercised: which courts will have to be abolished, as soon as the causes respectively pending before them, shall have been disposed of. This—to exclude complication, uncertainty, collision, delay, and useless expence.

3 That, these exceptions, and these the only ones, may be the following:—*military* judicatories, for the maintenance of discipline, land and sea service included: and *ecclesiastical* judicatories, for the maintenance of ecclesiastical discipline, on the part of ecclesiastical functionaries, belonging to the established church.

4. That, for taking cognizance of suits in the first instance, judicatories may be established in such number and situations, that, by an individual whose house is the most remote from the judicatory which is the nearest to it, the portion of time, during which in the day in question the justice chamber is open, may be passed by him therein without his sleeping elsewhere than at his own home: and that accordingly no individual may have more than twelve miles or thereabouts to travel in order to reach his own judicatory.

5. That, as in the existing principal court, there be not, in any instance, sitting at the same time any more than one single judge. This, for individual responsibility—the sole effectual—as well as also for saving expence and delay by mutual consultation and argumentation.

6. That, to obviate delay and failure of justice, every such judge be empowered and obliged to provide substitutes, styled as in Scotland, *deputes*, one or more, having for their sole remuneration the prospect of being constituted *judges principal :* and that when there has been time for a competent length of probation, no man, who has not served as depute, shall be capable of being constituted judge principal, in which way the provision of *judge power* will be as it were elastic, adjusting itself at all times to the quantity of the demand : judges, thenceforward, none but such as have served an apprenticeship to pure justice, and not to the indiscriminate defence of right and wrong, as at present.

7. That, seeing that, if the power of deputation be conferred as abovementioned, hands in number sufficient for every exigency, need never be wanting; every judicatory in the kingdom will

N

hold its sittings every day in the year, without exception, unless needless delay and denial of justice are not deemed more consistent with regard
for justice on some days than on others : and that
no exception be made by the *sabbath*, unless and
until it shall have been proved that the God of
justice is indifferent to justice, and that he who
was content that an *ox* or an *ass* should be delivered out of a pit, would be displeased at the ani-
mals being delivered out of the hands of a wrong-
doer; and that the sale of mackerel on that day
is a work of more urgent necessity than the gratuitous and uninterrupted administration of justice; lastly, that no exception be made by the
night time, unless, and until, a night shall have
been pointed out during which injustice sleeps;
in which so may justice likewise; seeing moreover
that to certain purposes, under the name of *police,*
justice is, in certain places, in that part of the
twenty-four hours, even under the existing system,
actually administered.

8. That, to each such judicatory, be attached a
competent set of *ministerial officers*, sufficient for
giving, in all ordinary cases, execution and effect
to its mandates : but, with power, as at present,
in case of necessity to call in aid all persons in
general, the military force included.   This, instead of the sheriff, that one man who, hitherto,
in despite of scripture and reason, has been employed to serve not merely two, but twice two
masters.   This, to exclude the complication, with
the consequent collision, litigation, useless expence, delay, and vexation, which from this cause
have place at present.

9. That, of these ministerial officers, such as
are now employed in the intercourse between

judges on the one part, and the respective subordinates, as well as parties and witnesses on the other part, such as are now empowered to use force, as well as to officiate without force, be distinguished by some such name as *prehensors* or *arrestors;* the others distinguished from them by the name of judiciary messengers, or, for shortness, *messengers:* and that for trustworthiness and economy, the business of *message-carrying* be, as far as may be, performed by the machinery of the *letter post.*

10. That the remuneration allotted to judiciary functionaries, ministerial as well as magisterial, be, the whole of it, in the shape of *salary;* and that, by no functionary belonging to the judiciary establishment, money or any other valuable thing or service, under any such name or in any such quality as that of a *fee*, be, by any judicial functionary, receivable on any occasion, on any pretence. This, to exclude the expence, delay, extortion, and vexation, which have ever hitherto been produced by the multiplication of judicial instruments and operations for the purpose, and with the effect of giving correspondent increase to the masses of fees.

11. That such remuneration be paid, the whole of it, at the expence of the public at large; no part of it at the expence of any individual or body of individuals interested: fines for misconduct as below, excepted. This, to avoid excluding of any person from the benefit of justice: every person who in the suit in question is not able to pay the whole mass of the fees exacted on the occasion of that suit, being at present, as well as having at all times hitherto been thus excluded: and because that which the rest of the community enjoy

without, litigants do not obtain otherwise than
by and with litigation, with its vexation and expence, the benefit of justice.

12. That, to obviate the danger and suspicion
of partiality through private connection, no judge-
immediate principal shall remain in the same judicatory for any longer term than *three* years, or
thereabouts : and that, for this purpose, an appropriate system of *circuiting* be accordingly established : but that, for continuing in an unbroken
course the business of recordation, or say *registration*, the functionary by whom it is performed be
stationary.

13. That, in every justice-chamber, for the better administering of that security, which it is in
the power of *public opinion* to afford, for conduct
apt in every respect on the part of judges,—commodious situation be allotted for two classes of
persons, under some such name as that of *judiciary
inspectors :* the one, composed of suitors, waiting
for their suits to come on, say *expectant suitors* or
suitors in waiting ; the other, of *probationary lawyers*, of whom presently.

14. That, in all sorts of suits, without exception,
a *jury* shall be employable : but, to lessen the
aggregate weight of the burthen of attendance,—
not till after an *original hearing*, before the judge
sitting alone, nor then but by order of the judge,
whether spontaneous, (for example, for the purpose of confronting such of the evidence as requires
to be confronted), or else at the requisition of a
party on one side or the other; in which case it
shall be obligatory on him to order and carry on a
fresh hearing, termed a *recapitulatory hearing*, or
say a *new trial*, before a jury, organized in manner
following.

15. That in cases of all sorts, one excepted, all functions belonging to the judge, one excepted, shall be exercisible in common with him, by the jurors : the *imperative*, or say the *effectuative*, being that on which the effect of the suit depends, being, for the sake of individual responsibility, allotted exclusively to the judge. Functions thus exercisible, these :—1. *Auditive*, applied to every thing that is to be heard. 2. *Lective*, applied to everything that requires to be read. 3. *Inspective*, applied to everything that requires to be seen. 4. *Interrogative*, applied to all questions that require to be put. 5. *Commentative*, applied to all observations which they think fit to make. 6. *Ratiocinative*, applied to whatever reasons they think fit to give for anything which they say or do. 7. *Opinative*, exercised by declaration made of opinion, in accordance or discordance with the opinion which, on the occasion of the exercise given to the effectuative function, is pronounced by the judge : exercised collectively, as by juries under the existing system, the *opinative :* exercisable individually all the rest.

16. That the class of cases, in which the *effectuative* function, as above, shall be exercisible by the jury, so far forth as to render of no effect a judgment of *conviction* if pronounced by the judge alone, shall be that in which the higher functions of government, as such, have, or may naturally be supposed to have, a special personal interest : for example—*treason, rebellion, sedition, defamation* to the injury of a public functionary, or set of public functionaries, as such, and the like.

17. That, for lessening the burthen of attendance on juries,—instead of a number so super-

fluous as twelve, a lesser number, and that for the
sake of a majority an *uneven* one,—that is to say,
three, or at the utmost, *five*,—be employed : by
which arrangement the practice of perjury on the
part of juries, in a number varying from one to
eleven,—perjury, to wit, by falsely reported unanimity, with torture for the production of it, will
be made to cease : for the better direction, one
out of three, or two out of the five, being of the
class of special jurymen : the foreman being to be
of this class.

18. That the institution of a *grand jury*, with
its useless delay, incomplete, secret, naturally partial, and inconsistently, though happily, limited,
applicability,—be abolished.

19. That, for receiving *appeals* from the decrees
and other proceedings and conduct on the part of
the abovementioned judges *immediate*, there be judicatories *appellate*, all single seated, in such number as experience shall have shewn 'to be necessary: if more than one, station of all of them the
metropolis : that being the central spot, to which
persons from all parts of the country have occasion
to resort for other purposes ; and at the same time
that in which the best-formed and most effective
public opinion has place — public opinion ! most
influential and salutary check upon the conduct,
and security for the good conduct, of these as well
as all other public functionaries : and, as below,
no evidence being proposed to be received other
than that which having been orally elicited in the
court below, and consigned to writing, no attendance by parties or witnesses will, on this occasion,
be necessary. And that, after the outset of the
here proposed change, no person being capable of

serving as judge appellate, who has not for a certain length of time served as judge principal immediate.

20. That, in each judicatory, as well appellate as immediate, for officiating in suits in which government, on behalf of the public at large is interested,—there be a functionary, under the name of the *government advocate*, with *deputation* and on the part of the principal, *migration*, as in the case of the judge : and superordinate to them all, a *government advocate general.*

21. That, for administering professional assistance to suitors who, by relative *weakness*, bodily or mental, are disqualified from acting as plaintiffs or defendants, for themselves,—or, by relative indigence, from purchasing assistance from professional hands,—there be in each judicatory a public functionary under the name, for example, of *eleemosynary advocate :* also with deputes, and migration, as above.

22. That, considering how opposite in their nature are the duties and habits of the judge and the advocate,— *impartiality* the duty of the one, *partiality* the duty, and purposed misrepresentation the unavoidable practice, of the other,—no functionary be transferable from one to another of these three lines of service.

23. That, at the head of the judiciary establishment, there be placed a single functionary, styled, as in other countries, *justice minister ;* at whose recommendation, subject to his majesty's pleasure, as at present by the *chancellor*, shall be filled up all other judicial situations.

24. That *accusations* or *complaints* made against a judge, immediate or appellate, on the score of official delinquency, or relative inaptitude from

any other cause, be heard and determined by the
justice minister.

25. That accusations or complaints, made for
the like cause, against the justice minister, be
heard and determined by the *House of Lords :* and
that, on that consideration, no person, during the
time of his officiating in the situation of *justice
minister,* shall be capable of sitting in the *House
of Lords* ; nor yet in the *House of Commons.*

26. That, considering the inherent and inde-
feasible comparative inaptitude of so numerous a
body for the purpose of constant and protracted
judicature,—in *all* cases, and the next to universal
habitual non-exercise of this function on the part of
their lordships in *criminal* cases ;—and that in
civil cases, their jurisdiction is, in so large a proportion, at present employed, nor could ever fail,
to be employed, as an engine of delay and expense, operating to all his majesty's subjects but
a comparatively few as a denial of justice,—it may
please their lordships to confine the exercise of
their judicial function to the abovementioned cases,
with the addition of such criminal cases, in which,
at present, a member of their own House is party
defendant :—thus making a generous sacrifice of
their uncontested rights on the altar of justice.

27. That, when it has been covered by a coating
of *legislature-made* law, the field of legislation be
preserved from being overspread by an over-
growth of *judge-made* law : for interpretation or
melioration, amendments proposed *in terminis* by
judges, on the occasion of the several suits, being,
by appropriate machinery attached to the code, of
course, unless negatived by a committee of the
one House or the other, and that, when these
arrangements have been made,—no reference, for

any such purpose as that of interpretation, to any thing said by a judge in any one suit, be permitted to be made in any other suit. Of this arrangement, another use will be—that of their applying the necessary preventive to the mischief, which might otherwise be produced, by discrepancy between the decrees of the several appellate judicatories, if more than one. This, when the field of law has been covered by *legislature-made law :* and, in the mean time, (though not equal facility,) equal necessity will there be, for the like provision, during the time that, to so immense an extent, the field has no other covering than that which is composed of *judge-made law :*—of judge-made law—that spurious and fictitious kind of law, if such it must be called, with the dominion of which, so far as it extends, all security is incompatible.*

So much as to the *Judiciary Establishment :* follows what we humbly pray in relation to *Procedure.*

28. That, as in former times, no suit shall receive its commencement, but by the personal appearance of some individual in open judicatory, which individual shall be responsible for his conduct in relation thereunto : and, to that purpose, shall, before he is heard for any other purpose, make declaration—not only of his present abode, but of such abode or abodes, at which any mandate issued by the judge, may be sure to reach him, at all times, down to that of the termination of the suit : that, for the purpose of all ulterior judicial processes, every missive addressed to him

---

* Drawn up for this purpose, a complete plan of operations, expressed *in terminis,* is already in existence.

be considered as having reached him: except in
case of any such accident as, without blame on his
part, may come to be alleged by him for the purpose of *excuse:* saving to such applicant the faculty
of changing such address, from time to time, on
giving timely information thereof.

29. That, exceptions excepted, the person so
applying be a party whose desire it is to be
admitted in the character of pursuer: of which
exceptions, examples are—1. Giving simple information of an offence, appearance on behalf of
any person or persons.—2. Purpose of the appearance, giving simple information, without desire to
be admitted *pursuer:* say pursuer, in all cases,
instead of plaintiff in civil cases and prosecutor in
criminal cases, as at present.

30. That for non-compliance with judicial mandates, an all-comprehensive system of appropriate
excuses be looked out for, and on the supposition
of the verity of the alleged facts, allowance given
to them.

31. The person by whom the matter of excuse
is submitted, will in general be the person to whom
the mandate is addressed: but, in several cases,
such as sickness, absence, &c. from other persons,
excuses for him must of necessity be accepted.

32. That the institution of *excuse-giving* which,
under the name of *casting essoins,* had place in
former days, when the attendance of parties,
instead of being as now prevented, was compelled—
be, for this purpose reviewed: and the extension
which the exigence of justice requires, be given
to it.

33. That, on every occasion, the proceedings be
regulated by regard paid to *convenience,* to wit,
the mutual convenience of all individuals con-

cerned, parties and witnesses: this being a matter which, they being on all occasions in the presence of and under examination by the judge, can, on each occasion, be ascertained: whereas, under the existing technical system, the rule being framed, without the possibility of knowing anything of the distinguishing circumstances of individual persons and things, the necessary consequence is—that, in a vast majority of instances, the convenience of individuals, some or all, is made the subject-matter of a needless and reckless sacrifice.

34. That, all judicatories being sitting every day in the year without intermission, evidence, in so far as indication of its existence has been afforded by the applicant, when admitted as pursuer, be, in such order as in each suit shall be indicated by the exigency of the individual case, from each source, as soon as obtainable, called for and elicited: and this without distinction, as between co-pursuers, co-plaintiffs, defendants, and extraneous witnesses on both sides.

35. That to the institution of *security-finding* in general, and that of sponsorship, or say *auxiliary bondsmanship* in particular,—be given the whole extent, of the application and good effect, which the nature of things allows to be given to them.

36. That, accordingly, all the sorts of *occasions* on which, and all the *modes* in which, it is capable of being employed, be looked out for:—for the purpose of employing, on each individual occasion, that mode which may be employed with the most advantage to all interests concerned.

Of *modes* of such security capable of being employed, examples are the following.

I. Intervention of *bondsmen,* stiled *auxiliary bondsmen,* one, two, or more, according to the

magnitude of the sum regarded as requisite, and
their capacity of contributing to make up such
sum; each individual contributing such part as his
circumstances enable him, and his inclination dis-
poses him, to contribute: as to the party's joining
in the bond, it would, under the here proposed
system, be a needless and useless ceremony, the
judicatory having his property as effectually at
command without it as with it.

II. *Deposit* of *money* by the *party* in the hands of
the registrar of the judicatory.

III. *Deposit* of *money* by these same *bondsmen* in
the hands of the registrar.

IV. *Deposit* of any *moveable* subject matter or
subject matters of property of considerable
value in small compass, in the hands of the
registrar.

V. *Impignoration*, or say *pledging*, of any *immoveable* or any incorporeal subject matter or subject
matters of property belonging to any such auxiliary
bondsmen.

VI. With *consent* of the party, *ambulatory confinement* of his person, he staying or going where he
pleases, so it be in the custody of a person or
persons appointed for that purpose.

VII. Under the same condition, stationary confinement in a *place* other than a prison.

VIII. At the instance of the party himself, imprisonment. Notwithstanding its afflictiveness, it
may happen to this security to be necessary; for
example, in a case where, security being deemed
necessary to be exacted of the other party, and
the finding of that security highly afflictive, the
party in question is by strangership, relative indigence, or bad character, disabled from finding any
security less afflictive.

37. Of *occasions*, requiring that such security be exacted, examples are the following :

i. At the charge of a defendant, need of security to a plaintiff, the defendant being on the point of *expatriating* either his person or his property, or both, and the value of what is demanded at his charge bearing a large proportion to his property : at the same time that, supposing the demand groundless, or the security needless, the wrong done to the defendant, if either his person or his property were detained, might be ruinous to him : as for instance, the whole of it being on the point of being expatriated on a commercial speculation in a vessel engaged by him for that purpose, and he about to embark for the purpose of superintending the disposal of such his property.

ii. On the occasion of the establishment of a mode of *intercourse* as above, with the judicatory during the continuance of the suit, want of trustworthiness may produce the need of the exaction of security, at the charge of the individual in question.

iii. Whenever, for any purpose, it may be requisite that security be exacted at the charge of a party on either side of the suit, need may also have place for the exaction of a counter-security, at the charge of the party applying for it.

Note here that of the infinite variety of *occasions*, on which the need of *security-finding* is liable to have place, the practice of *bailing* is but one, and on each occasion the chances of its being the least inconvenient one are as infinity to one.

38. That, in regard to *evidence*, whether the *source* be *personal, real,* or *ready written,* no distinction be made between *parties* and *witnesses* who are *not* parties—say *extraneous witnesses :* that is to say,

that from both, it be alike receivable and exigible :
seeing that so it is in the existing *small debt courts*,
in the aggregate of which more suits have place
than in all other courts put together : in regard to
exaction, penal suits not excepted : seeing that, in
the equity courts, such exaction has place, though,
by means of it, the richest proprietor may be di-
vested of the whole of his property ; and instances
are known, in which rather than submit to such a
loss men have sustained imprisonment for life.

39. That the mode employed in the elicitation
of evidence, (under which appellative is included
every averment made either by an applicant or by
a party on either side) be, in each individual suit,
according to the demands of that same suit, in respect of general convenience, one or more of the
three modes following : to wit, 1. The *oral*, elicited
in the originating judicatory ; 2. The *oral*, elicited
in another, say a *subsequential* judicatory, to which,
for the convenience of a party resident in the territory thereof, the inquiry is, for the purpose of his
examination, transferred : 3. The *epistolary*, by
means of interrogations approved of by the judge
of the originating judicatory.

40. That no response in the epistolary mode be
received, otherwise than subject to the eventual
examination of the respondent in the *oral* mode, at
any time, should demand have place for such examination, in the judgment of the judge.

41. That, instead of being applied, as in equity
practice, without necessity, and to the exclusion of
the *best*, that is to say the *oral* mode, the *epistolary*
mode of eliciting evidence be no otherwise employed
than for one or other of two causes : namely, 1.
Either for exclusion of preponderant evil in the
shape of delay, expence, and vexation. 2. Or of

necessity, elicitation in the oral mode being im-
practicable: as for instance, where at the time in
question the residence of the person addressed is
in the one or the other of the sister kingdoms, in a
distinct dependency, or in the dominions of a
foreign state : in all which cases the expence
and delay of commissioners sent to the places in
question will thus be saved.

42. That for avoidance of perjury and abolition
of the encouragement given to falsehood, by the
distinction between statement upon *oath*, and statement to which, though made without oath, efficiency, equal to that which is given to statement
upon oath, is, as above shewn, in many cases given,
—no oath shall, on any judicial occasion, or for
any eventually judicial purpose, be in future administered. But that every statement made on any
such occasion, or for any such purpose, shall be
termed an *affirmation,* or *asseveration ;* and that, for
falsehood in respect of it, whether accompanied
with evil consciousness, or say *wilfulness,* or with
temerity, or say culpable heedlessness, any such
punishment purely temporal shall be appointed, as
the nature of the case may be deemed to require :
consideration in each case had, of the nature of
the offence, to the commission of which such falsehood shall have been deemed subservient: and
that, as often as, in the course of the suit which
gave rise to the falsehood,—all the evidence that
can bear upon the question of falsehood has been
brought forward, conviction and punishment may
have place, even on the spot, without the formality
and expense of an additional suit on purpose, just
as, at present, in the case of an act, styled an act
of *contempt,* committed in the face of the court.

43. That, for rendering substantial justice, and for avoidance of needless multiplicity of suits, statements, and other evidence, relative to the whole of a series of wrongs, be elicitable on the occasion of one and the same application : such satisfaction, in so far as it is in a pecuniary shape, being adjusted to the state of pecuniary circumstances on both sides : this, where it is on one side only, that complaints have place : and that, where there are two parties, between whom, for a greater or less length of time, a quarrel has had place, each, in the way of recrimination, may elicit evidence of divers wrongs, of different sorts, at different times, from the other, in which case what, on the aggregate, on the score of compensation, is due from the one forms a *set-off* to what is due from the other,—satisfaction be accordingly allotted for the balance : as also, on one of the parties, or both, if, in the judgment of the judge, the case requires it,—a fine be imposed for the benefit of the public, on the score of the portion of the time of the judge and his subordinates, which, at the expense of the public, has thus been occupied.

44. That, with the exception of suits, in which, by reason of their comparative unimportance, it is purposely left unpreserved,—all evidence, elicited in the *oral* mode, shall, under the care of the *Registrar* of the judicatory, be minuted down as it is uttered : and that of this, with the addition of any such evidence as may have been adduced in the *ready-written* form, or elicited in the *epistolary* form, be constituted the main body of the document, which, under the name of the *Record*, shall, in case of *appeal*, be transmitted from an immediate to the appellate judicatory : and that;

for this purpose, the mode in which the minutations are made, may be that in which, under the name of the *manifold* mode, is already in use, and in which legible *copies*, say rather *exemplars* to the number of eight or more, are written at once: whereby all danger of error, as between one such exemplar and another, and all expense of the skilled labour requisite for revision, are saved.

45. That, towards defraying the unavoidable costs, in the case of persons unable to defray them,—a fund be established, under the name, for example, of the *Helpless Litigant's Fund.*

46. That all factitious costs being struck off, and unavoidable costs transferred on the revenue,— and professional assistance, in so far as needed, provided gratuitously as above,—*fines*, or say *mulcts*, be imposable on any party in proportion as he is in the wrong; in which imposition may be, from a degree of amplitude, far beyond any which, under the existing system would be endurable, if added to the burthen at present indiscriminately imposed under the name of *costs* on the injurer and the injured: and that of these fines the produce may constitute the basis of the *Helpless Litigant's Fund:* in the case of the wrong-doer, the requisite distinction being all along made, between evil consciousness and rashness, or say, culpable heedlessness, not accompanied with evil consciousness: and that, for any incidental misconduct manifested in the course of the suit, such fines be moreover imposable, even on a party who, on the main point, is in the right: so also on an extraneous witness: not forgetting, however, that where the case presents to view a party specially injured, no such fine can with propriety be imposed, unless more be needed on the score of punishment, than

o

is due on the score of compensation : forasmuch as the burthen of compensation produces as far as it goes, the effect of punishment : the effect—and, commonly, even more than the whole of the effect : forasmuch as by the consideration that from his pain his adversary is receiving pleasure, will naturally be produced a chagrin, which cannot have place in the case when the profit goes into the public purse.

47. That, as well of the judiciary establishment code, as of the judicial procedure code, the language be throughout such as shall be intelligible to all who have need to understand it : no word employed but what is already in familiar use, except in so far as need has place for a word on purpose : and that, to every such unavoidably-employed word, be attached an exposition, composed altogether of words in familiar use : and that, throughout, the *signs* thus employed be, of themselves, as characteristic as may be of the *things* signified.

Now for the general character of the two opposite systems : that which is in existence, and that which is herein, as above, humbly proposed as a succedaneum to it.

Behold first the existing system.

Justice, to Judge and Co. a game ; Judge and Co. the players : stake, in different proportions, the means of happiness possessed by the aggregate of all litigants.

Established a universal chain of tyrannies : established, by power to every individual to tyrannize over every other, whose circumstances are to a certain degree less affluent: in every case, instrument of tyranny; utter ruin: utter ruin, by the enormity of the expence.

Alike well-adapted to the purpose of the oppressor, that of the depredator, and that of him who is both in one, is this same instrument. This in hand, a man may oppress, he may plunder, the same person at the same time.

Considered with reference to its real ends, could any more accomplished aptitude — considered with reference to its pretended ends, could any more accomplished inaptitude be obtained by a premium directly offered for the production of it?

So much for the existing system. On the other hand, such, as hath been seen in brief outline, is the system of arrangements dictated by a real and exclusive regard for the happiness of the community, in so far as it depends upon the application made of the power of judicature. We invite the well-intentioned,—we challenge the evil-intentioned,—to elicit and hold up to view, all proofs and exemplifications of its inaptitude. Whatsoever alleged imperfections have been found in it, will of course, in case of adoption, be removed by the constituted authorities. But, considered as a whole, we cannot but flatter ourselves, that, in quality of a subject matter of adoption after such amendments made, no arguments will be found opposible to it, other than ungrounded assertions, vague generalities, narrow sentimentalities, or customary and already exposed fallacies.

Now for an apology: an apology for the freedom with which the vices of the existing system has been subjected to exposure, and its utter inaptitude for its professed purpose, we trust, demonstrated. In this inaptitude, coupled with the aptitude of the proposed succedaneum, will be found the best, and we humbly hope a sufficient apology for this boldness, how striking soever the contrast it forms with accustomed usage.

Another apology we have to make is, that which is so undeniably requisite for the freedom with which, in addition to the character of the system, that of the class of persons concerned in the administration of it is held up to view. For this liberty, our plea is that of indispensable necessity. For unhappily, the state of manners considered,—on their part, at any rate on the part of the great majority, it is not in the nature of man that this or any other system should be received by this class, otherwise than with opposition, and that opposition hostile and strenuous in proportion to the serviceableness in the thus exposed system, and the disserviceableness of the here proposed system, to their respective real or supposed particular interests: on which occasion, what again is but too natural, is, that beholding with serenity, and even delight, the torments out of which, and in proportion to which, their comforts are extracted by it, the unction of their panegyrics will continue to be poured forth upon the thus exposed system, in proportion to its need of them, which is as much as to say, in exact proportion to its mischievousness.

Thence it is, that the doing what depended upon us, towards lowering, as far as consistently with justice may be, the estimation in which their authority is held by public opinion,—because, how painful soever, an indispensable part of this our arduous enterprise:—assured as we could not but be, of its finding that so influential authority, in its whole force, with all its weight, on every point pressing down upon it.

Of an imputation which will of course be cast upon the line of argument thus taken by us, we are fully aware. This is—that the weakening the force and efficiency of the whole power of the law is a natural effect—not to say the object—of these our humble endeavours.

To this charge we have two answers.

One is that, from this cause, no such consequence will really follow: the other is—that, while by this same cause, the power of the law will not be diminished, the security for its taking its proper direction will be increased,

First, as to the apprehension of the evil consequence. Produced by a superficial glance, natural enough this apprehension must be acknowledged to be: by a closer view, it will, we trust, be dispelled.

That which produces the effect aimed at by the law, what is it? Is it anything other than the expectation, that, on contravention, the inflictions at the disposal of the functionaries in question will accordingly be applied to the contraveners? But of any such infliction, when the decree for it has passed, will the application depend upon public opinion? No surely: on no such fluctuating basis does public security rest: the persons on whom it depends for its efficiency, are, in the first instance, the judges themselves; in the next place, in case of need, the supreme authority, with the whole force of the country in its hands. When a judgment has been pronounced, is it in the power of this or that individual or individuals in any number whatsoever, to prevent the execution of it ? No assuredly.

Now, as to the desirable good consequence. This consists in the giving strength to the limitative check, applied to the power of the judge, by the power of *public opinion*—sole source from which, on the several individual occasions, this so necessary and from all other hands unobtainable service can be received. Yes; we repeat it—sole source. True it is that, in theory, and by the practice of times now past, *impeachment* is presented in the character of an oppropriate remedy : hands by which it is applicable, those of the Honourable House. But, in fact, only in appearance is it so. On no other condition than that of leaving—and that to an indefinite degree—inadequately done or even altogether undone, its superior and altogether indispensably *legislative* duty,—could be undertaken by the House, this judicial, and as such inferior and comparatively unimportant function. Witness the testimony so amply afforded by experience : witness the Warren Hastings impeachment : witness the Melville impeachment. Take away the check applied by the tribunal of public opinion, here then is the power of the judge, nominally and theoretically controlled, really and practically uncontrolled : and of this same uncontrolled power what sort of use has been made, and so long as it continues upon its present footing, can not but continue to be made, has, we humbly trust, been sufficiently seen already.

Well then : of the power of public opinion in consequence of the information hereby afforded to it, what is the application reasonably to be expected ? The universal power of the whole country

—will it employ itself against itself? But, the lower the trustworthiness of these same functionaries is in the scale of public opinion, the less efficient, on each occasion, will be capable of being made its resistance to this indispensable check :— the only one, as hath been seen, from which any control can be experienced by it.

Undangerous in perfection, gentle in perfection, continually improving, self-improving,—what other power can be so completely incapable of being abused as this? Only by the check applied by it can the efficiency of a judge's sinister leanings be lessened: only by the force of reason can the direction taken by this guardian power be determined.

As to any such fall as that just mentioned,— whatsoever may be the sensation produced by it,— in their predecessors and themselves, these functionaries may behold the original authors whom they have to thank for it. Instead of being what it has ever been and continues to be, and never can but be,—had the use made of their power been the direct reverse of what it has been,—no such state of the public mind,—no such sensation in the individual mind, could have had place.

While speaking of this same downfall, it is not without unfeigned regret that we can contemplate the hurt, which, by this our humble Petition, cannot but in a greater or less degree be done to the interests and feelings of individuals: and this, not only eventually by the establishment of the here proposed system, but actually and immediately by the picture here drawn of the causes by which the demand for it has been produced.

But well-grounded, as these their apologies cannot be denied to be, no reason will they afford

why the exertion necessary to the putting an end
to the abuses apologized for should in any way
be slackened. The surgeon, with whatsoever concern he may behold the sufferings of the patient
under the necessary caustic, cannot hold himself
exempted by the consideration of them from the
obligation of putting it to its use.

Nor yet under these regrets, for this hardship on
individuals, is alleviation, independently of that
afforded by the contemplation of the all-comprehensive benefit to the public, altogether wanting.

Classes, the interests of which would be affected
by the proposed reform, these two :—the professional and the official.

As to the professional class, not to near so great
an amount, if to any, as at first view might be
supposed, would be the detriment to their pecuniary interests. For, long would it be before their
situation could be in any way affected by the
change. Suppose the matter already before a
committee of your Honourable House. Long would
it be, before the reforming process would, by a
bill brought in in consequence, so much as take
its commencement: long, beyond calculation, notwithstanding the utmost possible exertions employed in giving acceleration to it, would be the
time occupied in the continuance of that same
process: long, even supposing both houses unanimous in their approbation of the measure considered in a general point of view : and how much
further could it fail of being lengthened, by the
exertions which it would be so sure of finding
everywhere opposed to it—opposed by the best
exercised and strongest hands ? Such is the length
of time during which all such professional men as
the bill found already in possession of business

would be enjoying the fruits of it, without diminution or disturbance.

So much for that class. All this while, all men who, but for the apprehended fall off, would have engaged in the profession, will have had before their eyes the prospect of it, and the notice and warning given by that prospect. On the other hand, in like manner will these same eyes have had before them the augmentation (and it has been seen how ample a one) given to the number and value of the aggregate lists of judicial situations. Correspondent will accordingly be the number of those whose destination will, by that prospect, be changed from the indiscriminate defence of right and wrong, in the capacity of professional lawyers, to the pure pursuit of the ends of justice, in the situation of judge. Moreover, proportioned to the amount of this secession would be a further indemnification to those already in the possession of business : so many men whose course has thus been changed, so many competitors removed.

The class upon which, chiefly, the loss would fall, is the *attorney* class. A certain class of suits there is by which, on the present footing, business with its emolument is afforded to the attorney, none to the advocate class : business, for example, begun, altogether without prospect of successful defence, and thence carried through actually without defence : action for example, with or without arrest for indisputable and certainly procurable debt. Barristers not deriving any profit from the present existence, would sustain no loss from the cessation of these actions.

But as to the length of the interval before commencement, as also the exclusion put upon competition, in these advantages the attorney class would possess an equal share.

As to the official class, nothing whatever in a pecuniary shape can any of its members have to apprehend from the change: from all such apprehension they stand effectually secured by the application so constantly made of the *indemnification* principle, to the interest of men of their order at any rate, whatsoever ground of complaint, on this score, may, in but too many instances, have been felt by functionaries belonging to lower orders.

After all, of all regrets from such a source the complexion, would be, what it would be if the sufferings, instead of these, were those of medical men from improvements made in the state of general health and longevity: improvement such as that made by the substitute of vaccination to inoculation: imaginable improvement by discovery made of a never-failing specific, for example, against the ague, the rheumatism, the gout, the stone, the cholera morbus, the yellow fever, the plague, or by the universal drainage of all pestiferous marshes.

Now as to the effect produceable on estimation and thence on feelings. Altogether unavoidable, and indispensably necessary to the establishment of the everlasting good, upon the all-comprehensive scale on which it is here endeavoured at,— has been the production of the transient evil upon this, comparatively minute scale. Before the running sore, kept up at present under and by the existing system, could with any the least chance of success, be endeavoured to be healed, it was necessary it should be probed, and the sinister interest in which it has had its cause, brought to light and held up to view.

Now, in the case of the class of persons unavoidably wounded, so far as regards damage to
estimation, are alleviations, and those very efficient ones, by any means wanting? In the first
place, comes the consideration, that what is important to them, so far from being peculiar to
them, is nothing more than what has place
incontestably and confessedly in all other classes of
men whatsoever. In the minds of the men here
in question, indeed, but no otherwise than in
those of all other men, with the exception of the
heroic few, prevalence of self-regard over all other
regards, and this on every occasion, is among the
conditions of existence : place all regard for the
interest of A. in the breast—not of A. but of B. and
so reciprocally, the species can not continue in
existence for a fortnight. True it is, that in this
or that heroic breast, on this or that occasion, under
the stimulus of some extraordinary excitement,
social feeling upon the scale of such an all-embracing charge, may, here and there, be seen to tower
above regard for self: but, to no man can the not
being a hero be matter of very severe reproach.
When, therefore, as here, interest from the very
first—interest real or (what comes to the same
thing) imagined—has been made to clash with
duty, sacrifice of duty is, with exceptions too rare
to warrant any influence on practice, sure, and as
such ought to be calculated upon, and taken for
the ground of arrangement and proceeding, in all
political arrangements.

Men are the creatures of circumstances. Placed
in the same circumstances, which of us all who
thus complain, can take upon himself to say or
stand assured—that, in the same circumstances,
his conduct would have been other and better

than that which, on such irrefragable grounds, he
is thus passing condemnation on, and complain-
ing of?

Of the existing race, whatsoever may be the
demerits, they have at once, for their cause and
their apology, not only the opposition in which, in
their instance, interest has been placed with reference to duty, but the example set them in a
line of so many centuries in length, by their predecessors: and in ancestor worship, how this our
country has at all times vied with *China*, is no
secret to any one.

The concluding observation how small soever
may be the number of the individuals to whom it
will be found to have application, is—that, to the
imputation of hostility to the universal interest, by
perseverance in the preference given to personal
interest, it depends upon every man to remain
subject, or liberate himself from it, as he feels inclined: and the more powerful the temptation, the
more transcendant will be the glory of having sur-
mounted it: and whatsoever may have been the
strenuousness and length of his labours in the
augmentation of the disease, ample may be the
compensation and atonement made, by his contributions to the cure of it.

Such are the considerations, from the aggregate
of which our regrets for the manner in which the
feelings of the individuals in question cannot but
be affected, have experienced the diminution
above spoken of. But were those regrets ever so
poignant, our endeavours for the removal of the
boundless evil of the disorder would not be, (for
will anybody say they ought to be?) in the
smallest degree diminished, by the consideration
of the partial evil thus attendant on the applica-

tion of the sole possible remedy: assuredly ours will not; nor will, as we hope and believe, the accordant endeavours of the great majority of our fellow subjects.

On this occasion, a circumstance to which we cannot but intreat the attention of the Honourable House is the uniform and almost universal silence, in which, by professional men, in bringing to view, or speaking of proposed reforms or meliorations, this universal cause of all the wrongs and sufferings produced in the field of law, has, as if by universal agreement entered into for the purpose, been, as far as depended upon them, kept out of sight. Of the several elements of appropriate aptitude as applied to this case,—intellectual aptitude and active talent are, on this occasion, assumed to be the only ones, in which any deficiency in the appropriate aptitude of the law itself in any part, has ever had its source: the only ones on which the degree of this same aptitude depends: the only ones, of a deficiency in which there can ever be any danger. As to appropriate moral aptitude, —on every such occasion, exclusively intent on the interest of the public, without so much as a thought about their own interest, in any respect, and in respect of profit in particular,—that all persons in this department sharing in the possession of power, and with them all persons engaged in the exercise of the profession, are and at all times will be, —this is what is tacitly, but not the less decidedly, assumed: assumed? and with what reason: with exactly the same as if the assumption were applied to all persons engaged in trade. Now then, in this state of things, while on every occasion universally thus referred to the wrong cause, what can be more impossible, than that the disorder should ever receive from the sole true *recipe*, deduced from the knowledge of its true cause, its only possible remedy?. Vain, however, how extensive soever, vain at any rate, so far as regards us your petitioners—will henceforward be this so decorous and prudential silence, the nature and magnitude of the mischief, and the nature of its cause, being at length alike known to us.

As to this silence, the decorum attached to it notwithstanding, we humbly trust that in the Honourable House it will not any longer be maintained : for so long as in that sole source of appropriate relief, it has continuance, so long will all possibility of effectual remedy be excluded ; and so long as the disorder continues unremoved, by no silence anywhere else can our ears be closed, or our tongues or our pens be stopt.

Yes ; as to us your petitioners, the film is now off our eyes : thus wide open are they to the disorders of which we complain, and to the urgency of the demand for the remedy, which, at the hands of the physicians of the body politic, we thus humbly, but not the less earnestly, entreat the application of the only remedy.

To some it may be matter of no small wonder, how such sufferings as at all times have been experienced, should at all times have had for its accompaniment, such almost universal patience. But, in this case, patience has been the natural fruit of ignorance ; the language in which these torments of the people have in this case had their instrument, being about as intelligible to the people at large, as is the gibberish spoken by the race of gipsies.

We beseech the Honourable House to ask itself whether, of the enormities above brought to view, one tenth would not suffice to justify the practical conclusion here drawn from them? whether of a system thus in every part repugnant to the ends of justice, and injecting into every breast, with such rarely-resistible force, the poison of immorality in so many shapes, the mischief can be removed otherwise than by the entire abolition of it, coupled with the substitution of a system directed to those ends, and pure from all such corruptive tendency? whether the inaccessibility of justice be not of the number of those enormities? and whether the House itself will, henceforward, be anything better than an enemy to the community, if with eyes open, and hands motionless, it suffers that inaccessibility to continue?

For our parts—respectfully, but not the less earnestly, we conclude, as we began, with the continual, and, till accomplishment, never about to cease cry—" Holy! Holy! Holy! Justice! accessible Justice! Justice, not for the few, but for all! No longer nominal, but at length real, Justice!"

ABRIDGED

PETITION FOR JUSTICE.

---

*To the Honorable the House of Commons in
Parliament assembled.*

1. JUSTICE! justice! *accessible* justice! justice,
not for the *few* alone, but for *all!* No longer *nominal*, but at length *real*, justice !—In these few words
stand expressed the sum and substance of the
humble Petition, which we, the undersigned, in
behalf of ourselves and all other his Majesty's long-
suffering subjects, now at length have become
emboldened to address to the Honorable House.
The case we accordingly take the liberty to state,
followed by a prayer, humbly suggesting a plan
for the removal of the grievance, is this—

2. That, of the *expense* without which application
to judges, for the *service* which, as such, they are
appointed to render, cannot be made, nor if made
continued, the effect is such—that, in cases called
civil altogether, and in cases called *penal* to a vast
extent, justice is not only sold at a dear price to
all the few who have wherewithal to purchase it,

B

but utterly denied to all who can not; and that those who are thus oppressed are thus subjected to wrong, in all shapes, without redress.

3. That the *delay* is such, that, in many cases, in which, under a proper system, a few minutes would suffice,—and even under the system established does in cases to a narrow extent actually suffice—more than as many years elapse before a man can obtain possession of what, at the end of that interval, are universally seen to have been, and to continue to be, his manifest and indubitable rights.

4. That, while thus unapt for *redress* of wrong, it is exquisitely well adapted for the *commission* of wrong : for, such is the mode in which commencement is given to suits, that is to say, without security given for compensation for wrong if done by means of the suit, that, without so much as imagining himself to have any just ground of demand whatsoever—any man, who is able and willing to pay a certain price, may, as we shall shew, stand assured of effecting the utter ruin of any one of from nine-tenths or ninety-nine hundredths of the whole body of the people.

5. That this state of things has for its *cause* the undeniable fact,—that, from first to last, the interests of all persons concerned in the administration of justice has been in a state of opposition, as direct as possible, to their acknowledged duty, and the interests of the community.

6. That this oppositeness had for its original cause the *penury* under which government at that time laboured ; it not having, in its then existing state, wherewithal to pay salaries ; and being thereby laid under the necessity of allowing the functionaries of justice to exact, for their own use,

payment in the shape of *fees* : payable for processes carried on in the course of the suit : for processes carried on,—that is to say, either for instruments (*written instruments*) communicated, or thereby or otherwise, *operations* performed.

7. That, under and by the influence of the sinister interest thus created—has been generated the existing system of judicial procedure : a procedure, having for its ends—instead of the ends of justice—the swelling, to its utmost endurable amount, the evil composed of the expense, delay and vexation, for the sake of the profit extractable out of the expense, to the use of the several partners in the said sinister interest : to whom, taken in the aggregate, may accordingly, without injurious misrepresentation, and with instructive and beneficial application to practice, the style and title of Judge and Co. may be allotted.

8. That, though, by a late act, in the case of the judges of the supreme Westminster Hall courts, salaries have been substituted to fees,—yet, this substitution, not being extended to those their subordinates, of whose situations they have the patronage, the comparative *sinister interest*, in unabated efficiency, still *continues : gift* being still allowed; and gift being, in all cases, a source of proportionable benefit to the giver : in some cases of even greater pecuniary profit than *sale* is : as in the case of the gift made of the next presentation to an ecclesiastical benefice by the patron to his son : and that even were this same supposed remedy effective against further increase of the grievance,—which however it is not in its nature to be,—still the system of factitious expense, delay and vexation, offspring of the sinister interest, would remain as it does in all its mischievousness.

9. That the boundless weight of human suffering thus imposed is not, in any part of it, as some suppose, natural and unavoidable, but in the whole artificial: as also in the whole removable; as, in and by the suggestion contained in the prayer of this our humble petition, we will humbly shew.

10. That, amongst others, of the *devices* which, in consequence, and by means, of the Norman conquest, have been contrived and employed, for the compassing of this same sinister object, the results are these which follow—devices, some of them first employed at and during that same period, others at different successive periods, grafted on or employed in fertilizing, the first devised radical ones.

11.—I. *Device the first—Exclusion of the Parties from the presence of the Judge.*

This, at the very outset of the cause, down to the last stage: that thereby, parties in general, and the most opulent in particular, may be, as they accordingly are, necessitated to employ in all, even the most simple cases, as substitutes, a class of men whose profit rises in proportion to expense, delay, and vexation; and who, exercising their profession under the dominion of the sinister interest, which they have in common with that of the judges, have the benefit of their support towards the reaping and encrease of this same sinister profit: a master device this, serving as a necessary instrument of the employment given to most of the hereinafter ensuing devices.

12. A collateral mischief is—that, by this exclusion, the door is shut against evidence from that which is commonly the most instructive source, and thereby decision necessarily given in

favour of the side in the wrong, in every case in which no other than the thus excluded evidence is obtainable. This in some cases : while, in other cases, by a glaring inconsistency, the thus excluded evidence is admitted.

13. In particular, in the judicatories called *equity courts*, in which the plaintiff is admitted, in and by his bill, to extract evidence, through the medium of the pen, from the bosom of the defendant : in which state of things, the defendant,—unless his professional assistants are deficient in appropriate aptitude—moral, intellectual, or active,—slides in, in and by his answer, whatsoever averments present in his and their joint opinion, a probability of operating in favour of his side.

14. Not but that, for two distinct purposes,—in so far as may be without *preponderant evil* in the shape of delay, vexation, and expense, is necessary to justice the thus excluded attendance : 1. for bringing to view all facts which are of a nature to operate in favour of any party on either side : 2. to serve as a check upon the sinister interest, whereby their respective professional assistants are prompted, as above, to swell to its maximum that same *evil*, for the sake of the profit extractible out of the expense.

15. Note also that, so far as it can be effected without preponderant evil as above, not less needful is this attendance on the part of *principals*, or say intended *benefitees*, (for example, wives, children and their offspring, wards, and members of associated companies), for the protection of their interests, against misconduct on the part of their respective *trustees :* that is to say, husbands, fathers and other progenitors, guardians, and agents of various denominations ; with or without collusion with their several professional assistants in the suit.

16.—II. *Device the second—Language unintelligiblized.*

Instead of the mother-tongue of the parties, the
language, originally employed in word-of-mouth
discussion, being the language of the conquerors ;
that is to say, *Norman French:* and the language,
employed in written instruments, the *Latin.*

17. Thence was created the necessity of employing these so little trustworthy trustees, not
only as assistants and advocates, but even as interpreters between the *English-speaking* parties and
the *French-speaking judges.*

18. Out of these two foreign languages, in conjunction with the mother-tongue, has been made
up the jargon, by which, to so great a degree, the
same continuance has been given to the same design ;—the translation, at length made by order of
parliament, notwithstanding : whereby, to so great
an extent, false and delusive lights have been substituted to total darkness.

19.—III. *Device the third—Written Pleadings worse
than useless, necessitated.*

By this means, justice was *denied* to all who
could not afford the expense of hiring the manufacturers of this sort of ware—sold to all who could
and would be at the expense : and, even now, such
continues to be the case : and, being paid in proportion to the quantity, thus it is, that, by this
sinister interest, they stand engaged to give every
practicable increase to it.

20. Now then, as to the supposed necessariness
and usefulness of these same instruments. Really
necessary are, and in every case, on the plaintiff's
side,—statements, 1. of the *demand* made, by him ;
2. of the *ground* of it in point of *law;* 3. of the ground

of it in point of *fact;* and, 4. of the evidence by which it is supported: 5. of the *persons* on whom the demand is made. These are, 1. in the first instance, as above—the *defendant;* 2. on failure of compliance on his part, by performance of service demanded at his hands—the judge; the service demanded at his hands then, the correspondent service, rendered by bringing about that which was demanded at the charge of the defendant, or what is regarded as an equivalent to it. In like manner, in case of non-compliance on the part of the defendant, correspondent statements in justification of such non-compliance.

21. Of all this matter, what is there in these same written pleadings? Answer—Really and distinctly expressed, nothing: nothing but a confused and redundant, yet imperfect hodge-podge, composed of more or less of it.

22. Moreover, for procuring custom, at the hands of individuals who know they are in the wrong,—as well as for giving increase to the quantity of jargon which parties are constrained to buy,—a distinction has been made between *pleadings* and *evidence;* and this, in such sort that, while on the one hand, of statements, to which the name of *evidence* is given, *punishment*, under the name of *punishment*, is in case of wilful falsehood, made the consequence,—on the other hand, to those to which the name of *pleadings* is given, no such consequence is attached: and thus it is that to all such left purposely unpunished falsehood, allowance, or say license, is given:. at the same time, to these same masses of falsehood, which are not so much as pretended to be entitled to the name of evidence, is given a surer effect, than to any the best and most satisfactory evidence: since, when

the party on either side has come out with one of
these pleadings, the party on the other side, if he
fails to encounter it with a correspondent mass, is
visited with the loss of his cause : and thereby
with a suffering, which may be any number of
times as great as that produced by punishment
under the *name* of *punishment* would be : and thus
it is, that the license so given to mendacity
operates as encouragement to, and reward for, the
commission of it.

22. Now then, this same failure when it takes
place, what has it for its efficient cause? His
being in the wrong, and at the same time conscious of being so, answer Judge and Co.: if both
these fail, his inaction is *circumstantial* evidence;
and to this we give the effect of *conclusive* evidence.

23. Such is the conclusion : now as to the just-
ness of it. Not to speak of others,—one circumstance which the failure is not less likely to have
had for the efficient cause is—want of wherewithal
to pay for this same thus necessitated mass of surplusage : and, the greater the quantity of it, the
more probable this fulfilment of the dishonest
suitor's wishes : and thus it is that by continuance
given to the length of the mass, any man may
make sure of consigning to utter ruin, any other
man, whose circumstances are to a certain degree
less affluent : and, under the name of justice, the
faculty of oppression is sold to the best bidder.

24. Addressed to the supporters of the existing
system, follow a few plain questions :—

If, in relation to any point, it were on any occasion your wish to learn the truth of a case of any
sort from a child of yours, or from a servant of
yours—

I. Would you refuse to *see* him?

2. Would you send him to, or keep him at, a *distance* from you?

3. Would you insist on his not answering otherwise than *in writing*?

4. Would you, on the occasion of such his writing, *insist* on his coming out with a multitude of *lies*, some *stale* and notorious, others *new* and out of his own head?

5. Would you so much as *consent* to his mixing up *false* information, in whatever quantity he chose—and *that* in an undistinguishable manner—with whatsoever true information it was that you had need of?

6. Would you establish an interval of four or five months' forced silence, between statement and statement, question and answer, or one answer and another?

7. Would you take any such course, if you were acting as *chairman of a House of Commons committee*, making inquiry into the state of things in relation to any subject, for the information of the *legislature*?

8. Would you, if acting in the character of a *justice of peace*, whether singly, or as chairman, at a meeting of a number of justices of the peace, sitting in special sessions, and making inquiry into the matter of a question of any sort, civil or penal, coming within your competence?

25. Well, then, this, however, is, all of it, the exact description of what has place, as often as the process of delivering *written pleadings* is carried on; carried on, as it is, under the eye and by order of all the judges: and this, as well in the equity courts as in the common law courts. This is what, in the common law courts (to go no higher), has place from beginning to end; has place until the suit

reaches the jury-box :—not to go along with it any further.

26. Now, then, on the part of those by whom this was the course in which judicial inquiry was ordained to be carried on, can you, now that that course is thus laid open to you,—can you for a moment suppose that *justice* was ever the end in view? Can any man of common sense suppose it? Can any man of common honesty declare himself to suppose it? Can it really be believed by any man, that *despatch* is promoted by an inexorably *standing still* for four or five months?

27. IV. *Device the fourth—Mendacity licensed, re-warded, compelled, and by Judge himself practised.*

Of the manner in which, by and for the benefit and profit of Judge and Co., falsehood has begun and continues to be *licensed, rewarded,* and on some occasions *compelled,* it has been necessary to give some intimation under the head of *written pleadings;* falsehood, wilful or not, as it may happen, on the part of the *utterers,* wilful at any rate on the part of the judges—the *suborners.* Follow, under the present head, instances of *compulsion* more manifest and avowed, as also of the *practice* of it by themselves.

28. First, as to *compulsion.* In the proceedings of the courts styled *courts of equity* in contradistinction to courts of *common law,* it is—that features of *compulsion* are in a more particular degree prominent. After the process which has the effect of a *summons*—the instrument, with which the suit begins, is a paper called *a bill,* commencing with a *case,* or say a *story,* and continuing with a quantity of *interrogative matter,* by which *answers* are called for: answers, to a string of *questions,* grounded on

the several *statements*, or say *averments* or *allegations*, contained in the case. To these averments is given, on this occasion, the name of *charges*.

29. Now then of this same *case*, what is the composition? Falsehoods, in a more or less considerable proportion, it can not but have; and in the larger proportion it commonly has. Penalty, on non-insertion of them, refusal to impose on the defendant the obligation of giving answers to the question; in which case, they will not be of any service to the plaintiff's purpose; they will not be contributory to his obtainment of his right: the evidence sought for by them at the hands of the defendant remains unelicited.

30. Seat and source of the falsehood, this: into the composition of the *case* or *story*, enter commonly two distinguishable *parcels* of alleged facts, all supposed to be *relevant* to the matter in question, and *necessary*, or at any rate *conducive* to the purpose of constituting an adequate ground for the demand made at the charge of the defendant, by this same instrument of demand: object of it, a *service* in some shape or other, at the hands, and at the charge, of the defendant; and, eventually, in default of compliance on the correspondent part of the defendant, the service at the hands of the judge; namely, the production of such compliance, or some other service regarded as an equivalent for it.

31. Contents of one parcel of these same facts, such of them as, without any information from the defendant, are (so the plaintiff conceives) known to him (the plaintiff), as also to some other person or persons, regarded by him as having had perception of them, and being able and about to be willing to declare them: or, at any rate, as being

in some way or other in his power to make proof
of: this, in whatever degree of *particularity* is necessary to constitute the requisite ground: call
these the *already known* facts.   As to this parcel,
all that is wanted at the hands of the defendant, is
admission: seeing that by this, the need of application to any other person for the purpose of *information*, will of course be superseded.

32. Contents of the other parcel, such supposed
facts as, in contradistinction to the foregoing, may
be styled *unknown* or *sought-for facts:* sought, to
wit, at the hands of the defendant: the case being,
that, for making proof of them, *information*, such
as it is in his power to afford, and perhaps in his
alone, is regarded as requisite: in relation to these
facts, all that, in the plaintiff's mind, in a form
more or less particular and determinate, has place,
being a *conjecture*, or say *suspicion*, of their existence.

33. Now then as to these same *sought-for facts*,
for what reason is it that by the plaintiff they are
thus *sought* for?   *Answer.*—For this very reason,
because they are *not* known to him.   Yet, in relation
to the facts thus unknown to him, is he obliged to
make declaration that they *are* known to him:
which declaration is constantly the offspring of the
inventive genius of his professional advisers and assistants.   Without such false declaration, from them
—writing in the plaintiff's name,—no information at
all will the learned judge suffer to be attempted to
be elicited from a defendant.   Purport of the rule
expressive of the obligation, this—Every interro-
gatory must have a *charge* for the support of it.

34. Plaintiff, for example, creditor of a person
deceased; defendant his executor.   To some
amount or other, property in some shape or other,

is left by the deceased : but, to what amount, and in what shape, this is what the plaintiff is altogether ignorant of; for information in relation to it—information in such shape as shall constitute an adequate ground for the demand made of the debt, this is what is thus *sought for* by plaintiff at the charge and at the hands of the defendant. Well then : to a question, asking whether property of the deceased to the amount requisite is in existence, and if yes, what it consists of, and so forth, will a judge compel any answer to be made? Not he indeed : otherwise than *upon condition*. And this condition—what is it? *Answer*—That, in the bill, a multitude of declarations, or say *averments*, *assertions* or *statements* shall be inserted—statements, giving an account more or less particular, of the several abovementioned *unknown* facts : facts, by the supposition unknown to the very individual, who is thus compelled to assert that he knows them, on which occasion, the learned draughtsman finds himself under the not altogether unpleasant or unprofitable obligation, of bringing to the view of his lordship (who will never see it) a statement of every sort of thing, which, it is regarded as possible should in the aggregate mass of the property in question have been contained; and, the richer the quantity of this poetry in prose, the richer the reward to the industry of the firm of Judge and Co. in all its branches.

35. Note, by the bye, in the case where no *information* is wanted at the hands of the defendant, the *consequence* of resorting to him, in *this* mode, for *admission*, instead of to a non-party, say an extraneous witness—for information, and thereby for proof. Consequence naturally expected (that is to say, by a man who has never

looked into equity procedure) delay and expense saved : for, to the defendant application (says he) must be made at any rate for payment of the debt. This (continues he) being necessary, when you are about it, add to the demand of the money due, a demand of the information necessary to the proof of its being due,—the information being thus obtained, and from the defendant himself, saved thereby is the delay and expense of the endeavour to obtain it from sources in number and distance altogether indefinite. Such as to delay and expense is the economy in appearance. How stands it in reality? *Answer*—In *natural* procedure it would have place; but in equity procedure, what the plaintiff gets by it, if the defendant (being rich enough) so pleases, is—in regard to delay, substitution of years to minutes, and in regard to expense, hundreds or thousands of pounds to shillings.

Is this handwriting yours? Yes, or no? For the answer to a question to this effect *spoken* by a justice of the peace less than even a *second* of time would serve; and by an answer in the affirmative would be decided many a suit which, under equity procedure, while questions and answers are *written*, occupies *years*.

36. So much for *licence, remuneration,* and *compulsion* of mendacity; now for the practice of it: practisers, as well as compellers of mendacity, never, for a moment, let it be out of mind, the judges themselves. *Fiction* is the appellative, by which the sort of falsehood, thus by judges coined in their own mint, has at all times been distinguished. Nor was the choice thus made of the appellative a *blind* one. Established they found it in a situation of favor in the public mind,—esta-

blished, by means of the application made of it to the purpose of designating *poetry* and *romance:* and thus it was, that into a portion of the favor, associating with those always agreeable and sometimes useful productions of the imaginative faculty, they thus contrived to let in these constantly not only useless, but enormously mischievous ones. So much for the nature of this species of poetry.

37. Now for some accompaniments belonging to it.   In every case, of the utterance given to these falsehoods, *evil consciousness,*—styled in their language *mala fides,*—has on their part been an accompaniment: *fraudulent obtainment,* the *object:* subject-matter of the obtainment, money: to wit, either immediately, that is to say, in the shape of *fees,* or mediately, through the medium of power, parent of fees: *persons thus wronged*—in so far as the subject-matter was composed of *money*--the people, in the capacity of *suitors:* in so far as it was composed of *power,* the fellows and competitors, of these same judges, as also in various indirect ways, the *people* again: one way, the being, in the course of the scramble between judge and judge, consigned to imprisonment; and through imprisonment, frequently to utter ruin, as, under the head of *groundless arrests* for debt, will be found distinctly visible.   So much for the *morality* of the *practice.*

38. Now as to the *effects* of it.   Beneficial effects, none: mischievous effects, these.

i. Mischief the first and most prominent, depredation and oppression, as above: on each individual occasion, at the charge of *assignable* individuals in the capacity of *suitors.*

39.—ii. Mischief the second, *arbitrary power,* acquired and exercised.   Allow a man to assume the existence of a matter a fact,—of an event, or state of things, by which, supposing it really to have had existence, the assumption and exercise of power would have a justificative cause,—allow him this, what is the power which you do not thus allow him to assume? Of this indirect mode of assumption in preference to the direct, what is the consequence—any diminution of the evil? No : but, on the contrary, an addition to it: namely, the evils produced, as will be seen, by the nature of the *instrument* thus employed.

40.—III. Mischief the third: birth given to a particular instrument of arbitrary power: an instrument to which exposition and exposure have been given elsewhere, under and by the name of the *double fountain.* Mechanism thus alluded to, a vessel invented by *jugglers;* contained in it, wine of two sorts and colours; out of it, come the one or the other at the word of command. Whenever any one of these. fictions has been established, thus is it with truth and falsehood. On the individual occasion in question, to this or that sinister purpose of the judge, which of the two is it that is most suitable? Is it the falsehood? Out comes, as usual, the established falsehood, and on this it is that the proceedings are grounded. Is it the truth? Back goes he to the original truth; and on this are the proceedings grounded new. Consequence to juggler's reputation what? At the hands of the people, anything in the way of censure? Oh, no : they look on and stare. Instead of censure, comes in either case praise : on this occasion, as on every other, praise at the hands of Judge and Co. and their dupes,— praise without stint, for everything, be it what it may, which by these same hands, is done. Whichever be the ground taken by the decision, praise, appropriate in shape and quantity, stands prepared for the reception of it. Is it the falsehood? Topic of eulogy, strictness of the regard manifested for *established* rules : for the precept expressed by the words *stare decisis*. Is it the truth? Topic— liberality and paramount love of truth and substantial justice : who shall blame the holy love of substantial justice? Of the *double fountain*, one form this : under the head of " *Decision on grounds foreign to the merits*," will be visible another.

41. Thus it is, that, on each occasion, according as it happens to him to feel disposed, disposed by whatsoever motives, whether by corrupt profit to himself, by sympathy or antipathy towards individuals or parties, the judge has it in his power to determine the suit in favour of the one side or the other : and thus, without any the smallest danger, either of punishment at the hands of government, or so much as censure at the hands of public opinion.

42.—IV. Mischief the fourth. In the minds of well intentioned judges, generated by the incongruous mixture, confusion, thence relative intellectual inaptitude—one efficient cause of misdecision, on the part of the judge, delay in the proceedings, with expense and vexation at the charge of suitors.

43.—V. Mischief the sixth. Of that part of the rule of action, which continues in the aerial shape of *common*, in contradistinction to *statute* law,—the texture vitiated, and the all-persuading and incurable inaptitude increased : and this, as well in the *substantive* as in the adjective branch of the law : it being through the machinery of the *adjective* branch, or say the system of *procedure*, that the

c

cobwebs, of which the substantive branch or *main body* of the law, in so far as manufactured by judicial hands, is composed : and thus it is, that in the minds of the manufacturers, the confusion and intellectual inaptitude, and in the work the consequential inaptitude, extends itself over the whole fabric : which, by this means is manufactured into an opaque mass, into which the most learned among lawyers have no better than an indistinct insight, and we, the people at large, next to none : at any rate none such as enables us, of ourselves, to guide our course by it. Witness, in particular, the law of *real property*.

44.—VI. Mischief the sixth. By the example set by a class of persons who, by all these devices, hereinbefore mentioned, and hereinafter mentioned, have hitherto succeeded in rendering themselves objects of almost universal respect and confidence, and by means of those sentiments, in addition to their uncontrolable power, masters of our conduct, the public mind has been and continues to be, to a deplorable degree, impregnated with the poison of mendacity in this so highly corruptive shape : and thus it is that *demoralization* and *disintellectualization* go hand in hand.

45.—V. *Device the fifth.—Oaths for the establishment of the Mendacity, necessitated.*

As intimated on the occasion of the *written pleadings device*, mode in which the ceremony of an oath has there been employed as an instrument of mendacity, and as will be seen maleficence in so many other shapes, the following : to assertions, on the occasion of which the ceremony is employed, the distinctive appellation of *evidence* is applied, and to wilful falsehood contained in such

assertion, punishment is attached : while, to falsehood, the assertion of which is not accompanied
with the performance of this same ceremony, no
punishment is attached.   In mendacity has been
seen an instrument by which such enormous increase is given to the evil produced to suitors,
thence to the good produced to Judge and Co.
by *written pleadings*.   In the ceremony of an
oath may now be seen an instrument, by the
use of which the production of the mendacity is
effected.

46. *Purposes* for which this ceremony is employed, two : 1. securing veracity at the hands of
witnesses : 2. securing fulfilment of duty at the
hands of functionaries, more particularly on the
part of *jurymen*. 1. *Mischievous*, in both instances,
we trust, it will, on examination be seen to be :
thus efficient to evil purposes ; 2. *inefficient*, and 3.
endless to all good purposes, in both cases.

47.—i. First, as to its application to *testimony*,
and on that occasion, as to its mischievousness.
1. Abundantly sufficient to warrant and necessitate
abolition would surely be its abovementioned property of producing mendacity, were it the only
one.

48.—2. But to this is added another of most appalling magnitude.   Yes : the giving impunity to
crime in every shape, the most obvious not excepted,
in the hands of every man,—the most worthless
and mischievous not excepted,—does it place the
power of producing this effect : thus sharing with
the sovereign the prerogative of *pardon*. Called into
the witness-box, *conscience* (he declares) will not
suffer him to bear a part in the ceremony.   Not
unfrequently have instances of such refusal made
their appearance: none, in which punishment, in

any shape, has been attached to it: the insincerity; howsoever real, not being manifest nor proveable, punishment for the refusal would be *persecution;* and *that* persecution, happily, too odious to be endurable.

49. Without the ceremony, for this long time, in *civil* cases, now of late in criminal cases, admission has been given to the testimony of *Quakers* and *Moravians.* " *I am a Quaker,*" or " *I am a Moravian,*" (suppose) is in purport the averment made by the person thus called upon :—this said, who shall gainsay it?

50. Suppose even punishment applied, how would the matter be mended? Applied it could not be, till after the impunity had been effected.

51. Moreover, even were the inflictions sure, it might be made worth a man's while to undergo it.

52. So, in any case called a *civil* case, may he in like manner give or sell success to either side.

53. Murderous robbers might thus go on in impunity, for any length of time, in the commission of the crime. Is the number regarded as requisite they join in it; a reward, a high amount with pardon, as usual, being offered to any one of them for information, some of them in one or more, proffering testimony against the rest: trial coming on, they declare themselves Atheists, whereupon they refuse to bear a part in the ceremony: true it is that in this case conviction not taking place, pardon is not earned; nor need it, for no testimony being delivered, acquittal follows of course: acquittal on the part of the prisoners, for no evidence is there against them: on the part of the informer for no evidence is there against him. But (says somebody) by simple and direct refusal to swear, unaccompanied with any such declaration of

opinion, will not the same effect be produced? and is it not produced accordingly? Natural enough this question: but to find an answer to it belongs not to the present purpose.

54. Yes, Atheists; of Quakerism or Moravianism, declaration can no longer serve; but *Atheism* remains as good as ever: power of pardon, a share in the king's prerogative, remains the reward for it.

55.—II. Secondly, as to its inefficiency, still as applied to testimony: to a mode of punishment, which might, in an almost unexampled degree be efficacious, it substitutes a mode in an extraordinary degree inefficacious. For contempt of court, when, in any other shape committed in court, commitment to prison being an instantaneous consequence, the same consequence might be attached to such contempt in this shape. Under the name of *evidence*, testimony, when orally delivered, not being received without an immediately previous oath-taking; thus it is that mendacity, whenever it is thus committed, is committed in the shape of perjury; and in this shape this mode of proceeding against it has been—if not employed, at any rate threatened: in which case no *individual* is there, on whom the expence and vexation attached to the character of *prosecutor*, would be imposed: accordingly, what in relation to this matter we shall have humbly to propose is —that in every case in which it is seen that the whole of the stock of evidence which the suit affords, is brought out at the time of the perjury, punishment for it may instantaneously follow.

56. So much as to efficiency when the ceremony is not employed: how stands it now that the oath is so almost universally employed? Punish-

ment none without the concurrent testimony of two witnesses: nor then, but at the expence of a separate prosecution, commenced at a distant point of time, and with such disadvantageous prospects as to success. Proportion, of the number of cases in which prosecution has place to the number in which delinquency has place, at what shall it be set? Say, for example, at a venture—out of ten thousand scarcely so much as one. So much as to inefficiency.

57. Thirdly, as to needlessness. For a complete and conclusive demonstration of this property of the ceremony, we humbly beg leave to call on the testimony of the Honourable House. Compared with the importance of the legislative, what is that of the judicial function? When, for the formation of a ground for a legislational proceeding, *evidence* is called in, in what instance is employment ever given to this ceremony by the Honorable House?

58. Thus efficient to bad purposes, inefficient and needless to any good purpose whatsoever in particular,—in particular to that of giving execution and effect to the law,—far indeed is it from being so, to the sinister interest of Judge and Co.

59. Already mentioned has been its needfulness, with relation to the profit by *written pleadings*.

60. Add to this, the encouragement and invitation given to dishonest plaintiffs and defendants, by the chance which it produces of failure on the part of honest ones; and thence the addition of dishonest to the aggregate of honest demands and defences; the profit to subordinate judicial functionaries, by the fees, partly in the direct way, partly in various indirect ways, necessitated; and to judges their *superordinates*, correspondent profit

in the shape of *patronage,*—all by the clumsy and complicated machinery which, to so large an extent is, on this occasion, employed.

61. See the country over, for example, *attornies* converted into *masters extraordinary in chancery,* and for no other purpose.

62. Note now the consequence as to delay, and *non-decision* and *misdecision:* or in one word, *failure* of justice. No machinery at hand, no oath capable of being administered ; and the testimony, how important soever the purpose, lost, and the purpose frustrated : frustrated—always for a time; not unfrequently for evermore.

63. So much for its effect when employed on a judicial *occasion,* as well as for a judicial *purpose.* Now as to its effect when employed on *an occasion not* judicial, (there not being any actual suit in the case): only for an *eventual* judicial *purpose,* to wit in case of prosecution for perjury in respect of it. Under this head, in proof of its inefficiency, the bare mention of the words *Custom-house oaths* might of itself be amply sufficient.

Other instances, in which the quality of it is demonstrated and the number ascertained might be adduced, but the range of them being less extensive, respect for religion and its teachers commands our silence—one observation alone excepted; namely, that to oaths, whether assertory or promissory, the *sanction* is the same.

64. So much for *testimonial* oaths. Now as to *official.* Various are the *occasions* on which, correspondently various the *purposes* for which, under the existing system, the obligation of giving employment to this ceremony has place.

Principal occasion that of *entrance* upon office : *declaration* with relation to *opinions*—*promise* with relation to *conduct*. On neither of these occasions is punishment as for perjury, or punishment in any other shape, attached to what is regarded as a violation of the oath. In all these cases, whatsoever good consequence is looked for, from the solemn promise with the oath attached to it, would (we humbly contend) be equally obtained by a promise declared with like solemnity, unincumbered by the oath.

65. In all these cases, intended or supposed effect of it is—its operating as an instrument of *security* : real effect, operating as an instrument of deception and consequent insecurity : reliance being placed on this inefficient security, others that would be efficient and applicable, remain unlooked out for and unapplied.

66. Take, for example, the fee-fed judge: whatsoever line of conduct—conformable to justice or adverse—that it happens to be agreeable to him take,—pronounced with appropriate emphasis, out come the words—" *My oath !*" *His oath*—does he say? what oath? who ever saw him utter any form of words under that name? And if uttered, what would it be found to amount to? Just nothing. Some vague generality, vying with cobwebs in effectively binding force.

67. Enter now upon the stage *jurymen's* oaths —and with them the everywhere abundant and perennial crop of jurymen's perjuries. The exercise of this important function, indispensable obligation of bearing the supposed effective and so much relied on part in this ceremony, stands attached : at the same time, for the production of declared unanimity,—truly or falsely declared as it may happen, continuance in one and the same apartment without respite or refreshment, except

by permission of the judge, though death by inani-
tion, with the antecedent course of torture, be the
consequence : torture to such a length, at no time
ever endured or endurable.

68. Here then as to the consequence in the
shape of perjury. Declaration of opinion it is,
opinion itself it is not, in the power of torture to produce. Here then, as often as diversity of opinion has
place, here are two antagonizing forces applied to
one and the same man, at one and the same time:
here is the oath to make him speak true, here is
the torture to make him speak false: the torture—
this altogether irresistible instrument, employed
in the manufacture of perjury.

69. First, as to the prevention of mendacity.
To this altogether needless, on inspection, will
be seen to be this ceremony, with the perjury
thus essentially sticking to it : thrown away the
price—and it has been seen how dear a one—paid
for the use of it. Look in the first place, to *natural* religion. If mendacity, independently of this
or any other ceremony, does not stand prohibited,
—prohibited, which is as much as to say, visited
with punishment, what else is there that does?
What then is the additional security that it affords?
No other can it be than that which would be
afforded by some extra punishment apprehended
in the future life, at the hands of the Almighty,
as about to be undergone on the score of the thus
supposed aggravation, over and above that which
would be apprehended, if the ceremony were not
employed.

70. Now then for this supposed additional security, what is the price paid? An assumption is
made and acted upon ; and what is it? That, to

the purpose in question, the power of the Almighty is at the disposal of any and every man, who for any purpose chooses to employ it : of any man, howsoever bad, for any purpose howsoever bad, the Creator an instrument in the hand of every one of these his creatures! an instrument, on the part of which compliance is more assured, than it can be on the part of a slave : the Almighty more surely obsequious to the will of the most wicked man upon earth than a sheriff is to that of the judge !

71. Look lastly to *revealed religion.* On this score, we humbly beg that, now at length, by the constituted authorities, and in the first instance by the Honourable House, it may be taken into consideration, whether, in addition to these considerations, or even without the aid of them, the words *Swear not at all,* in more passages than one, attributed to the holy Author of our religion, might not suffice to put an end to *swearing,* in compliance with compulsion, imposed by those same authorities.

72. As to mendacity, the production of this so abundantly thus produced commodity—is this then the object? neither to this purpose is it at all needful. Legislators, if simple mendacity will content you—mendacity without perjury for a zest to it—abolish the ceremony, there remains the torture, which is quite sufficient to produce the thus desired effect.

73. Note here, the effect of the torture in the production of mendacity belongs not precisely to the present head. It is however too influential on justice, and the efficiency of the main body of the law, to be suffered to pass without notice. It is—the placing the decision, and thereby in so far the

lot of the parties—the placing both under the command of the strongest will : in other words, of the most long suffering and persevering stomach.

74. Of this ceremony, such as it is, is what is called a violation, a sin? So many times as, being employed, it is violated, so many are the sins created, not to say committed : abolish the ceremony, the manufacture of these sins is at an end : and sins, in number altogether infinite, saved from being committed. Such the security supposed to be thus given against mendacity. True it is that times were, when—not merely on a certain *occasion* for a certain *purpose*,—not merely in conjunction with other securities for veracity,— but singly, and to the exclusion of all such other securities,—this ceremony, having been instituted, was frequently performed.

75. Witness the so stated *wager of law*. *Occasion*, demand of money on the score of debt : *purpose*, the obtaining a discharge from the demands. *Witness*, the defendant himself; testimony, assertion in general terms, denying that the money forming the subject matter of the demand, is due. With this witness came a *chorus*, consisting of twelve others styled *compurgators; subject matter* of *their* testimony, their belief that what their principal and leader of the band— the defendant—had been saying, was true. But these times, what were they? Times of primæval and grossest ignorance, superstition, and barbarism.

76. In conclusion, as to the whole of this momentous subject, and our respect for the time of the House not permitting us to do anything like complete justice to the importance of it, we humbly beg leave to give intimation to the Honorable

House, that the form of a petition, in which fuller consideration is given to it, is in print, and universally accessible.

77. That, in no case this part of the institution is productive of good effects, is more than we take upon us to affirm. On it depends, for its existence, the latent, but not the less efficient, virtual *veto* possessed by the jury, and thus by the *strongest stomach* among them, over the laws. If, on any point of law to which jury trial applies, the statute law and common law together, is in a state of opposition to the welfare of the community, in this respect, beneficial, in so far, is the effect of jury trial in its present shape: and on this part of the institution, we beg it may be considered, whether that liberty does not depend—the liberty of the press to wit—on which everything else, which, in a peculiar manner, is good in the form of government, depends. But to this and the other cases, in which the constituted authorities have a particular interest, more or less adverse to the general interest, such as treason, sedition, and the like, this feature may be preserved, without its extending to any other cases.

78. In any case, to produce whatsoever good effect is expected from the ceremony, the substitution of the word *affirmation*, (or, to give indication of *deliberateness*) *asseveration*, to the words *swear*, *oath*, and *maketh oath*, might, we submit, most fully and effectually suffice.

79. To conclude, neither to the prevention of mendacity, nor, (if such should be the pleasure of the King in parliament) to the preservation and augmentation of mendacity, (or as it is more familiarly called, *lying*) is the preservation of this cumbrous and dissention-sowing ceremony necessary.

This we have already taken the liberty to observe and shew: and we humbly trust, that to the pre-servation of that *veto*, which, as above, so long as the government of this country continues in its present form, is so indispensable,—this same cere-mony will not be found to be, in any way more necessary.

80.—VI. *Device the sixth.—Delay, in groundless and boundless lengths, established.*

Delay is, so long as it lasts, *denial:* and we invite and challenge any person to say why, though it be but for an hour, *denial of justice* should have place.

81. In the process of judicature,—of the various *sources*, or say *causes* of delay—all of them factiti-ous—the work of Judge and Co.—samples (will it please the Honorable House to behold them?) the eight here following :—

I. *Source the first, vacations.*—The year split into *terms*—four in the year—with intervals be-tween them, styled *vacations:* during which last, so far as could be contrived, *denial of justice* remains established.   Terms, four : vacations, as many.

In the whole year of 365 days, aggregate num-ber of days allotted to administration of justice, 91 : to denial of justice, 274 : add Sundays in term time, 13; total, 287 : to justice not so much as a fourth part of the time allotted to injustice.

82.—II. *Source the second, circuits.*—For country causes, no *trial* but on *circuits;* circuits, in the year, at the most no more than three; till the other day, but two : in some counties, now two : till the other day, no more than one.   In these cases, what is the *crime* for which denial of jus-tice—in a word, *outlawry* (for this it is so long as it lasts) thus made the penalty? Is it the crime of living at so great a distance from the metropolis? If not on the account of *crime,* on what other account is the condition of one part of his majesty's subjects, of all ranks, rendered in so essential a respect to such a degree inferior to that of all besides?

83.—III. *Source the third, fixt days.*—Between one proceeding and another, intervals established by *fixt days,* of which, further on, under the head of *Blind Fixation:* days the same, length of interval the same, for every individual suit: say, for example, of a *fortnight,* whereas necessary will be, in some cases, no interval, in others a day, in others again a year or years: none, where upon plaintiff's own showing, his demand is ungrounded; a day or less (for notice) when the residence of both parties is in the near neighbourhood: years one or more, when, at the moment, defendant's residence is, for example, at Australia.

In this latter case, if, as in the established mode, inaction on the part of a defendant, is by the judge acted upon as if it were conclusive evidence of the justice of the demand, and judgment and execution take place accordingly,— here delay gives place to what is still worse: namely, *precipitation* (of which presently) with misdecision and misconduct for its certain consequences.

84.—IV. *Source the fourth, written pleadings.*—Of these, above. If, a mass of written allegations being exhibited, loss of cause is, as under the existing system established, as a penalty for the non-exhibition of correspondent counter-allegations,—allowance of time for framing them is necessitated : and, on each individual occasion, time, adequate to the need, delay in indefinite quantity, is made necessary to justice.

85.—v. *Source the fifth, mischievous removals. Needless transference* and *bandying of suits, trans- ference* of a suit from the judicatory in which it has been commenced to a different one in which it is to receive termination or continuance, as to which under the head of *Device the tenth, mis- chievous transference, &c.*

86.—vi. *Source the sixth, equity procedure.*—The mode which has place in the judicatories called *courts of equity :* a mode altogether different from that which has place in the judicatories called the *common law courts;* and in the shape of delay, as also of expense in a prodigious degree still more productive of torment.

87.—vii. *Source the seventh, court christian,* alias *spiritual court,* alias *ecclesiastical court,* procedure. Of this mode, differing again from both the others,— and, in lengthiness of delay and expense vying with that of the equity courts,—mention is made only to shew that it has not been overlooked : for, though, in delay as well as expense, it vies with the most dilatory of the two,—yet, the number of suits carried on in it is to such a degree compa- ratively small, that the use derivable from the picture of the additional torment produced by it, would not, on the present occasion, pay for the space of time and labour it would necessitate.

88.—viii. *Source the eighth, procedure in appeals :* that is to say, demands made to a super-ordinate judicatory, for reversal or other change, in the *judgments,* otherwise styled *decrees,—ultimate* or *in- termediate,* styled *interlocutory,*—pronounced in the judicatories,—original, or say *immediate,*—in which the suits respectively took commencement or received continuance.

89. For procedure in equity courts and on appeals, development is to the present purpose necessary, and here follows :—

First, as to *equity procedure.* Endless would be the task of giving anything like a correct and complete sketch of the system of delay, of which the judicatories, styled, as if in mockery, *courts of equity*, present the scene : a few slight touches are the following :—

90.—I. In regard to elicitation of *evidence*, modes in one and the same suit, three : namely, the epistolary, or say written mode ; and two varieties of the oral, or say word-of-mouth mode.

91.—Epistolary mode. Employed at commencement, *questions* styled *interrogatories*, put by plaintiffs to defendants : name of the instrument of which they form a part, the *bill.*

92. Between each such string of interrogatories, and the correspondent string of answers (name of the aggregate, *the answer*) an interval of months. In one amply extensive parcel of the whole number of these suits, the end in view, as prescribed by interest, is, on the plaintiff's side, the maximization—not of dispatch, but of *delay* : that *interest* being accompanied with the *faculty* of multiplying those intervals of delay by an unlimited number. Sufficient of itself is this state of things to spin out into years, a suit, to which, by an interview between the parties, in the presence of the judge, as in the case of procedure before a justice of the peace, termination might be given in the same number of minutes : debt, for example, on a note of hand, whether for forty shillings or forty thousand pounds.

93. To elicit, *per contra*, for the benefit of the defendant, whose *self-differing* evidence has thus been elicited, the like evidence from one who is plaintiff in this same suit, another such suit, commenced by a bill styled a *cross bill*, is made necessary. Thus, lest the abovementioned delay should not be sufficient,—what, in a common law court, would be but *one* suit, is split into *two*.

94. Note, that as yet not a particle has been elicited, of that which comes from the only source from which a common law court will suffer any evidence to be elicited; namely, the testimonial or other evidence capable of being furnished by *extraneous* witnesses; *extraneous* on the present occasion, so called of necessity, to distinguish them from parties where, as above, information is received from them, or called for at their hands; say accordingly *party-witnesses*, or *testifying parties*: and, before the elicitation of any such evidence is so much as commenced, money, to the amount of hundreds, or even thousands of pounds, may, at the pleasure of the plaintiff, if rich enough, be extorted from the defendant, if he has it: and thus is his utter ruin produced.

95.—II. Oral mode employed subsequently in the elicitation of the evidence of extraneous witnesses, and sometimes in the elicitation of ulterior evidence from the defendant. Scene, the *Examiner's office*: mode of examinations, *secret*.

96.—III. Oral mode employed in addition to the above, in the elicitation of evidence relative to matters of *detail*. Scene, the office of the subordinate judge, styled a *master in chancery*. For attendance at this office, not more than an hour at a time ever allowed in the same suit: and by any one of these *actors*, of all of whom it is made the

D

interest to maximise the delay, the hour may be cut down to a time too short for the doing any part of the business.   Nor does any such meeting take place till after *three* appointments, with an interval of several days between the second and the third. For these actors, if so they may be called, for every one of them, fees, extorted by the power of the superordinate judge, the chancellor, as if they had all attended: the *master* establishing this mode of obtaining money under false pretences, and sharing largely in the profits of it.   Of late years, the salaries of these functionaries have received large increase: and this and all their other modes of depredation left undiminished.   Had the enactment made by Parliament (it is that of the 22 G. 2. ch.   § 1.) been applied to them, as it would have been had they not been in a public trust, not one of the judges by whom, for several generations, these situations have been occupied,—not one of them who would not, over and over again, have been either whipt, pilloried, or transported; for only by power, and consequent impunity and complicity with judges of a still higher order, not by innocence, are they distinguished from those delinquents, who, under the name of *swindlers*, are every day so dealt with.

98.—IV. By these judges, *vacations* made for themselves: some, of not less than seven months out of the twelve: witness, declarations made by men of the first eminence in the profession: made in print, years ago; and confirmed by the confession implied in uninterrupted silence.

99. All this forms as yet no more than a part of the length of delay established in equity procedure.

In the greater number of the individual suits

carried before the superior common law courts,— *after* the common law suit has been made to run its length, still farther length may be added to it; added by any defendant, who, being rich enough, has an interest in so doing; namely, by a suit styled, as above, an *injunction*.

100. In the year 1824, April 25, year 5th of the present reign, issued a commission: *purpose* of it, (so therein declared) introduction of *improvements* and *changes: subject matter*, declaredly confined to *equity courts* and their proceedings. Five years, within a trifle, have elapsed, and in all this time, no *improvement* made; in consequence, no *change* made but such as, in comparison with the abuse, was, in *extent*, conspicuously trifling, and in *quality*, has proved to be worse than none.

101. In addition to this, another commission instituted in the year 1828, composed of a different set of commissioners, subject matter expressly confined to the superior common law courts and their proceedings, as if, in the practice of two sets of courts, with their branches of jurisdiction, to such a degree entangled throughout the whole field,—it were possible to make any substantial improvements—improvements in either,—without *change*, and for that purpose, all comprehensive *scrutiny* applied to the other.

102. We humbly entreat the Honourable House to consider whether it be in the nature of man that a separation of this sort, thus deliberately made, by, or by the advice of, persons perfectly conversant with the whole of the business, could have had any better object, than the giving perpetuity to a system of depredation and oppression thus portentous.

We shudder at the bare idea of the Honourable

House rendering itself an accomplice of such enormities, by remaining silent and inactive, after
receipt of this our humble petition, and forbearing
to apply either the remedial system, which we
shall take the liberty to suggest, or some other not
less effectual, if any other such there be.

103. Now for the remaining source of delay—
appeals and writs of error. Omitting particular
cases, in endless variety, when, on the ground of
alleged *mis-decision*, a suit is transferred from a
relatively inferior to a relatively superior court,—
if it be in equity procedure, *appeal* is the name—
the name given to the operation, or the instrument, by which the transference is effected : if it
be in common law procedure, *writ of error* is the
name. *Appeal* is the term thus put foremost, as
presenting, to an unlawlearned mind, a clear idea;
writ of error, a confused one.

104. Note, that only for alleged misdecision,
that is to say, either at the conclusion, or during
the continuance of the suit, are either *appeals* so
called, or *writs of error* received. But, not more
effectually done is injustice by *mis-decision* than by
non-decision : by non-decision, whether *after* a
suit instituted, or for *want* of a suit instituted.

105. Causes of such *want* any one of these
which follow. On the minds of persons wronged,

i. Opinion of the relative inaptitude of the
system.

ii. Opinion of the relative inaptitude of the
judges, one or more, employed in the application
of it.

iii. Fear of being, at any time after commencement, and before conclusion, sunk into the gulph
of ruin by the weight of the purse on the other
side.

IV. Or, in other situations, relative indigence, such as to produce an utter incapacity of giving so much as commencement to the suit.

106. In some instances, in the case of a *writ of error*, the appeal goes immediately from the four-seated court in Westminster Hall to the *House of Lords*: in other instances, another and more numerously-seated Westminster Hall judicatory of appeal is *interposed*, under the name of the *Exchequer Chamber*,

107. By an *appeal*, in which and whatsoever way denominated—an additional mountain of delay is set down upon the mountains above sketched out. But of appeal, in both cases, there are stages upon stages, mountains upon mountains, set down, one upon another.

108. For an example of the *stages*, or say *stories* in this pile—behold in Blackstone the following: sorts of cases to which they apply, those called *civil*.

109.—I. From various "inferior courts," to the Common Pleas (iii. 40.)

110.—II. From the Common Pleas to the King's Bench (iii. 40, 56.)

111.—III. From the King's Bench to one of the three courts, all confounded under the name of the Exchequer Chamber, composed of so many different lists of judges (iii. 56.)

112.—IV. From the Exchequer Chamber to the House of Lords (iii. 56.)

113. Note well the organization of this chaos. From the four judges of the Common Pleas, appeal to the four judges of the King's Bench: from these, back again to those same four judges of the Common Pleas: who are thus expected, every one of them, to pronounce condemnation on

his own act, with the addition, however, of the
four judges styled *barons of the exchequer:* which
same Court of the Exchequer is " inferior in rank
(says Blackstone, iii. 43) not only to the court of
King's Bench, but to the Common Pleas also."
Thus, to apply conviction to an alleged error in
one court, the business of two others is put to a
stand-still. To complete the confusion, nothing
more is wanting, than to give an ulterior appeal
from the Exchequer Chamber, immediately, or
through the medium of the House of Lords, to a
court composed of the judges of some one or more,
or all of the judges of the courts herein just mentioned, under the name of the " inferior courts."

114. Of the gradation here exhibited, was ever
any instance exemplified in practice? Probably
not. But why not? *Answer.* Because the rapa-
city and wickedness of judges—creators and preservers of this system—have to such a degree
outrun the wickedness of their pupils, the attornies, and the opulence of individuals, whom they
have thus employed in the endeavour to convert
into dishonest suitors.

115. Now as to appeal and its stages in the so
called *equity* courts.

116.—I. When the suit is in the first instance
brought before the chancellor, stage of appeal but
one—appeal to the *House of Lords.*

117.—II. When the suit is in the first instance
before the vice-chancellor, each party has the op-
tion between an appeal immediately to the House
of Lords : or first to the chancellor ; then from him,
as in the instance of this same appellant, or of the
party on the other side, a further appeal may be
made to that same Right Honourable House.

118.—III. So, where the suit is in the first instance brought before the other subordinate equity judge, whose title is the *master of the rolls:* a functionary who under this absurd title has for centuries exercised the functions of a substitute to the chancellor, in a word, those of a vice-chancellor, though without the name.

119. In equity procedure, stages of appeal have place, disguised under different denominations.

120.—i. Under the name of exceptions to report, appeal from the judicatory of a master in chancery, to that of the chancellor, the vice-chancellor, or the master of the rolls, as the case may be.

121.—ii. Under the name of a *rehearing*, appeal from any one of those functionaries to his successor.

122.—iii. Under the name of a *rehearing*, appeal from any one of them at one time, to himself at another time : for, thus are two sorts of proceedings, so different in tendency, disguised under the same name.

By the master of the rolls or the vice-chancellor a definite decree (suppose) has been pronounced : plaintiff or defendant, losing his cause by it, proposes to himself to take, by means of appeal, another chance. To which then of the two judicatories shall the appeal be made ? The Chancellor's Court, or the House of Lords? For answer —the solicitors of the losing party takes the soundings of the two purses, of his client's and of the adversary's; if in his client there is depth enough for both courts, he recommends the chancellor's as the most eligible court: namely, that from thence if, without reproach to himself, he has the good fortune to succeed in making his client lose his case a second time, he may carry it into

the House of Lords, in which there being no ulterior judicatory, it will be his interest, for reputation sake, and accordingly his endeavour to gain
rather than lose it : from the chancellor to the
House of Lords, that is to say, from the chancellor
under the name, to him, said chancellor, under
another name.

This course, it being that which, in the situation
of a solicitor, it is every man's interest to take, is
that which with a view to legislative arrangements
every man, unless prevented, ought to be expected to take; and as to a solicitor, so should
this expectation apply itself to every dishonest
plaintiff or defendant, who being in the wrong,
and knowing that he is so, has formed a plan for
purchasing of the judges in question the faculty of
acquiring or retaining the estate in question, by
the ruin of the destined victim, thereby availing
himself of the offer which, though not in words, is
not the less in deeds, held out by the several
members of the learned brotherhood to all who are
respectable enough to be able to give acceptance
to it : yes, respectable enough : for, in the language of the opulent, opulence and respectability
are names of the same thing.

119. A word or two as to the particular sources
of profit : profit to Judge and Co. from the delays
manufactured as above.

1. By the delay are produced, as above, dishonest suits and defences, which otherwise would
not have place : the evil hour is thus staved off to
the last moment. To a dishonest defendant, the
delay produces, for a time, if he be solvent, at any
rate common *interest of money* correspondent to the
duration : add, if in trade, profit of trade ; if he be
insolvent, the faculty of converting the whole to

his own use. Of this profit, what part, if any, shall be *net*, depends upon the proportion as between debt and costs of suit. Of the costs, one constant portion is—that which is laid hold of by Judge and Co., the dishonest man's partners and accomplices; laid hold of in the first instance, and before so much as a farthing's worth is paid to any one of those to whom the debt is due.

120.—ii. When the debt is such, that the interest amounts to still more than the price paid to Judge and Co. for the delay, the delay follows of course.

121.—iii. Delay breeds incidents; incidents, fees. Who shall number the varieties of these prolific incidents?

iv. Bred out of one incident—namely, the incident of death—one inducement to delay is, in cases to a large extent, the extinction put upon the suit, by the death of a party, on one side or the other, —and, on either side or each side, deaths of parties may have place by dozens and scores. Invited by Judge and Co. for joint profit, the injurer, by delays made when in the situation of defendant, helps to consign the, injured plaintiff to a lingering death, the result of vexation, Judge and Co. having taken care to exempt from the obligation of making compensation the murderer's representatives. "A *tort* is a sort of thing that dies with the person:" such is the expression given to the rule, in the lawyer's dialect of the flash language.

122.—v. When these factitious delays were first instituted, the minor portions of the year sufficed for as many suits as money could be found in the country to pay for, in fees.: the major part being consecrated to ease: in proportion as opulence has increased, *ease* has been exchanged for *fees*.

123. In the business of the department of justice is factitious delay useful, and as such justifiable? If so, apply it to the finance and defensive force departments: apply it to the military departments, land service and sea service: in particular in time of *war:* not more indefensible is it in those than in this.

124. Whence this difference? *Answer.* In these cases, were any such factitious delays established, government would fall to pieces: in these cases accordingly they are not established: in the justice department, government, however badly, can go on, the delay notwithstanding: in these accordingly they *are* established.

So much for government. Now for surgery. To a patient who wants to be cut for the stone, does the surgeon ever say, wait with the stone in your bladder till I have nothing else to do? No: by the medical man, no such thing is ever said: by the fee-fed judge it is in effect, as often as he makes a plaintiff wait for his money, when wanted for making payment to the surgeon. Whence the difference? *Answer.* From this—To produce the delay without losing the customer, is not in the power of the surgeon: it is in the power of the judge: and, so far from losing, he is a gainer by it.

125. On this occasion, as unhappily on so many others, *religion* is pressed into the service of injustice. To St Hilary, a Catholic saint—to St Michael, a Protestant as well as Catholic saint—to Christ Jesus—to wit, by the word *Easter,* nay, even to the whole incomprehensible *Trinity,* as St Athanasius so truly styles it,—does this misery-making employment stand assigned.

126. Out of the sabbath is made another pre-

tence, " which of you shall have an ox or an ass fallen into a pit, and will not straightway pull him out on the sabbath-day ?" By whom this is said, may it please the Honourable House to consider. If, when it is by mere accident that the damage has been produced, worship of the God of Justice is no sufficient warrant for delay of justice, how much less when it is by injustice? by groundless distress, for rent (suppose) or by robbery? By the worship of the God of Justice, would not an appropriate overture be furnished to the oratorio of judicature?

127. Wives converted into widows, children into orphans ; both by slow murder rendered destitute ; depredators fattened upon the substance of these victims, Judge and Co. contrivers and sharers in the booty,—such is the scene presented by the fruit of this wisdom of this branch of ancestor wisdom : the branch to which we are indebted for the plantation of judge-made law.

> " When sleeps Injustice, so may Justice too :
> Delays, the wicked make ; the injured rue."

These two memoriter verses it is our humble wish to place in the memory of the Honourable House.

128.—VII. *Device the seventh.—Precipitation necessitated.*

Excess on one side is thus made the parent of excess on the opposite side. By delay is produced precipitation : and, reciprocally, by precipitation, more delay. Grand and principal instrument of precipitation, *Jury trial,* as hitherto conducted : but, to its efficiency vast addition made by circuits.

129. Of the suits out of which a pretence for recurring to this mode of trial is manufactured, classes two: one, composed of those which, by the very nature of the case, are rendered incapable of receiving their termination from a judicatory so composed.

130. Instance, *account:* a case in which, under the name of one single suit, may be included suits in a number altogether indefinite; suits, as many as the account contains *items*, each with a separate batch of evidence belonging to it.

131. The other class of these indeterminable suits, is composed of those which are rendered such by *accident*, that is to say, by the magnitude of the aggregate of the evidence. In the case of Elizabeth Canning, prosecuted for perjury,—time, about the middle of the last century, seven days passed before the trial was concluded. Since then, instances of still longer duration might, perhaps, be found.

132. In the interval that has place at present between circuit and circuit, what limit can be assigned to the number of suits that might present themselves, if the door, shut against them by this institution were thrown open?

133. Behold now Judge and Co., syringe in hand, forcing and injecting the whole mass of all the suits into a compass of *three* days, or in some counties *two* days. What is the consequence? On condition of their being heard badly,—in regard to some portion of the whole number, possibility of being heard has place, and accordingly heard they are: in regard to the rest, even under that condition, no such possibility has place.

134. On those which remain in hand is stamped the appellation of *remanents* or *remanets*. For

Judge and Co. the more *remanets* the better: the more fresh suits for redress of one and the same wrong.

Not that the number of these disastrous effects is—at all times, or even commonly—altogether as great as that of the efficient causes: for, commonly by the postponement, some, in number more or less considerable, are at this stage of their existence, prematurely killed: cause of death, deperition of evidence, or death of a party: more frequently perhaps than either, on the part of the injured plaintiff, exhaustion of the power of finding the matter of fees. But for this, *remanets*, in swarms, might go on, begetting one another to the end of time.

135. When one of these indeterminable suits comes to be called on, brought to view then is the discovery—that, from the first, such it was in its very nature. Re-discovered on every circuit is this discovery: re-discovered for centuries past. But, the jury box is not the less worshipped. Why? *Answer*—Because, as at present constituted, trial *by* jury is, in every instance, trial with lawyers.

136. Fresh suits produced by precipitation are 1. in an immediate way, *new trials*: 2. in an un-immediate way, namely by means of *remanets, arbitrations.*

137.—I. First, as to *new trials*. Greater in this case may to the parties be the expense, greater accordingly to Judge and Co. the profit, than by the original suit. For, preceded always is the new trial by motion for ditto: which said motion is one sort of suit, carried on for the purpose of determining whether another suit shall be carried on or not: shape of the evidence on which the original suit is determined, the best shape: shape, in which the excretitious suit is sometimes determined, the worst shape—namely, affidavit evidence. Barristers necessarily employed as well as attorney : whereas, in the original suit, it may have been carried down to trial, and perhaps most commonly is, without the intervention of argumentation by barristers : commonly, that is to say where the *general issue* (as the phrase is), being pleaded, no demand has place for written pleadings of more than a determinate and comparatively short length.

138. II. Now as to *Arbitrations.* Of the disadvantages this sort of suit labours under, with correspondent advantage to Judge and Co., samples are these—

1. Power for the attainment of evidence comparatively inadequate: not comprehending the power of obtaining it from all places : not ascertained whether in it is universally comprised any power for rendering attendance on the part of witnesses effectually obligatory.

139. II. If not, then, on many occasions, the body of the evidence will be not merely *incomplete*, but in the sinister sense of the word, *partial :* admitted, and perhaps exclusively, witnesses, with a *bias* on their testimony, "*willing witnesses*," as the phrase is : and these, biassed all of them in favour of the same side : of which state of mind the very fact of the willingness affords some, although not conclusive, evidence.

140. III. *Evidence of parties.* *Admitted* it cannot be without giving up as completely adverse to justice, the general exclusionary rule; *excluded*, not without substituting misdecision, or denial of justice, to right decision, in a large proportion of

the whole aggregate number of the suits, demand for which has place. Yes, *denial of justice:* for, in so far as it is foreknown that by the exclusion put upon evidence necessary to success, all chance of success is excluded,—in so far the suit will not be instituted.

141.—IV. Professional persons, if chosen as arbitrators, must be paid : here,—be the payment ever so moderate and well-regulated—here, will be a vast addition to the expense : the remuneration being over and above that which, at the expense of the whole community, is given to the *permanent* judges—*judges* so styled and intituled.

142.—V. But, in cases thus disposed of, the mode of payment is in a flagrant degree corruptive and adverse to the professed end : it is payment *by the day;* a mode, by which a *premium* is given for the maximum of delay and extortion : corruption, delay, and extortion which it is not in the power of human sagacity to prevent, punish, or so much as discover and hold up to view : corruption, which it is not in the power of flesh and blood to remove.

143.—VI. These professional judges, who are they? naturally such, of the choice of whom, self-regarding, or sympathetic interest is more likely than regard for the interest of justice, more likely than appropriate aptitude—to have been the cause. In the train of the judge come always, along with the brief-holding, briefless barristers. Of the choice made, cause not unfrequent, and certainly none so natural, as recommendation at the hands of the judge. Proportioned to the value of every situation is that of the patronage by which it is conferred : and, recommendation taken, patronage is exercised.

144.—VII. Question, which of the suits shall be *tried*? which, by being left *untried* converted into *remanents*? This will depend upon the result of the conflict of interests. Yes: but of whom? the suitors? No: but of learned lords and ditto gentlemen. By sinister interest full is the swing enjoyed in this case: into it, is it possible for the eye of public opinion, in any degree to penetrate?

145. In respect of *favour*, manifest it is here, upon how different a footing stand the *forced* arbitrations brought on in this *circuitous* mode, compared with those *spontaneous* ones which *originate* with the *parties*. So many spontaneous arbitrations, so many usurpations upon the authority of learned judges. Moreover most commonly the arbitrators will be *unpaid*, or at any rate, *unlaw-learned*, individuals: whereas, on the circuit, a suit will not only have already brought grist to the learned mill, but have moreover brought with it a superior chance for finding learned arbitrators.

146.—VIII. *Device the eighth.—Blind fixation of times for Judicial operations.*

I. Only in relation to the exigencies of the case, and the interests of the sincere among suitors, not in relation to Judge and Co.'s profits, will, in this case the blindness be seen manifested.

147.—II. Blindness to the exigencies of the case? Yes, to all exigencies: to all differences between time and time, to all differences between place and place.

148.—III. Between *dishonesty* and *insanity*, on the part of the creators and preservers of this arrangement,—that is here the question.—What?

For holding intercourse with the judicatory—for paying obedience to its mandate—appoint, in all cases, the same day for every individual subject to its authority? On whatever spot, wherever at the time he happens to be, whether within a stone's throw of the justice chamber, or at the Land's-end, and whether in England, or in Australia, in Peru, or in Nova Zembla? Except for the purpose of deception, is it in the nature of man that any such arrangement shall have presented itself to a sane mind? No: not of honest blindness is this the result; but of sinister discernment on the part of the contrivers, taking advantage of that blindness which, on the part of the people, has, with such deplorably successful industry, been organized.

So much for the policy of *dishonesty*.

148. Behold now the policy of *common honesty* and common *sense :* yes, and everywhere, but in the land of chicane, common *practice*.

i. No suit ·being (suppose) ever commenced, but by application made to you (the judge) in your justice-chamber, by a proposed plaintiff,— or, in case of necessity, a substitute of his,—settle with him before you let him depart, the *means of intercourse* with him during the continuance of the suit, the further obligation being at the same time laid on him, of continuing the line, or say chain or series of those *means*, by timely information of every such change as shall eventually have place : reference being moreover at all times made to such other individuals, whose assistance to these purposes may eventually become necessary.

149.—ii. Learn from him, as far as may be, the like means of intercourse, in the first instance, with all *other* individuals, whom his examination presents to view in the character of *defendants*,

E

extraneous witnesses, or *co-plaintiffs*, or say *co-pursuers*.

150.—III. At the first attendance of each such
other individual, make with him the like set-
tlement.

151.—IV. Should any subsequent attendance
on the part of the same or any *other* individual be,
for the purpose of the suit necessary—accident
and other exceptions excepted—let the time fixt for
it be as *early* as, without preponderant evil in the
shape of expense and vexation it can be.

152.—V. Accidents: for example, death, sickness, impassableness of ways, calamities, casual-
ties, confinement, or transference by force, by
fraud, or the like.

153.—VI. Correspondent arrangement as to
inspection: inspection of things *moveable*, requisite
to be inspected by you, in the character of sources
of *real* evidence.

154.—VII. So as to things *immoveable*.

155.—VIII. So as to *persons*, by sickness or infirmity, rendered immoveable.

156. So, as to instruments in *writing:* whether
already written; or, for the purpose in hand, *requiring* to be written, allowance made in this last
case for the quantity of time likely to be made requisite by the quantity, or the quality of the matter.

157.—IX. As to the requisition thus to be made
of the maximum of dispatch, note the exceptions
following :—

1. When, of two individuals, attendance *at the
same time* is requisite, the residence of both or either,
—from each other and from the judgment-seat,—is
at the time, at a certain degree of *remoteness :* in
this case, for the attendance of him whose residence at the time is nearest, postponement :—that

is to say, to the earliest time, at which attendance can be paid by him whose residence is most remote,—is necessitated by the exigency of the case.

158.—II. So, in regard to any *greater number* of individuals, on whose part conjunct attendance is necessary.

159.—III. So, when the exigency of the case requires the attendance of one individual to be postponed till *after* attendance paid by this or that other.

160. With each individual, with whom, for the purposes of the suit, intercourse is holden,—*places* for intercourse, and in that respect *modes* of intercourse, two:—1. The justice-chamber; 2. other places at large: in the justice-chamber, by attendance of the individuals there: other places, in extraordinary cases by visitation, *transition*, or say *migration*, thither on the part of the judge. Thus far, for intercourse in the *oral mode*. For intercourse in the *epistolary mode*, in ordinary cases it will be carried on by transference made of the written instrument or other source of evidence, from place to place; transference of letters, by the post, for example: included, from and to the justice-chamber, will be this transference, in most cases.

161. In this way will conjunct provision be made for the exigencies of each individual suit, and for the convenience of each individual concerned;—delay, expense, vexation—all minimized. So much for the policy of honesty.

162. Return we now to the policy of dishonesty, as it presents itself to a closer view. On the part of each such individual, requisite will be the performance of some *operation*, and, included

under the head of *operations* is that which is performed by the exhibition of some *written instrument* or other moveable source of evidence, as above.

163. Behold now the course, which, in regard to each such operation, and each such instrument, the dishonest plan prescribes.

For each such operation, on the part of every individual concerned,—fix one and the same day. Then to *the minimization* of the evils in question—the evils to wit of delay, vexation, and expense, you will substitute maximization : for, in each individual instance the chances, against the so fixt days being a proper day, are as infinity to one.

164.—1. In regard to operations, it will be your care to maximize the number of those by which birth is given to written instruments; for in this case superadded to the profit—profit in the operation is the profit upon the instrument.   On this occasion reciprocal generation has place: operation produces instrument; instrument, operations.

165.—ii. So, the length of each such instrument.

166.—iii. So the number of the instances in which, for the performance of the several operations, days are appointed on which the performance of those same operations respectively is impossible : for by the impossibility the need of ulterior operations and ulterior instruments will be established.

167.—iv. So, and thence, the number of instances in which need of *application* for *further time*, and application accordingly, shall have place; in particular the number of those in which the allowance of such time shall be a subject matter of *contestation*.

168.—v. So accordingly, of the instances in which the *notices*, without which compliance cannot have place, shall *not* have been received.

169.—vi. So accordingly, of those in which the notice shall not have been *given*.

170.—vii. So likewise of those in which whether the notice *has* or has *not* been received and given respectively,—shall be the subject matter of *contestation.*

171.—viii. So likewise the expense of *special messengers*, employed by professional assistants (in this instance chiefly of the attorney class) in making communication of such notices,—the expense, to wit, for the sake of the profit extractable out of the expense.

172.—ix. So accordingly the *number* of such *journies*, and the *length* of and *difficulties* attendant upon each.

173.—x. So likewise, in regard to the journies employed in the making *seisure, definitive* or *provisional* and instrumental, whether of *persons* or *things*, for the purposes of justice : that is to say, whether for *execution* and effect to be given to a decree of the judge, or for *evidence* to be elicited for the purpose of constituting a ground for it.

174. Admirable, under the existing system, is the equipment made for this species of *chase :*—*party-hunting*, to wit, and *witness-hunting :*—a chase in which the fox, instead of being the *huntee*, is the *hunter*, and his object is to catch—not as *early*, but as *late*, as possible, and through as many turnings and windings as possible.

175. Behold here an example. For the purpose of obtaining, at the hands of the defendant, the service he stands engaged for—say the money he stands engaged to pay—engaged, to wit, by a

bond, to which his signature stands attached, adequate ground for regarding it as being his signature, is necessary. This defendant the judge sees standing or sitting in court. Shall this same judge say to same defendant, "Is this your hand-writing?" Not he, indeed: no, nor any person by word of mouth. Never since the Conquest was any torment thus barbarous inflicted. By word of mouth nobody. The hardship of saying *Yes* or *No* would be unendurable. In writing Yes, so it be by the plaintiff and by a bill in Equity, length from half a dozen pages to any number of sheets of ordinarily-sized letter press: as to time, at the end of years five or more as it may happen. Yes, or by word of mouth, so it be by learned counsel to a witness who has been hired to come, say from Australia for this purpose, if there be no person, whose residence is less remote, and by whom the information can be afforded. Both those resources failing, the defendant, by the hands of Judge and Co., pockets the money: the right owner loses it.

176. Think of a judge, with this spectacle before his eyes, turning them aside from it—lifting them up to heaven, and proclaiming, in solemn accents, his love of justice.

177. By the arrangements hereinafter submitted, put down altogether would be this pastime.

178. As to *fees,* inexhaustible is the source of them, thus created by *chicaneries about notice.*

179. Under the existing system, to this relatively so desirable state of things, with what consummate skill and success, and not less consum-summate effrontery, the *blank fixation* device has been adopted, may now be, with sufficient distinctness, visible.

180. To all these sinister purposes, it has been

seen how indispensably necessary was the primordial, radical, and all-producing device—*exclusion of parties*, severally and collectively, from the presence of the judge.

181. So will it presently be seen, to all these same purposes, how exquisitely well adapted is the system of *mechanical*, substituted as far as possible to *mental*, judicature.

182. Nor yet, for reconciling the public mind to this host of enormities, and of sufferings produced by them,—are *pleas* altogether wanting: pleas with which pleasing or imposing ideas stand associated: words, such as they are, have been found in *uniformity*, *regularity*, and *strictness*: pleas furnished by the ascendancy so extensively prevalent of imagination over reason.

183. Uniformity? what uniformity? *Answer*— That produced by the fabled arrangement in which, between the bed and the men reposing on it, uniformity in length was produced by cutting off the redundant part of each body which was longer, and stretching out to the requisite length each body which was shorter, than the bed. Here is *uniformity;* and, this being done according to rule, here is moreover *regularity;* and, for the display of the heroic strength of mind, requisite and produced by this branch of the gymnastic exercise, added not unfrequently is the word *strictness:* strictness in the observation of justice-killing and misery-begetting rules.

184.—IX. *Device the ninth.—Mechanical, substituted to mental, judicature.*

In so far as, in the production of any effect, *machinery* is employed instead of *human labour*, machinery is employed instead of *mind:* for example, in the shape of a man, an *automaton* figure, such as has been seen, forming writings with its hands.

185. Origin of this device, a problem: a problem from the beginning, proposed to one another by Judge and Co. Purport of all this—how to administer justice without a thought about the matter: reward for solution,—trouble, time, labour, responsibility,—all minimized: meaning always by *time*, Judge and Co.'s time: ditto, profit of course, on this, as on all other occasions, maximized. Nowhere in Euclid is to be found any problem more skilfully and effectually solved than by Judge and Co. this.

186. For proof as well as elucidation, one example will supersede all need of recourse to others. This is—the operation styled *signing judgments*. Machinery and mode of operation, this.

187. Machine, a pair of scales, invented by the dæmon of Chicane, in derision of the scales of Justice. Kept in one scale, papers styled *judgments*; kept vacant the other, for the reception of fees. Drop into it the appropriate fee, up rises the appropriate judgment. This the attorney (the plaintiff's attorney) takes in hand, and off it goes to the sheriff, for execution. Such is the way in which money, to the amount of hundreds of pounds, thousands, or tens of thousands, is made to pass from defendant's pocket into plaintiff's. His lordship, under whose *auspices* this *leger-de-main* is performed, what knows he of all this? Exactly as much as his learned brother in Calcutta.

188. To such perfection is the invention brought —so complete the mechanism produced—not so much as even in pretence is it by the *judge* that the effective operation is performed. " *I have*

signed judgment," quoth plaintiff's attorney. Nor yet is so much as this true. What *is* true is —that it is by a journeyman of the chief justice's that the signature is performed: all that the attorney has done is the paying him for so doing. And the journeyman—what knows he about the matter? *Answer*—That an instrument, which, on the *blind fixation principle,* as above, should by defendant's attorney have been put in by a certain day, had not been put in by that same day.

189. Now for a reason for such judicature: where shall it be found? Without so much as a particle of blame on the defendant's part, or even on his attorney's part, in how many cases may it not happen that the failure took place?

190. In a system having for its end the ends of justice, in a word, in the here proposed system, cases forming so many grounds of excuses, would, as in the infancy of English jurisprudence, received under the name of *essoigns,* be looked out for, and a list formed of them. But, suppose even *blame,* and to any amount, might not *compensation,* if to the same amount, suffice? compensation instead of the ruin, of which execution given to the judgment may be productive?

191. " Persons ... obtaining money ... by false pretences ... may be punished by fine and imprisonment, or by pillory, whipping, or transportation." These words stand part of the marginal abridgment of the first section of the statute 30 Geo. II, ch. 24, § 1, in the statutes at large; which statute, is in Ruffhead's edition of the statutes, referred to under the head of *Cheat, Swindler,* as the name by which, in common parlance, persons so offending are designated. Seeing this, we humbly entreat the Honorable House that it

may be considered whether, by the high-seated functionaries by whom fees are obtained by warrants for attendance paid before them, although such attendances were never paid nor intended so to be, money has not at all times been obtained by false pretences: as also to consider whether if there be, either in a *legal* or a *moral* sense, guilt in the obtaining money by such means, the guilt is lessened by the power by means of which such obtainment is effected: whether, if functionaries so seated in those and other judicial situations, were not, to every practical purpose, in this respect, above the law, obtainment by such means would not be an act of extortion, and, as such, a crime; and whether, by the addition of extortion, and, on the part of a suitor, the impossibility of avoiding to comply with the demand so made, the moral guilt attached to the idea of *chicanery*, or say swindling, is in any degree lessened. We acknowledge that it is in the power of the Honorable House, with the assent of the House of Lords and his Majesty in Parliament, not only by connivance, but by express enactment, to give impunity and encouragement to the above and any or all other persons, who, being constituted in authority, obtain money by false pretences; and this, while persons not constituted in authority are, for obtaining money on false pretences, punished in manner above-mentioned: and moreover, that it is fully in the power of that authority of which the Honorable House is a branch, to give impunity and encouragement to every enormity, to whatever extent maleficent, and by so doing to cause the act not to come with propriety under the name of a *crime*, nor the actors to be, with propriety, denominated *criminals;* and accordingly, to cause to be punished, as for a libel, all persons speaking of these under that name : which, accordingly, we forbear to do otherwise than hypothetically, as above : but we humbly entreat the Honorable House to consider whether it would not be more for their honour and dignity to endeavour to repress maleficence in this, as well as in every other shape, than in this, or any other shape, give impunity and encouragement to it.

192. If instead of this mechanical, mental were the mode of judicature, how would the matter have been managed ? *Answer*—Of each individual case, of each individual person concerned, the circumstances would be looked to, of each individual person the feelings taken for objects of sympathy and consideration ; respite upon occasion granted ; pecuniary circumstances, on one side as well as the other, taken into the account : claims of other creditors not neglected, though not parties to the suit, nor privy to the *application* by which it was commenced.

193.—X. *Device the tenth.—Mischievous transference and bandying of suits.*

Instead of transference and bandying, the one appellative *removal* might better have been employed : removal—that is to say, of a suit from one judicatory to another.

194. Removal may be, and is, either,—1. Established ; or, 2. Incidental : *established*, when by usage it takes place in every individual suit of the sort in question : *incidental*, when it does not take place but in consequence of some extraordinary operation performed by some person for that pur-

pose; some person usually, if not exclusively, a party on one side or the other of the suit.

195. Under the existing system, when it has place incidentally, a *certiorari* is the name of the written instrument by the issuing of which the removal is produced : of this further on.

196. Subject matter of the established removals two : namely—i. Incorporeal the *operation*, performed on the occasion of the suit; corporeal the written instruments, brought into existence, or into the custody of the judicatory, in consequence of the commencement given to the suit : including every such account, or say history, as happens to be given of these same operations : as also any such other *things moveable*, if any, as happen to have been presented, or intended to be presented, to the view of the judges, in the character of sources of evidence—that is to say, *real* evidence.

197.—ii. In case of *removal*, whether established or incidental, the suit is by some other judicatory *received :* call this the *recipient* or *subsequential :* and for distinction, call the first-mentioned judicatory the *originating, original,* or *primordial.*

198.—iii. If, after removal, the suit *does not* return to the primordial judicatory, call the removal *transference,* or *simple transference :* if it *does* return, *oscillation* or *bandying :* in case of *bandying,* the transference is followed by *retrotransference.*

199.—iv. Emblems—of oscillation, a *pendulum :* of bandying, *battledore and shuttlecock.*

200.—v. Where oscillation has place, returns are in any number secured by what has been called *pre-established harmony :* at battledore and shuttlecock, to every return a fresh application of mental power is indispensable.

201.—vi. As to *recipient judicatories,* they have place of course in a number correspondent to that of the oscillations of the pendulum, or the strokes of the battledore.

202.—vii. From the operation here termed *removal,* distinguish that designated by the word *appeal.* Under every system, *appeal* is for *cause assigned,* namely, on the part of the judge, of the originating judicatory, either *mis-decision,* or *non-decision* productive of the same effect as misdecision: misdecision, either ultimate or *interlocutory,* or say *interventional*: in any case, *misconduct.* In the case of what is, here meant by *removal,* no allegation or supposition of any such misconduct has place.

203.—viii. Under the here proposed system, incidentally, both simple transference and removal have place. But in every case it is for cause specially assigned: thence in the way of *bandying;* not in the way of *oscillation.*

204. Under the existing system, in no case will the removal be seen to have any good cause assigned or assignable. Good cause, none: but as *effects,* bad effects in abundance; bad in relation to the interest of the community and the *ends of justice:* thence, herein, as above termed, *mischievous:* good, at the same time, in correspondent abundance, relation had to Judge and Co. and their particular and sinister interest: and thence in relation to the actual ends of judicature.

205. To return to the *here proposed* system: and to the good effects which under it are deducible from the removal in question, and would accordingly be deduced from it. *Execution, evidence, intercourse;*—to one or more of these objects will be found referable everything that can be said

of the *operations* or *instruments* which have place in judicial procedure.

206.—I. *Execution*, to wit, of the enactments of the *substantive* branch, or say the main body of the law: under which head is comprised everything that does not belong to the *adjective* branch, or say *procedure:* enactments, really existing in the case of legislation-made, imaginary in the case of judge-made law.

207.—II. *Evidence*, for the purpose of forming a ground for what is done in the way of *execution*.

208.—III. *Intercourse*, to wit, between the judge and all other persons concerned, for obtaining evidence and effecting execution: including the securing the means of such intercourse from the commencement to the termination of the suit.

209.—IV. Giving, to all these several objects, accomplishment, with the minimum of delay, expence, and vexation, to the individuals concerned.

210.—I. First, as to *execution*. For this purpose need of removals—of removals in a number altogether unlimited—may have place. In proof of this, a single example may suffice. *Judge-shires* (as herein proposed) say two hundred. For whichsoever purpose—say satisfaction to a party wronged or punishment—seizure and sale of defendant's effects requisite: within any number of these judicial territories so many portions of these effects may happen to be situated. In this case, even though perfect intercommunication of jurisdiction was to have place between the judge of each judge-shire and the judge of every other; still preponderant convenience might require that for this purpose employment should be given to the power of the judge of this or that *subsequential* judge-shire.

Originating judge-shire, or say judicatory, suppose in London : of the effects, one parcel in Liverpool. Of seizure and sale, the purpose might perhaps as conveniently be fulfilled by mandate from the London judge-shire. But, for the discovering what they are, and in whose possession situated, suppose *evidence* necessary, and that evidence composed of the testimony of a person resident in Liverpool: here, expense and delay in no small proportion will be saved, if it be by a Liverpool judge instead of the London judge that the examination of the Liverpool witness is performed.

211.—II. As to *evidence*. In regard to evidence, what is desirable is, that, in each individual case, whatsoever evidence the case affords, be obtainable, in whatever part of the globe it happens to be situated; whether in England, Ireland, Scotland, a distant dependancy, or a country under foreign dominion: obtainable with the best security for its completeness and correctness and with the least delay, expense, and vexation: with least delay, and accordingly from persons and things in any number, at the *same time*.

212. Good effects in this respect obtainable from removal and not otherwise, these—

I. Obtainment of evidence not otherwise obtainable.

213.—II. Obtainment of it in the *best shape*, that is to say, that which it assumes when elicited in the *oral* mode : when, otherwise, it could not be elicited but in a less instructive shape; namely, when elicited in the *epistolary* mode.

214.—III. Obtainment of it from its several sources, namely persons and things, in any number at the same time, for the purpose of the same suit; and, in each instance, in that one of the two modes, which, on that individual occasion, is best adapted to the aggregate of the purposes of justice.

215.—IV. Accomplishing the elicitation, not only with the minimum of delay and vexation; but that minimum laid, in each individual instance, on the shoulders best able to bear it: namely, those of the public at large, in so far as practicable without preponderant evil in the shape of addition made to the expense.

216. For all these several purposes, removal of the suit from the originating judicatory to some other or others, is eventually necessary: that is to say, in so far as the means necessary for the accomplishment of these three several objects respectively in the best mode, fail of being in the power of the *originating* judicatory, and at the same time are in the power of some other, which accordingly is constituted the *subsequential* and *recipient* judicatory.

217. Of the benefit in all these shapes a necessary instrument will be seen to be the division of the local field of judicature into the above-mentioned compartments, styled on this account *judge-shires*: extent of each judge-shire limited, in such sort that, the *justice-chamber* being in the centre, every inhabitant, not disabled by infirmity, may, during the sitting of the judicatory, be in attendance therein, without passing the night elsewhere than at his own home.

218. Mode of elicitation oral or epistolary: places, the originating or subsequential judicatories, in any number, according to the exigency of each individual case.

219. Eventually subsequent to epistolary, oral elicitation: now for the first time this arrange-

ment : object of it, check upon, security against, falsehood.

215. Where, for correctness and completeness of the whole body of evidence, the confrontation, of all persons speaking to the same fact, is regarded as necessary,—confrontation accordingly : not otherwise : place, either the original, or some subsequential judicatory.

216. So, order in respect of time of elicitation as between the several examinands : that is to say, co-plaintiffs, if any,—defendants, and other persons at large, in the character of extraneous witnesses.

217. Now, as to *retrotransference* and *retroreception*, or say, return of the suit to the originating judicatory. Demand for it will in some instances have place, in others, not : purpose of it, continuation of the series of *operations*, by which commencement had been performed.

218. By all these arrangements taken together, minimized will be seen to be the burthen of the expense : that is to say—1. By minimization of the extent of the judgeshire, the quantity of the expense, of journies and demurrage : 2. By transferring to the letter-post the conveyance of such of the written instruments as are contained within the compass of an ordinary letter, expense of intercourse in so far minimized :—3. By laying on the shoulders of government, and thereby of the public at large, that same expense, together with the whole of the remuneration of all judicial functionaries,—minimized will be the *hardship* of the burthen, by its being laid on the shoulders best able to bear it. Thus provided for by far the greatest part of the expense : other part, by fines for delinquency on the part of defendants,

F

where there is no individual specially wronged, and for *misconduct* in the course of the suit, on the part of suitors on both sides : particularly if in the shape of falsehood : always remembered, that the burthen of compensation has the effect, and even more than the effect, of money to the same amount exacted, and applied to the use of the public, or in any otherwise disposed of.

219. By the *evidence-holder*, understand the person whose testimony is requisite, or who is in possession of the *writing*, or other *thing* which is the source of the evidence. When of this evidence-holder, the residence is at the time in the dominion of a *foreign* power, elicitation in the epistolary mode may be practicable or not with advantage, according to circumstances. Practicable it will be in so far as, by any means, he happens to be in effect subject to the power of the judicatory : means of such subjection, subject matters of property, whether *moveable* or *immoveable*, in possession or expectancy, certain or contingent, so circumstanced as to be susceptible of seizure by the judge. So, as to subject matters termed *incorporeal*, that is to say *rights* of all kinds. From the impracticability of making this mode of elicitation available in some cases, no reason assuredly can be deduced, for the not employing it in any case in which it can be made available.

220. In so far as, for any of the above purposes, on any of the above occasions, removal in each of the two modes, with or without retrotransference to and retroreception on the part of the originating judicatory, has not place,—manifest it will now (it is hoped) be, that the jurisdiction of the whole territory cannot but be as the phrase is—*lame :* and in what a multitude of its organs and muscles juris-

diction is under the existing system lame, and to all good purposes impotent, will be manifest to every person, in proportion as his conception of that same system is correct and complete.

221. For extraordinary removal sole case this. By a judicatory, or by a tribunal of exception, cognizance taken, (suppose) of a suit, which lies not within its competence; here will be a case— either for the *extinction* of the suit altogether, or for the *removal* of it into the sort of judicatory, to which (those exceptions excepted) cognizance is given of all sorts of cases. Tribunals of exception these;—*military* judicatories for the establishment of appropriate discipline among military functionaries, in both branches—land branch and sea branch—of that service: *ecclesiastical* functionaries (in a country in which an ecclesiastical establishment has place) for the establishment of discipline among ecclesiastical functionaries.

222. Removal in both shapes will, in some cases, of necessity, have place in the same judgeshire; for example, as between the judge *principal* and judge *depute*,—in case of death, simple *transference:* in case of temporary inability through illness,—perhaps simple transference, perhaps oscillation or bandying may be the more eligible course.

Only that it may not be supposed to be overlooked is this need mentioned.

223. Enter now the existing system. Short account of it, as to this matter, this: The *purposes* for which,—the *occasions* on which, so as to be conducive to the ends of justice—say in a word *useful,* the removal will take place, have been seen. Under the existing system for none of these purposes, on none of these occasions, has it place: on

none, but where (the rare case—that of applying a check to usurpation) alone excepted,—it is worse than useless.

224. Intricate is here the complication, vast the labyrinth constructed by it: to let in upon the whole expanse the full light of day would be an endless enterprise : only, by way of sample, upon a hole-and-corner or two, can a few rays be endeavoured to be cast.

225.—1. Sample the first. Mode of established removal, the simple transference mode. 1. Class of cases and suits, that called *criminal*. Species of cases, that called by the nonsensical term, *felony:* thus denominated from the sort of punishment attached to it : nonsensical, because no idea does this denomination afford of the *nature* of the evil ; nor therefore of the *cause* for which it is thus dealt with.

226. Course taken by the suit in these cases, this.

Case the first :—Judicatory in which the suit is tried, the original common law judicatory, having for its seat, in a country cause, the assize town.

i. Originating judicatory, that of *justices of the peace*, one or more, acting otherwise than in general sessions, as above,

ii. First recipient judicatory, the *grand jury* for the county, sitting at the place where the trial is about to be performed.

iii. Second and last recipient judicatory, that in which the *trial* is performed, as above. In this case it is in that same town that the judgment is pronounced. Place of execution varying ; but no return in any case to the originating judicatory.

227. Note that, in the case of *homicide* a crime belonging to this same class of *felony*,—an origi-

hating judicatory, taking cognizance antecedently to the above, is the court called the Coroner's Inquest: judge, the *coroner*: with a jury called the *inquest jury*.

228. Of these removals, note now the consequences in regard to *evidence*. Short account this: Shape in which the evidence is elicited, more or less different in all these cases; the mass elicited on the first occasion made no use of either in the second or the third: the mass elicited in the second made no use of in the third: the two first masses—after the expense, labour, and time employed in the elicitation of them, thrown away.

229. Even of this third mass no use is made for any purpose subsequent to the *verdict*. For, being elicited in the oral mode, it is not committed to writing, by authority. Only by accident, that is to say by this or that individual, by whom the profit on publication is looked to as affording a sufficient return for the labour and expense of *minutation*.

230. In one class of cases, the suit does receive its termination, in the same judicatory in which it has received its commencement:—these cases are of the number of those consigned to the cognizance of a justice of the peace acting singly, or two or more in conjunction, out of general sessions. Now then, supposing the judicatory aptly constituted, why (except in the cases provided for under the herein proposed system as before) why should it not so do in these, and in a word in all other cases? And where is the case, in which the judicatory should be otherwise than aptly constituted?

231. In the originating judicatory—namely, that of the justice of the peace acting singly,—some-

times a *part* only of the stock of evidence which
the individual can afford will have been elicited,
sometimes the whole of it, as it may happen; but
where the whole of it does happen to be elicited, the
suit is not the less sent in to those other judicatories.

232. Moreover, where, after the whole of the
evidence which the suit affords has been heard,
including the evidence on the defendant's side,—
be this evidence in its own nature ever so satisfactory, and as against the defendant conclusive,
yet, thereupon, when the suit has been transferred
to the secret judicature,—the grand jury, it is
liable to be, and not unfrequently is, decided the
opposite way, on evidence heard on one side only :
meantime evidence-holders have had from a day
to half a year given to them,—to go off of
themselves, or to be bought off,—and, in prison, the
defendant, guilty or not guilty, that same time, for
contaminating, as the phrase is, or being contaminated, or both; if not guilty, there to moan under
the oppression, thus, for the benefit of Judge and
Co. exercised on him ; and, whether he be guilty or
not guilty, the country is made to suffer under the
expense of keeping him in a state of forced idleness.

233. Cases in which removal in the oscillation
or bandying mode is employed, these.

I. All suits termed *civil*, commenced in any one
of the three common law Westminster-hall courts.

234. In Westminster-hall, they take their commencement without elicitation of evidence : their
commencement, viz. in the office of a clerk; mode,
the mechanical mode, as above; the judges not
knowing anything about the matter : applications,
incidental and accidental, excepted ; for example
for *leave to plead*, or for *putting off the trial*.

235. For elicitation of evidence, in a country

cause, off goes the suit to an assize town, there, as the phrase is, to be *tried;* to wit, by the elicitation there performed, by a judge dispatched thither from one of the Westminster-hall courts, with a petty jury.

236. The trial performed, back it comes to the judicatory from whence it had emanated; and there it is that, in the mechanical mode as above, it receives judgment..

This done, then back again it goes to the same county for *execution;* but, for execution, the office it goes to is—not any office belonging to the court in which it originated, nor that in which the trial was performed : it is the office of the sheriff, of the county in which the suit was tried.

237. Such is the operation of the *judgment,* when it has for its subject matter, a *person,* or a *thing moveable* or *immoveable :* whereupon the officer causes hands to be laid upon the person or the thing ; and, in the ordinary course, does by that same person or thing what by the judgment he has been bid to do. But, in some cases, the suit has for its subject matter nothing on which hands can be laid ;—nothing but a fictitious entity—an incorporeal thing—to wit, a *right,* or an *obligation;* in which cases, as *execution* consists in the extinction of the obligation or the right, *words* contained in the judgment suffice—words, without acts and deeds, for the performance of it.

238. Now for removal upon an almost universal scale—removal by *certiorari.*

Exceptions few excepted, from all courts a suit is, at any stage, removeable into the King's Bench. Instrument of removal, a writ styled in the Judge and Co.'s dialect of the flash language, a *certiorari:* in the language of honest ignorance, a *sisserary :*

witness the threat—" I'll fetch you up with a sisserary."

239. Eminently mischievous to the community at
large, correspondently beneficial to Judge and Co.,
is this same monster. Mischief it does in two ways:
1. by its operation when not killed: 2. by its dead
carcase when, by a clause in a statute, killed. Of such
as are let live the effect is—from a less expensive,
and comparatively to Judge and Co. unprofitable,
judicatory, to send up the suit to a more expensive
and more profitable judicatory : as to the *carcases*,
they are those of the *certioraris*, killed in embryo
or *endeavoured so to be*: that is to say, in and
by every statute, by which additional jurisdiction
is given to a justice of the peace, or other sum-
marily acting judicatory. In this case, one of two
things :—either by the insertion of the clause by
which the death is produced, so much rubbish is
shot down into the statute-book, or else danger of
inefficiency is left by the non-insertion of it.

Note by the bye, that in every such statute, this
is but one of a string, of efficient causes of inefficiency, which must be thus dealt with, or the
like effect will follow.

240. Yes, *endeavoured* to be : for, (as law books
shew) not in every instance has the endeavour
been successful : on this occasion as on all others,
in comes the established habit of Judge and Co.:
when a clause of an act of the legislature is
brought before them, they pay obedience to it, or
run counter to it, as they feel inclined; *moulding* the
law is among the phrases on this occasion employed.

241. Now for the *instrument* and *document*,
which, in case of *removal*, whether *established* or
incidental, is the corporeal subject matter of this
same operation; the *suit* being the incorporeal subject

matter of it.   Of this instrument the proper contents will be composed of a *statement*, or say
history, of the several *proceedings*, carried on in the
course of the suit: proceedings,—that is to say appropriate operations performed, and written instruments, framed and issued or exhibited: contents,
for various purposes *proper :* for the purpose of
appeal, and in so far as that is in contemplation,
altogether indispensable.

242. Of this history, by far the largest, the
bulkiest part, will consist of an account of the
evidence : to the evidence which by this means, for
this purpose, has, in the course of the suit,
by the correspondent operations been elicited in the
word of mouth mode :—the expression given to it
by the pen, by the *taking it down*, as the phrase is,
or in one word *the minutation* of it, will constitute
a *written instrument*.

. 243. Hereupon, in the instance of each individual suit will arise two questions:—1. Shall the
minutation be performed? 2. When it is performed, shall the result be, for any and what length
of time, preserved?   To both these questions,
the proper answer will depend—upon the proportion between the *profit* in the way of *use* elicitable
from the document, and the *loss* composed of the
expenses : always understood—that, wheresoever
appeal is in contemplation, *preservation* will of
course not be less necessary than *creation*.

. 244. As to all matters besides the evidence, so
small in comparison will in every instance be the
bulk of them, that of what is necessary to either of
these operations, of no part can the expense be
grudged.

. 245. Obvious as may seem these observations,
not so obvious are they as to be superfluous : for

by them will judgment have to be pronounced on the practice of the existing system in relation to the subject matter of them.

246. Enter now accordingly, the existing system. To the difference between courts of record and courts not of record, prodigious is the importance attached by it. Mountains, in the survey taken of them, the courts of *record:* mole hills, the courts *not* of record.

247. Now as to the treatment given by the two sorts of courts to the mass of evidence belonging to the suit.

In the record of the courts of record, not a syllable of this same evidence is ever inserted: and in particular, in those of the Westminster Hall courts —the King's Bench: the Common Pleas, and the common law side, of the half common law, half equity court—the Court of Exchequer.

248. In the records of the courts not of record, every syllable of the evidence elicited. Witness —1. The Chancery Court: including its subordinate branches, the vice-chancellor's and the master of the roll's court.—2. The courts held by the bankruptcy commissioners, and which are also courts subordinate to the Chancellor's Court.— 3. The equity side of the Exchequer Court.

249. Between the real state of things, and the pretended state, as intimated by the denomination thus given,—whence this seemingly strange difference? *Answer.*—By the common law court it is that this nomenclature was framed. Courts to which the depreciatory denomination was attached by them, the shops of their rivals in trade: rivals, with whom for a length of time they had fierce battles; till at last an accommodation was come to:—of course, at the expense of customers, and

of those who should have been, but by the expense were kept from being customers.

250. Of the particulars contained in the instrument styled the record, as framed in the courts self-styled courts of record, what shall be the account given? Short account this.

i. Written pleadings, which ought not to have been exhibited.

ii. Mendacious assertions, by word of mouth and in writing, which ought not to have been uttered.

iii. Delays such as have been seen, which ought not to have been made.

iv. Ulterior delays—fruits, such as have been seen, of the precipitation established.

v. Products, of the blind fixation as above—days appointed, for operations, which it was foreknown could not on those several days respectively be performed.

vi. Operations, which, in pursuance of the system of mechanical, *vice* mental judicature, are stated as having been performed by the judge, though, if performed at all, it is not by him that they have been performed.

vii. Removals made, which ought never to have been made.

251. Prefaced the whole by a fabulous history of *apparitions:* statements asserting *appearances* as having been made by unhappy defendants (and in these courts what defendants are not unhappy?) who from beginning to end never did appear; they not knowing, nor having it in their power to know, what to do had they appeared; and knowing but too well that, had they appeared, their appearance would have been of no use.

252. As to the written pleadings,—note, that

though otherwise than in an eventual, indirect, and disguised way, as above, the effect of evidence is not given to them,—not unfrequently more voluminous are they than the evidence is, or would have been if properly elicited.

253. As to *suit* and *record* taken together,—under the existing system, general conclusion, as intimated at the outset, this : To any useful purpose, removal none : to purposes worse than useless, removal in abundance.

254.—XI. *Device the eleventh.—Decision on grounds avowedly foreign to the merits.*

☞ For the matter belonging to this head, reference may be made to the Full-length Petition.

255.—XII. *Device the twelfth.—Juries subdued and subjugated.*

☞ For the matter belonging to this head, reference may be made to the Full-length Petition.

256.—XIII. *Device the thirteenth.—Jurisdiction split and spliced.*

In the Full-length Petition (pages from 125 to 128) have been seen, the sorts of courts, splinters from the one original *Aula Regia*, each with a different scrap of jurisdiction. Number, not less than thirteen : without reckoning others which in process of time came to be superadded. Number of *judges* in these respectively, from *one* to an undefinable greater number : species of functionaries, acting in various ways in *subordination* to the judge, in one alone of these same thirteen sorts of courts (as per Full-length Petition, page 154) more than twenty; not to speak of the other sorts of subordinates acting in the *other* sorts of courts : all these species, in-

stead of the four or five, which, in every court
would (as per page 178) with the addition of no
more than two or three others in some special
cases, be sufficient.

257. That confusion may be still worse confounded, behold now a sample of the diversifica-
tion, which, in these same judicatories with their
additaments, the denomination given to the character of *judge* has been subjected to : the function belonging to that character being disguised,
under and by most of those several denominations :
a sample only—not a complete list : for the labour
of making it out would have been unrequited, and
unendurable.   Here they are—

1. Lord high chancellor.
2. Lord keeper of the seals.
3. Lord commissioner of the great seal.
4. Master of the rolls.
5. Vice-chancellor.
6. Lord chief justice of the King's Bench.
7. Lord chief justice of the Common Pleas.
8. Lord chief baron of the Court of Exchequer.
9. Puisne (pronounced puny) justice of the
King's Bench and Common Pleas.
10. Puisne baron of the Exchequer.
11. Master in chancery.
12. Master of the crown-office.
13. Prothonotary of the Common Pleas.
14. Remembrancer of the Court of Exchequer.
15. Commissioner of bankruptcy.
16. Commissioner of the insolvency court.
17. Justice of the peace.
18. Chairman of the quarter sessions of the
peace.
19. Recorder.
20. Common serjeant.

21. Commissioner of the court of requests.

22. Privy counsellor.

23. Chancellors of the duchy of Lancaster: of the bishoprick and county palatine of Durham.

24. Vice-chancellor of a university.

25. Lord delegate.

26. Dean of the arches.

27. Chancellor of an episcopal diocese.

28. Surrogate of a diocese.

29. Commissary of an archdeaconry.

30. Assistant-barrister (in Ireland).

31. Grand juryman.

32. Constable of the night.

33. Annoyance juryman.

34. Coroner.

35. Steward of manor court.

36. Warden of the stannaries.

37. Warden of the cinque ports.

38. Vicar-general of the preachers. (Quere whether judicial?)

39. Official principal of the court of arches.

40. Master of the prerogative court.

41. Master of the faculty office. (Quere whether judicial?)

42. Official principal to various deaconries and archdeaconries.

43. Commissioner of the hackney coach office.

44. Commissioner of excise.

45. Commissioner of the customs.

46. Commissioner of the audit office.

47. Auditor-general (of Greenwich Hospital).

48. Commissioner of a court of claim.

258. As to the confusion on which the enumeration thus made of them is involved,—so far from being a *blemish*, it may be stated as a *merit:* serving, as it does, to render the portrait the more

appropriate and perfect a representation of the original.

259. Behold another evil, produced by the jurisdiction-splitting, and not brought to view in the Full-length Petition. This is—the all-pervading denial of justice, produced by the exclusion put upon one or other of the two remedies which wrong in every shape calls for: namely, the *satisfactive* and the *punitive*. Modes of procedure, the *fissure* makes two :—the one styled *civil*, the other *criminal :* in and by the *civil* you may demand the *satisfactive ;* in and by the criminal, the *punitive :* in some cases you may have the one; in other cases, the other: but with scarce an exception, both together,—either by one and the same suit, or by two different suits,—you cannot have. As to courts,—the *satisfactive* remedy, you are admitted to demand at the hands of either of two courts— the King's Bench or the Common Pleas; not to speak of the Exchequer: the *punitive* you are not admitted to demand in more than one of these two courts, namely the King's Bench. Moreover, there is another sort of court in which in some cases you may demand the *punitive*, namely the provincial court—the *quarterly-sittings* justice of peace court: whether, after obtaining in this court the *punitive* remedy, you can take your chance for obtaining in one or other of the two metropolitan courts, the *satisfactive*,—say who can; never yet (it is believed) has the experiment been made. Moreover, from this *local* court, the suit may, without reason assigned, by means of a sort of a *crane* termed a *certiorari*, (as per 239,) be raised up into one or other, of these two higher and more expensive courts : and this, either by the author of the wrong, or by you—the party wronged.

260. Of this severance, by co-operation and a sort of tacit concert between Judge and Co. on the one hand, and the rest of the ruling and influential few on the other,—advantage was taken, to give additional strength to their power of exercising depredation, as well as oppression, at the expense of the subject many. By the high price put upon the chance of receiving the article at the hands of Judge and Co., the satisfactive remedy, in so far as not obtainable but by procedure in the *regular mode*, was effectually denied to the vast majority of these same subject and oppressed many. So far as dependant upon *law*, these that were unprivileged were thus laid completely at the mercy of the thus privileged classes, in all cases to which the application of the *punitive* remedy did not extend itself.

261. Dear, it is true, was the price; still, however, in the eyes of a large proportion of those to whom the privilege was thus granted, the advantage was and is worth the purchase. By each man the privilege is possessed, and, whether exercised or no, exercisible at all times, all his life long, and to a certainty: whereas the inconvenience of paying for it, namely by the expense of going to law or being at law,—is a danger, the magnitude of which is, by each man's confidence in his own good fortune, concealed from his regards.

262. This being the imposed price,—how happened it that the intended victims were not deprived of the benefit of the punitive remedy, as well as of that of the satisfactive? Answer: This they could not be, without an all-comprehensive sacrifice of all security against wrong,—a sacrifice in which the sacrificers themselves, as well as the intended victims, would be included. To the security of the

privileged classes it was necessary that not only they themselves should be preserved from depredation and oppression altogether, but that the unprivileged classes should be preserved as far as might be, from depredation and oppression at the hands of one another: otherwise production would cease; and with the *subject matter* of depredation the *power* of exercising it. To this purpose it was therefore necessary, that application of the *punitive* remedy should, in a more or less considerable degree, be kept free, from the clogs, by the strength of which the *satisfactive* remedy had been rendered unattainable to the unprivileged and devoted many.

262. How to effect the severance was however the difficulty. Of this difficulty, the primæval *penury*, brought to view at the outset of the Full-length Petition, had been certainly *one* cause: the want of sufficient discernment and talent, perhaps, another. Whichever were the case, so it happened that the machinery employed in the application of the *punitive* remedy, was no other than that employed in like manner upon the *satisfactive:* whence it happened that the load of factitious delay and expense, laid upon the one, pressed also upon the other.

263. Without the fiat of a Grand Jury, for example, *caption* of the prisoner would not take place; and, except at the metropolis, no Grand Jury sat, but at the *assizes:* and the assizes were not held oftener than twice a-year in any county, nor than once in some counties: nor in any county did they last more than two or three days: and, suppose the *caption* effected, *trial* could not take place till the next assizes. What, as to offences, were the consequences? Abundant as they were

G

upon the continent, criminal offences operating by force, were in England in still superior abundance. In the time of Henry VI, Fortescue, then chancellor, takes notice of this superiority, and makes it matter of boast. In the reign of Henry VIII (as may be seen in Barrington's Observations on the Statutes) no fewer than 72,000 individuals suffered death by hanging,— about 2000 a-year upon an average : this, out of a population not half so great as at present.

264. Of the marriage of Queen Mary with Philip of Spain, one consequence was—the putting England, in this respect, upon a level with the continent. *Rome-bred* was the species of law, by which the continent was then, as now, principally governed : and, under Rome-bred law, persons accused of crimes might be apprehended *at all times.* By a statute of Philip and Mary, this power was given to justices of the peace. In the case of a criminal suit, thus was caption, with *commitment,* accelerated : still *trial* remained at an undiminished distance. But, how inadequate soever to the purpose of deterring others,—commitment made in this mode would, of itself, so long as the incarceration continued, give effectual security as against future offences on the part of the same delinquent : for, while a man is *in* jail, he cannot commit crime *out* of it. Sagacity neither was nor is wanting to perceive this incontestable truth.

265. With this arrangement, the contracting parties—Judge and Co. of the one part, and the rich and powerful of the other part—were, and continue to be well satisfied. True it is, that upon this plan, this so regularly and uniformly applied lot of suffering of about twenty-six weeks, or fifty-two weeks, applied without regard to quality of guilt,

is,—when, in consideration of quality of guilt, a few weeks, and not more, ought to be suffered,—applied in addition to those few weeks. True it is, moreover, that it is applied to the innocent who ought not to suffer at all. True it is, moreover, that all this while the innocent part of the thus forcibly *mixt company*, thus dealt with, are (as the phrase is) *contaminated*; and the guilty are occupied in contaminating as well as in being still further contaminated. " But what care I for all this?" says to himself noble lord or honourable gentleman; " none of it can ever fall upon me or any friends of mine. No danger is there of our being thus taken up, and if we were, we should be bailed of course. Then, as to the contamination, this could not be put an end to without innovation; and that would be out of the frying-pan into the fire. Besides, there is a satisfaction in having thus to talk of *contamination:* as it is the poor alone that are exposed to it, it gives a zest to the pleasure we feel in the contempt we pour upon them. It magnifies the great gulph which is fixt between them and us." Such is the almost universally established sentimentality and correspondent language in the upper regions: as if by far the most maleficent of contaminations were not that, of which (as hath over and over again been demonstrated) in these same upper regions, and in particular in the part occupied by Judge and Co. has its source.

266. Thus it is, that over and above the power of depredation, as well as oppression, which (from the nature of things) the rich and powerful, as such, unavoidably possess, at the expense of the poor and helpless,—they possess this vast additional

power, derived (how indirectly soever) from positive law.

267. By this confederacy it is, that the most powerful obstacle to law reform is constituted. Judge and Co. having, by the price put by them upon what is called *justice*, placed the satisfactive remedy out of the reach of all but the favored few,—noble lords and honourable gentlemen run in debt, under the assurance of having it in their power to cheat creditors: and thus by the higher orders are the lower orders spoiled, as by the Israelites the Egyptians. So completely, by a mixture of pride and cupidity is all sense of shame capable of being extinguished, that right honourable and noble lords have been heard to say; and without contradiction to insist, that for small debts, in this case, there ought to be no remedy. Why no remedy? Because affording a remedy against injustice encourages extravagance: as if, with this or any other encouragement that could be given to extravagance, the extravagant could ever be the majority: as if, without consent on his part, wrong in a pecuniary shape could not be done to a man in a variety of ways; as if dishonesty were not still worse than extravagance; as if, whatever were the amount, the loss of what is due *to* him were not a greater evil to any man, than the payment of what is due *from him* is to another.

268. In pursuance of this same policy, property, in a shape in which noble lords and honourable gentlemen have more of their property than in all other shapes put together, is exempted from the obligation of affording the satisfactive remedy—in a word, from the obligation of paying debts, while

property in these other shapes is left subject to it. Noble lords or honourable gentlemen contract debts, and instead of paying them, lay out the money in the purchase of land: land being exempted from the obligation of being sold for payment, creditors are thus cheated. Noble lord's son is too noble, honourable gentleman's son too honourable to pay the money, but not so to keep the land.

269. For the like reason, mortgages and other charges upon land, are not to be in an effectual way, by registration or otherwise, made knowable. Why? because, if they were, money, of which it were known that if lent it would not be recovered, would not be lent; extravagance would thus be lessened; swindling, as above, would thus be lessened: and, in a country in which a man who is rich and not honest receives more respect than a man who is honest and not rich,— obtainment of undue respect for opulence not possessed would thus be lessened.

270. For *Device* XIV. *Result of the fissure—groundless arrests for debt.*—See the Full-length Petition.

271 or 80. *Supplement to Device* V. *Oaths necessitated.* Full-length Petition, p. from 35 to 75. Abridged Petition, p. 29, art. 79. Consummation of the mass of evil shewn to be produced by this Device as above. By this one instrument, evil is capable of being produced more than by all others put together. For by it, besides the evil produced by itself, eternity is capable of being given to the evil produced by all those others.

273 or 81. Even without this addition, sufficient

for any ordinary appetite for the pleasure of maleficence, should be the power of the singly-seated
absolutist.   Infinite, however, is the addition,
which the power of imposing oaths is capable of
making to it.

273 or 82. Extirpation of all heretics—extirpation of all liberals,—conceive a Don Ferdinand,
conceive a Don Miguel, beat upon procuring for
himself these two gratifications—either of them,
or, which would save trouble, both together:—for
the accomplishment of these objects, added (suppose) the obligation of making re-application of
those tortures, the application of which used to be
common for some of these same purposes. Nothing
can be more easy. Two formularies for this purpose
are already to be had from geography and history.
He goes to work thus. An appropriate oath of the
promissory kind is framed.   All public functionaries take it : functionaries, administrational—judicial—military.   All schoolmasters and schoolmis-
tresses take it : they administer it—all of them—
to their respective boarders and scholars.   All husbands administer it to their wives.   All parents, to
their children, who by the form of it stand engaged to
transmit it to their children, and so on to the latest
posterity.   Behold here a sort of *estate tail*, for
the barring of which no *fine*, no *recovery* is available.

274 or 83.   Dangerous enough in an absolute
monarchy, of which there are so many examples,—
it is still more dangerous under a pure aristocracy,
of which there is one example, and under that
composed of monarchy and aristocracy, of which
there is another example. A monarch has caprices:
an aristocracy has no caprices.   By the monarch
of the day, the oath imposed one hour, may be

taken off the next hour. The oath imposed by the monarch of one day may be taken off by his successor—the monarch of the next day. Under an aristocracy, relief has no such chance. Long before the aristocracy-ridden monarchy of England had begun to lighten the yoke of religious tyranny on the necks of the Catholic subjects, Austrian monarchs had nearly removed it off the necks of their Protestant subjects.

275 or 84. To the *extent* of the evil produced by this instrument, addition may be made day after day: and, as to *duration*—if by it the existence of the evil can be secured for two days together, so may it be to the end of time.

276 or 85. Those, who are so fond of it, when employed, in giving support of their own sinister interests or prejudices, on one part of the field of law,—might do well to think, how capable it is of being employed against those same interests or prejudices, on another part of that same field. A radical, who wishes to see it continued to be employed against Catholicism, should have considered how capable it is of being employed against radicalism. Against radicalism? Yes: or against any the smallest melioration in the form of the government.

277 or 86. Lord Castlereagh and Lord Sidmouth, when they enacted the Six Acts, should, after making a few more such Acts—whatsoever were necessary to complete their plan—have taken this method of giving perpetuity to it. Without touching the invaluable *Coronation oath*, an amendment tacked to it, would have done the business at once. The heavier the yoke thus laid on the necks of the subject many, the more exquisite would then have been the tenderness of all royal consciences.

278 or 87. Will it be said—'' No : formidable as the instrument is, the application made of it will never be carried to any such lengths ?'' Let him that says so, say—at what point it is that the application will be sure to stop. Let him say—at what point the appetite for power will be sure to stop. This point found, let him say—whether, after having reached that point one day, it may not go on the next.

279 or 88. Observations these—which, by their importance, may, it is hoped, atone for the irregularity committed by the insertion in this place given to them.

MORE ABRIDGED

PETITION FOR JUSTICE.

To the Honourable the House of Commons;

THE PETITION OF THE UNDERSIGNED,

SHEWETH,

1. THAT, so far as regards the law in general and the constitutional branch in particular, the main object of attachment and veneration is—the law called *Magna Charta*, the earliest of all statutes now recognised as such; and upon occasion, as such it is spoken of by all legislators and all judges.

2. That, although, in large proportion, the happiness of us all does in truth depend upon the degree of observance given to a certain clause of it; yet in respect of that same clause, is this same fundamental law grossly, notoriously, and continually violated: violated by all judges who are styled *judges*, and that violation connived at by legislators.

3. That, though in and by this clause it is said

3

in so many words—" To no one will we *delay*, to no one *sell*, to no one *deny justice*:" meaning by justice, judges's service—the sort of service performed by a judge as such : yet is this same *justice*, in all common law, equity and ecclesiastical courts, wilfully *delayed* to all—*sold*, at a vast and extortious price, to those who are able to purchase it,—and *denied* to all those who are unable : in which sad case are the immense majority of the whole people.

4. That the sale, thus made of the service performed by a judge, was produced, and is continued, by the mode in which remuneration was made for such services : the matter of such remuneration coming out of the pockets of those by whom alone the benefit of such service was supposed to be reaped, and increasing with the number of the official operations, performed, or falsely said to be performed,—and the number and length of the written instruments framed, or falsely said to be framed,—on the occasion of such service : of which remuneration each distinct portion so received is styled *a fee*.

5. That, setting aside the case in which he is paid (as by salary money in the shape of,) without prospect of increase of pay by length of time,—there are two modes in which a workman of any sort is paid for the service done by him, or supposed to be done ; one is that in which he is paid for the quantity and quality of the *work*; done, or supposed to be done ; this is called payment by the job, and the work is called *job-work :* the other is that in which he is paid according to the *time*, during which he is occupied or supposed to be occupied in doing the work : this is

called payment by the time, and the work is called *time-work*.

6. That, for letting in operations upon operations, and written instruments upon written instruments, and applications for enlargement of the time,—a proportionate quantity of *delay* has been and is made necessary : and here may be seen the sinister interest in which the factitious part of the delay has its source.

7. That, in whichsoever mode the payment is made,—where, in official service, there are masters and servants (styled superior and subordinate) occupied or supposed to be occupied in the same work—there are two modes in which the benefit of such remuneration finds its way into the pockets of the superior—in the present case, the *judge :* one, according to which each fee is paid to himself; the other, according to which the fee is paid to the possessor of some office under him, of which he has the patronage ; and that thus, it being the interest, and put into the power, so has it been and continues to be the practice, of judges—to raise to the utmost the price paid, by the suitors, for the service of the subordinates of these same judges.

8. That the same community of sinister interests, which, in the case of the official class of lawyers, has place between superiors and subordinates, has place between the whole of the official class and the whole remaining class, (that is to say the professional,) their emolument being composed of payment made for service done, or supposed to be done, to their respective clients—the parties : the more suits the one class gets, the more suits the other gets ;

and the more money the one gets the more money the other gets upon each suit : and thus it is that, by the judges, to swell their own emoluments to the utmost, the suitors, who would be sufficiently vexed by the suit without being taxed, are taxed three times over : by payments to the judges, by payments to their subordinates, and by payments to the professional lawyers : the classes of whom are, for the same sinister purpose, multiplied without limit : and—not only without use to, but greatly to the detriment of, truth and justice.

9. That, while thus benefiting themselves by the *sale* of justice, the same judges—by the same means —produce benefit to themselves by the *denial* of justice; for that, in so far as a judge saves himself from being called upon to perform his appropriate service, without losing money by so doing,—he obtains *ease ;* and, as the total amount of the remuneration depends—partly upon the number of the suits, partly upon the amount of profit upon each suit,—and the number of the purchasers decreases as the price increases,—the price demanded will consequently *be* always as high as, without lessening the total profit, by lessening the number of the purchasers, it can be made to be. Here then, in the sale of what is called *justice*, as in the sale of *goods*, a constant calculation has, at all times, been carrying on ; and, that the price is no higher than it is, is owing to this—namely, that if it were higher, more would be lost by the number of the persons *prevented* from being customers, than gained by the extra tax imposed upon those who *become* customers.

10. That thus, although in point of morality it

is, and in point of law it ought to be *made*, the *duty* of a judge—to make the number, of those to whom his service is rendered, as great, and the service rendered to each, as great, and as cheap, as possible,—yet so it is, that it having, as above, been made his *interest*, as well as put into his *power*, to render the number of those to whom his service is rendered as small, and the service rendered to each as small, and dear, as possible,—his interest is thus, by these arrangements, put into a state of opposition to such his moral duty :—opposition, as complete as possible.

11. That, in respect of *expense*, such is the effect of this sinister interest, that, where money or money's worth is the subject of dispute,—in the common law courts, the least amount of the expense, is, on each side, under the most favourable circumstances, upwards of 30*l.* ; while, in cases to a large extent it amounts to hundreds of pounds, and in the equity courts to much more : and, by appeal from court to court, one above another, under different names,—it may be, and is, raised to thousands of pounds : in the equity courts to little if anything short of tens of thousands of pounds : and this, in cases in which, under the only mode of procedure really conducive to, or aiming at, justice (of which mode presently) the suit would be heard and determined, without any expense in the shape of *money*, and at an inconsiderable expense in the shape of *time*.

12. That, in cases of *bankruptcy* and *insolvency*, matters are so ordered, that,—in a great, not to say the greater, part of the individual instances,—the persons, among whom the greater part, not unfrequently the whole, of the effects are distributed, are

—not the creditors, but the lawyers:—the lawyers of both classes : and, as if to thicken the confusion, and increase the plunderage,—*insolvency* and *bankruptcy*, in themselves the same thing, are dealt with, by two different sorts of judicatories,—examining into the facts in two different sorts of ways, upon two different sorts of principles : every insolvent having moreover given to him the means of making himself a bankrupt.

13. That, in the courts called equity courts, matters are so ordered, that, when a fortune is left (for example to a female) by a last will,—so it is that, in cases to a large extent, she cannot receive it, till it has passed through an equity court; and the consequence is that, if the fortune—say 10,000*l.* —has fallen to her at a period of early infancy, and, upon the strength of it, she has made and received promise of marriage,—upon coming of age, when she should receive it, if at the end of eight years from the death of the testator, she has received so much as a penny for her subsistence, it is a favourable case : and, by an opponent, if he chooses to be at the expense, may this delay, (as witness a trustworthy writer*) be "*doubled* or *trebled:*" the proceeds being in the mean time swallowed up by the judges and their confederates.

14. That, by intervals of *inaction* between one part and another of the same suit—intervals of from eighteen to one hundred and twenty days between term and term, and, of six months or twelve months between assizes and assizes,—matters are so ordered, that, on the occasion of a penal suit, which,

---

* Cooper on the Court of Chancery, A° 1828, p. 91.

by proceeding as before a justice of the peace, would
have been heard and determined in a few minutes,—the accused, guilty or innocent, is confined in a prison for six months or twelve
months, there to linger, before the definitive examination called the *trial* is performed. Thus is
produced the so-much-lamented *contamination :* a
disease not least deplored, by those, to whose profit,
and those by whose indifference, it is suffered to continue. All this while, if for a single moment
injustice sleeps, why should justice? Even in
sabbath time, if the God of justice forbids not the
drawing of an ox or an ass, at that time, out of
a pit,—with what reason can he be supposed, to
forbid the drawing an innocent man, woman, or
child, out of a prison? or to forbid, for a moment,
any operation, necessary or conducive to the prevention, suppression, or punishment of crimes, or
to satisfaction for the suffering?

15. That, in an equity court, an answer,—which,
by proceeding as by a justice of the peace, might
be brought out in the same minute as that which produced the question,—may be made to take five years
or more to extract,—if he to whom it is put will distri-
bute among the judges and other lawyers, the price
put upon the delay ; and, in cases to a great extent,
when the answer is thus obtained, all the use made
of it is—the enabling a man to give commencement
to another suit—a suit at common law : the common-law judges,—whatsoever question they allow
to be put to a *witness* at the *trial*, that is to say
towards the *conclusion* of a suit,—not suffering any
question to be put to a *party*, at the *commencement*
of that same suit.—And why?—Even because, if
they did, suits in large proportion would, in less

than an hour, be each of them nipt in the bud;—these same individual suits, of which, in equity, the mere *commencement* may, as above, be made to last more than five years.

16. That, on pain of losing his right,—whatsoever may be the value of that same right,—this is the course, which a man may be obliged to take, in order, for example, to put it to another man to acknowledge or deny his own hand-writing: this being the only course which can be taken, when no third person—who has seen him write, or in any other way is sufficiently acquainted with his hand-writing,—can be discovered, and made to answer: common-law judges refusing to suffer any such question to be put, to any person who is a *party* to the suit: to insincerity thus scandalous, on the part of a suitor who is conscious of being in the wrong, affording in this way encouragement and reward.

17. That, on a proceeding before a justice of the peace, or in a small debt court, the matter of *law*, and the matter of *fact* on which the *demand* is grounded, are brought forward at the very outset; and, in many if not most cases, the *evidence* in support of it at the same time: and so, either at that same time, or on as early a day as may be, it is, in regard to the *defence*: And here, if, in any *one* case, this mode of proceeding is, in a greater degree than any other that can be employed, conducive—not only to the exclusion of needless expense, delay, and vexation, but moreover to *right decision*,—we humbly entreat the Honourable House, to consider, whether it can be any otherwise in any *other* case.

18. That, in the common law courts,—both in

cases called *criminal* or *penal*, and in cases, between man and man, called *civil*,—so lost are judges to all sense of shame,—that, not only do they carry on, but openly avow—yes, and in so many words—the practice, of giving "decisions" *not grounded on the merits:* that is to say, of deciding contrary to justice; for, by a judge, how is it that justice can be contravened, or injustice committed, if it be not by purposely deciding otherwise than according to the merits? And, to this dissoluteness is given the denomination, and the praise, of *strictness:* and, such is the blindness produced by the arts of delusion on the public mind,—that this abomination is, by non-lawyers commonly supposed to be, because by lawyers it is said to be, necessary, or at any rule conducive, to justice.

19. That, accordingly, it is without scruple that they give one man's whole property to another man, for no other reason than that some lawyer, official or professional, or some clerk in the employ of one or other of them or of some third person, has inserted, in some word, material or immaterial, in some writing, material or immaterial, a letter which is, or said to be, a wrong one,—or has omitted a right one.

20. That, by the same means, and on the same pretence, and without any the least symptom of regret, they give, habitually and constantly, impunity to crime in every shape: the most mischievous and atrocious not excepted

21. That, for example, it was but t'other day, that a man,—who, beyond all doubt, had cut off the head of a child, was, at the instance of a judge, and for no other reason than that a word in a written instrument had been wrong spelt, acquitted: by which same

means, with the approbation of all the judges, impunity may, at any time, by any man, in the situation of a lawyer's clerk, be given to any other man, for
any crime : and, under favourable circumstances,
the crime may be planned, and impunity secured
to it, beforehand.

22. That this practice is the more flagrantly inexcusable,—inasmuch as, while it is carried on by
a common law judge, it is not carried on by an
equity judge ; nor, unless by accident, and in
imitation of the bad example so set by superiors,
is it, by a justice of the peace, or by a small debt
court.

23. That, on any occasion, the same judge, who,
on this or that former occasion has framed his decision on grounds contrary to the merits, declines,
if he pleases, to pursue this course, and makes a
merit of so doing: that, in this way any set of
these judges may,—under the direction, as usual,
and in compliance with the will, of the chief,—give
the thing in question—the estate or the money—
to whichever of two men he pleases ; by which
means, without possibility of discovery, corruption
to any amount, may, on the part of judges in any
number, have had place.

24. That, by all judges who are commonly stiled
judges — common-law judges as well as equity
judges, (not to speak of others who are not so
stiled,) mendacity, in one shape or other, is—openly,
as well as habitually—licensed, rewarded, necessitated, and practised : and, by these same judges,
by such mendacity, is filthy lucre knowingly and
wilfully obtained.

25. That, by habit, to such a degree is all
shame for the practice of so scandalous a vice ex

tinguished,—that when a criminal who, conscious of his being guilty, confesses himself so to be,—the judge, as a matter of course, by persuasion purposely applied, engages him to declare himself *not guilty :* as if, supposing it desirable that other proof should be made, it could not as well be made without that lie as with it.

26. That, in like manner, what frequently happens is—that when, no one entertaining the least doubt of the man's guilt, he is accordingly by the jury about to be declared *guilty,*—the judge, by persuasion purposely applied, engages them to declare him *not guilty :* and—so wretchedly, by thoughtless excess in the punishment, has the law been contrived—the law, or that which passes for such—(meaning the common law in contradistinction to the statute law,—that, in the individual instance, more evil is perhaps excluded by abatement in that same excess, than produced by the immorality and the insubordination thus exemplified.

27. That, in common-law, under the name of *Judges,* and in equity, under the name of *Masters* in chancery,—judges have been, and habitually continue to be, in the practice of exacting fees, for operations never performed : for attendances (for example) never paid : thus adding extortion to fraud : at the same time, not merely admitting but compelling the lawyers of the parties to be sharers in the same guilt, thus multiplying the expense to the suitors, for the sake of the profit to the lawyers :—and this abomination—though brought to their view by evidence which they have caused to be printed,—the Commissioners, appointed for the purpose of perpetuating, on pretence of abrogating, abuses,—have, together with the above-

mentioned and so many other abuses, suffered to pass without calling for abrogation,—and without censure, or token of disapprobation.

28. That, under the system thus faithfully howsoever imperfectly delineated,—every man who is to a certain degree wealthy, has it completely in his power to ruin any other man who is to a certain degree less wealthy than himself: at the expense of a proprietor,—whether the property be in the possession of the one or the other,—gratification may thus be given by the wealthy man to his avarice : at the expence of any man, proprietor or non-proprietor, to his avarice, or to his groundless hatred or vengeance : the poorer the victim, the less time and money will the gratification thus afforded to the oppressor, cost him : in the lawyers of all classes, and more especially in the judges,—on condition of distributing among them the requisite sums in the established proportions, —he will, on this as on other occasions, behold and find his ever-ready instruments.

29. That, accordingly, under such judges and such laws, security for whatsoever is most dear to man—property, power, reputation, personal comfort; condition in life, life itself—is an empty name:—witness, in regard to all real property, the printed declaration of an honest lawyer, whose name is so happily to be found on the list of the Commissioners appointed to make report to the Honourable House on that subject. " No title" (says he in so many words) at present, can be considered as perfectly " safe :"*—and it is by the

* Suggestions sent to the Commissioners appointed to Inquire into the Laws of Real Property, by John Tyrrell, of Lincoln's Inn, Barrister, London 1829, p. 168.

sinister interest herein holden up to view, that this as well as the other portions of the law, have been brought to this pass.

30. That, to keep the door shut, as close as possible, against all endeavours to apply to that system of disorder and maleficence any effectual remedy,—pains are constantly taken, to induce the persuasion, that of all these disorders, the cause is to be found—not in human maleficence, but in the unchangeable nature of things:—but, in any such notion, what degree of truth there is, we leave it—after the exposure thus made,—we leave it to all men to imagine, and we humbly leave it to the Honourable House to pronounce.

31. That, should it be affirmed that this our humble representation is exaggerated, and in proof of its being so, should it be asked—how, if the provision made for the support of rights and exclusion of wrongs were no better than as above represented, society could be kept together;—should this be asked, the answer is—that it would *not* be kept together, but for three things: namely, 1st, the circumstance—that the man of law, though from delinquency in the shape of *fraud*, from which, in his view of it, he has little or nothing to fear, he has more to profit than to suffer,—yet, as to crimes of *violence*,—under the impossibility of providing protection for himself without extending it to the community at large,—he feels it his interest to do more or less towards the exclusion of them: 2nd, the guardian influence of *public opinion*, under favour of that liberty, precarious as it is, which the press is left in possession of;—3d and last, an expectation, —though produced by delusion in spite of experience,—that, on each occasion, will be done

that which ought to be done, or something to the like effect : on which last account we cannot but acknowledge, that it were better the delusion should continue, were it not that it is not possible that the disorder should, any further than it is laid open, receive any effectual remedy.

32. Finally, in regard to the so often-mentioned *summary* system, which is of course represented by lawyers, and thence regarded by others, as having nothing but *dispatch* to recommend it ; we humbly insert, and challenge them to disprove it, that, for rectitude of decision, and thence for giving execution and effect to the law in all its parts,—it is far better adapted—not only than the system stiled *regular*, but moreover than any other that can be named.

33. We therefore humbly pray—that, with such extensions and other amendments as may be found requisite,—this same system of summary procedure may be universally established—a *judiciary* establishment, suited to the application of it, instituted,—and the system stiled *regular* completely extirpated.

34. For further particulars of the grievance and the main cause of it, but more especially of the remedy,—we take the liberty humbly to refer the Honourable House to the forms of Petition, intituled *Full-length Petition for Justice, Abridged Petition for Justice*, and *Petition for Codification*,— all bearing the name of JEREMY BENTHAM, who thereby has made himself throughout responsible for the correctness of the statements therein contained : and to those who cannot find time for the perusal, we leave it to imagine and say,—whether a man, by whom a life of more than fourscore years

has been passed without spot, and more than sixty of them employed on works on legislation, which in every part of the civilized world are known and regarded with approbation,—would, on a subject and occasion of such importance,—in the face of that same world, lightly hazard any assertion without some substantial ground.

SUPPLEMENT

---

§. *Corruption—its imputability to English Judges.*

1. CORRUPTION is generally spoken of as the
ne plus ultra of depravity in a judge. By Englishmen, the English are commonly spoken of as forming, in respect of clearness from this stain, an
honourable contrast with the judges of other countries. After reference made to what is above, we
entreat those whom it may concern, and the Honourable House in more especial manner, to consider—whether, either corruption or something still
worse is not, beyond dispute, with few or no exceptions, but too justly imputable to English
judges. For—if *denial* and *sale* of justice, with
profit by the amount of the sale, be not corruption, or something still worse, what is?

2. Like other trades,—the trade, which may
with propriety be termed the *trade of corruption*,
may be carried on—either in the *retail* or in the

4

wholesale way: in the retail way, when it is at
the charge of individuals only that it is carried on;
in the wholesale way, when it is at the charge of
hundreds of thousands and millions, that it is carried on: by *sale* of justice at the charge of hundreds of thousands, with benefit in the shape of
pecuniary *profit:* by *denial* of justice, at the charge
of millions, with benefit in the shape of *ease.*

3. By the word *corruption*, only in that which
has just been styled the *retail* mode is the thing
itself commonly brought to view. In this case,
the conception formed of the magnitude of the evil
produced, is naturally much exaggerated. Cause
of the exaggeration, this: In so far as carried on
in the *retail* mode, whatsoever intercourse has place
on the occasion is of course carried on in secret:
by the secrecy, suspicion, and *that* on the most
incontestable grounds, is excited; facts, though
it were in small number, transpiring by accident,—
especially when other persons of note are concerned in them, or affected by them—suffice to
produce in the public mind the conception—that
the instances in which it has place are much more
numerous than in reality they are. Under governments, and in judicatories, in which means of corruption, producing profit by money or money's
worth received in the direct way, have place,—the
probable number of these instances is not very
great. Why?. Because in this case the receiver
must put himself in the power of the giver: and
because a proposed giver will not, without such a
sum in his hands as will (he thinks) suffice to outweigh the fear of the risk in the mind of the judge,
incur the risk of being delivered over to punishment by that same judge.

4. In a direct way in the shape of money, small indeed, comparatively speaking, is the probability, that, on the part of an English Judge, corruption should have place. Why? because, so far as concerns reputation,—by a Judge, a bribe could not be *received* in a *direct* way without his putting himself, as above, in the power of the *bribe-giver*. But, *indirect* ways there are, in which no such danger has place :—where, for example, it is not the Judge, but a connection of the Judge's, that receives the benefit in question ;—and *that* from a connection of the *party ;* especially if it be in the shape—not of money, but, for example, of a lucrative office, or a lucrative bargain.

5. Note here, that on the part of a Judge, as on the part of any other man,—where, in this or any other shape *misconduct* has place,—the amount of the evil in *all* shapes taken together being given, it matters not what has been the *motive*. In the case of a Judge,—besides *self-regarding* interest in respect of money or money's worth at the hands of individuals,—temptations to the operation of which his *probity* stands exposed ; are—*self-regarding* interest in respect of desire of the matter of good in that and other shape, at the hands of government, together with *sympathy* and *antipathy* as towards individuals or classes of any sort,—on whatever account—private or public. Now then—to corruption,—(if corruption is the name to be given to misconduct otherwise than from blameless misconception)—to corruption, in the *retail* mode, from all these sources; the probity of the judge stands more or less exposed,—in all countries, and in all judicatories. Why? Because, by all these efficient causes, misconduct, in any

shape, may, on the part of a functionary, in that
as in any other situation, be made to have place,
without need of intercourse with any other individual ; and this, unless circumstantial evidence
be received as sufficient, without possibility of its
being, for the purpose of censure, proved either
in a legal tribunal, or even in the tribunal of public
opinion.

6. Thus it is—that, in respect of corruption,
carried on by functionaries in all situations in the
retail mode, England is not much otherwise than
upon a footing with other countries: while, in
respect of the corruption trade, carried on by
judges in the *wholesale* way, as above, she is altogether unrivalled.

7. Without any the smallest fear of punishment,
—without even any considerable fear, if any at all, of
any such disrepute as he is capable of being influ-
enced by,—an English Judge, on a question in which
the ruling one or the sub-ruling few are supposed
by him to take an interest, may commit injustice to
any amount in favour of that side. Without danger
of any *such* disrepute, for two reasons. 1. Because,
at the hands of all with whom he is in the habit of
passing his time, or is in any particular way connected,—instead of disapprobation, approbation is
the sentiment he will make sure of experiencing.
2. Because, in the situation of a judge,—partiality
in favour of that side is so general, not to say universal, and is the result of influence notoriously so
irresistible, that, on the part even of those who
suffer by it, slight is the degree of disapprobation
which it calls forth : a mere nothing in comparison
of that which would have place, if it were by hard
money, to the same value, that it was produced.

8. In the case of an alleged *libel*, for example, against a Government functionary, as such,—what man is there that ever expects, that the chief justice will fail to do his utmost to procure the conviction of the alleged libeller? or, on the prosecution of a justice of peace, to screen him from punishment? If *indictment* be the mode, the jury will be directed accordingly; if *information*, the impunity will, as far as possible, be conferred at an earlier stage :—the *rule* will be refused : the established maxim about *motives*—(no conviction without *proof* of a corrupt motive)—being of itself equivalent to a statute law granting impunity to every abuse of power on the part of every individual placed in that same office. A justice of peace, supposing it possible that punishment be his desire, would not be indulged with it : for, by the example of *his* punishment, delinquency on the part of others—4000 and more, acting in that same office—might be more or less checked: not to speak of official men, in other offices, whether below him, on a level with him, or even above him. In as far as in that office a man is deterred from abuse of its powers—it is by fear—not of conviction (a disaster to which he does not stand exposed) but of *prosecution;* to which, whatsoever can be done for him, he cannot but remain exposed, at the hands of any such adequately opulent individuals, in whose breast *resentment* has so far got the upper hand of *prudence*.

9. As to *incorruptibility* and *independence*,—under matchless constitution, every judge is, on every occasion, acted upon by that same matter of corruption, of which the fountain springs from behind the throne: he alone excepted, who for

himself has nothing to wish for, nor has relation, friend, or enemy. What then, but either deceiver or deceived can any be, by whom, in the situation of an English judge, any such quality as *independence* is said to have place?

Two laws, *made*, both of them, by these same judges who " never make any law," two laws—either of them, much more both of them together, (not to speak of the fullest assurance at the hands of legislators, of which presently) suffice to keep banished from the mind of an English judge, all apprehension of punishment, in any shape, for any thing done in the exercise of his power. One is —that which enables a public man, to whom misconduct is imputed, to bring down punishment on the head of the imputer, without exposing himself, on that occasion, to any such unpleasant accident, as that of hearing the truth of the imputation proved, out of the adversary's, or any *other* mouth: the other is, that which preserves him from the still more unpleasant accident of hearing it proved out of *his own* mouth.

Where the procedure is by *information*, true it is—that, in some instances, the court has refused to grant what is called *the rule*, (namely, the rule by which it is suffered to go on) without an *affidavit*, denying the truth of the imputation. But, for preserving an *oppressed* complainant from being punished instead of the *oppressor*, what would this practice do, were it ever so sure to be adhered to ? Just nothing. Whether any judge, whose pleasure it has been to receive a bribe, will have received the bribe-giver, with a third person in his hand, to bear witness of the transaction, may be left to be imagined: and, without such third person the

evidence of the bribe-giver will go for nothing ;
for, forasmuch as to conviction in case of perjury,
two evidences are made necessary, a license is
thereby granted to every person to commit perjury,
wherever no evidence, in addition to the testimony
of *one* witness, has had place.

·But, suppose an extraordinary case : similar or
other evidence, not only in existence but obtainable, on the strength of which it is possible that
conviction may take place.   How stand the relative situations of the parties ? Against conviction
of the doubly guilty functionary, guilty of the
original oppression or depredation, guilty of the
perjury committed for the purpose of transferring
all punishment from the injurer to the injured, the
chances are several to one : while, to the oppressed or plundered accuser, or other prosecutor,
punishment is applied to a certainty : punishment,
that is to say, pecuniary punishment, and this to
an amount not ascertainable beforehand ; but frequently not less than some hundreds of pounds.
True it is, that, in this case, not *punishment* but
costs is the name given to it : but, whether by this
change of denomination any abatement be made in
the suffering produced by the thing denominated,
may be left to be imagined.

· ·True it is again—a mode there is, in which, if a
judge, or any other functionary or any other person by whom oppression, depredation, or any
other crime has been committed, wishes to see it
exposed to public view,—he is at liberty to put in
for the indulgence : this is the mode by *action :* for
in this case the alleged libeller—the defendant—is
left at liberty to prove the truth of the imputation ;
which if he does, the criminal, whose guilt has

thus been proved, obtains no *damages*, and perhaps pays *costs*. But, some how or other, a desire of this sort is not very commonly entertained.

Not that in all cases the guilt of the prosecutor is thus demonstrated by the mode of prosecution chosen by him. For where, as in the cases of *indictment* and *information*, the suit is of that sort in which punishment is applied under the name of *punishment*, to the *author* of the injury,—and no *compensation* given directly and avowedly to the *sufferer* by the injury,—in this case the testimony of the sufferer is admitted; and not only so, but as capable of being taken for sufficient, without corroboration from any extraneous evidence. But, in the case in question, extraneous evidence, and *that* adequate, never can be wanting. It is given by every man, by whom a copy of the alleged libel has been purchased.

Accordingly, if any such criminal act is imputed to a man: to any man, and in particular to a judge,—he will proceed by one sort of suit or another, according as he is guilty or not guilty. If not guilty, he proceeds by action: if guilty, he proceeds by indictment or information; by information—either in the ordinary way, or by information in the *ex officio* way: in the *ex officio* way, that is to say, by the mere act, if obtainable, of the attorney-general, without application for leave, made in public, to the court. This being the case,—if it be in any one of these three last-mentioned ways that he proceeds,—to what a degree he exposes his character to suspicion, not to say gives it up, is sufficiently obvious.

§ II. *Other sources of opposition to Law Reform.*

1. If it be of use, that, in the situation of judge, the opposition of interest to duty under the existing system should be held up to view,—not less so can it be, in the case of those, by whom the conduct of all judges is determinable.

2. On this occasion may be seen two conflicting interests, by which the minds of legislators are everywhere operated upon: legislators, and the ruling few in general: to which class belong of course the judges; whose case comes, on this account, a second time under consideration; of these same conflicting interests, the one acting in accordance with the official duty, the other in opposition to it.

3. First, as to duty in respect of the main end of justice: namely, maximization of the execution and *effect* given to the several existing laws, by whomsoever made. To the legislator for the time being, if to anybody, belongs assuredly this duty, in the character of a moral duty: necessary to the fulfilment of which, (as there has so often been occasion to observe) is prevention, not only of *mis-decision*, but of *non-decision*, where, and in such sort as, *decision* is necessary to the production of that same *effect:* so likewise in respect of the *collateral* ends of justice; namely, minimization of expense, delay, and vexation.

4. Thus much for *duty.* But, as to *interest*, unfortunately, in the breast of the legislator, as well as in that of the judge as such,—against that interest which is in accordance with duty, fight other interests which stand in opposition to it.

Interests in accordance with duty, those which belong to him, in common with all other members of the community; interests in discordance with and opposition to duty, all those which, being peculiar to the few, cannot be promoted but at the expense of those of the other members of that same community; in a word of the *subject-many*.

5. So much for conflicting *interests :* now for *law.* In the aggregate body of the laws, some there will always be, by which the promotion of the interests of both sections—that of the subject-many, and that of the ruling few—will have been endeavoured at, and in a greater or less degree compassed : others again there will be, by which the interests of the ruling few will be promoted, or be endeavoured to be promoted, at the expense of those of the subject-many : others again by which the interests of the subject-many will be promoted or be endeavoured to be promoted, at the expense of the particular interests, or supposed interests, of the ruling few.

6. So much for legislators at large. Enter now in conjunction, such of them as are lawyers, and lawyers at large, official and professional, both in one, and professional at large; looked up to, all of them, by legislators, as their advisers. These being the only persons, who can so much as profess to have any general acquaintance with the law as it is,—thence it but too naturally comes to pass— that, as often as any proposal for the amelioration of the system is brought forward,—the opinion by *them* declared is, as of course, referred to, as that on which the determination respecting acceptance or rejection shall be grounded. But, it being in

the highest degree their interest that it shall be in a state as opposite to the interest of the people in respect of the abovementioned ends of justice, as possible,—and, whatever it be, as little known as possible,—of course, so it is, that supposing any such change proposed, as affords a promise of rendering it conformable to the ends of justice, whatever knowledge each man possesses is applied—not to the promotion, but to the prevention of it; prevention of it—by any means, and in any way; in an open and direct way, or in a disguised and indirect way; in particular, by the promotion of such narrow improvements, apparent or even real, so they be—either by unadaptibility, or by their narrowness and the consequent length of time requisite for their establishment, obstructive of all adequate as well as beneficial change.

7. Accordingly when a plan has been brought forward, having for its object the establishment of an all-comprehensive, uniform, and self-consistent rule of action,—conducive, in endeavour at least, in the highest degree possible, to the happiness of the whole community, taken together,—and this at the earliest *time* possible,—little less than universal have been the anxiety and the conjunct endeavour to frustrate its design. For this purpose, silence, being at once the most commodious, and the most efficacious, has been the means generally resorted to : the most efficacious; forasmuch as by declared opposition, attention would be drawn to the subject, and to the validity of the arguments *in favour* of the plan; and the futility of the ablest and strongest arguments capable of being brought *against* it, would be the more extensively perceived.

8. Hence it is—that, under the existing system—

while, on the part of judges, not only acts of
wilful omission to give execution and effect to the
law have place, but acts are committed, by which
the authority of the will declared by the legislature is avowedly overruled,—so perfectly undis-
turbed is the tranquillity manifested by legislators.
In cases, in which no particular detriment to the
particular interests of the ruling few is percepti-
ble, as plenary as can be wished is the indulgence :
in these cases, these hired servants of the law are left
to obey it or break it, as is most agreeable to them.

9. Parliament enacts one thing : equity rules,
or acts, the opposite thing. The *Earl of Mans-*
field, ablest as well as most zealous absolutist that,
since the aristocratical revolution, ever sat upon
an English bench,—had for use, a word admirably
adapted to this purpose. According to him, statutes, singly or in any number, were on each
occasion, to be taken in hand and *moulded.*

10. Thus, on a *common-law* bench : and, in
equity, the *Earl of Eldon,* though without the use
of the *word,* was not backward in declaredly following the example.* As for apprehension, no
very strong sensation of this sort could reasonably
be entertained, by a Lord Eldon, sitting in his
court of equity, of the same, Lord Eldon sitting in
judgment on his own conduct in his House of
Lords. Now, for above these four years, has
indication of this mode of ruling, by vigour, over
the law, been before the eyes of the public.
There it is ; and who cares? Just as much the
tories out of place as the tories in place.

11. Connected with this prominent and undeniable interest, may be seen another particular and

* Indications respecting Lord Eldon.

sinister interest, which though so much less
extensively shared, will, by its latentcy, and the
consequent appearance of disinterestedness, naturally operate, in the sinister direction, with still
greater force.   This is the interest of the *ex-lawyer*.
Interest affected, and feared for, by the lawyer in
office or practice, pecuniary interest: interest
affected, and feared for, by the ex-lawyer, interest
created by regard for reputation, reputation of
appropriate wisdom.   Well-grounded altogether
is this fear, it must be confessed : for, proportioned
to the acknowledged beneficialness and extent of
any such beneficial change, will be sure to be the
real folly which has all along been covered by the
veil of apparent and boasted wisdom.   Occupied—
first in the study of this system, then in the acting under it, and all along in the magnification of
it, the labour of a long life,—and now, after all,
and all at once, a compound of mischievousness
and absurdity is found to be the character of it!
What a shock to vanity and pride !

12. Not merely in proportion to the change
effected, but as soon as the change is determined
upon, will the sad sensation be produced. Ill-
gotten wealth and power excepted, all that the
great man has been accustomed to be valued
upon, or to value himself upon, vanished!

13. In the train of these sinister *interests*, come
interest-begotten prejudice, and *authority-begotten
prejudice*.   But, of these sources of opposition to
whatsoever is at once useful and new,—in one
place or another, so continually recurring, has
been the need,—and, with the need, the act,—of
making mention,—that every further mention of
them *here* may well be spared.

14. Such being the exposure made of the oppo-

sing causes : now for its practical uses. Uses of
it may be seen two :—One is—shewing, that,
taking the existing system all together, no proof
of its fitness to exist is declarable from its having
thus long been in existence.

15. The other use is—shewing, that, against no
one distinguishable article of the here proposed
system, or of any proposed system,—to any declared opinion of any individual belonging to any
one of those same classes, so far as it seeks to
operate in favour of the existing system, should
any weight be attributed—any regard be paid. On
the contrary, it should be looked upon as an argument in *favour* of that system to which the opposition is made : in favour of it, and for this reason.
With this subject, as with every other, the better
acquainted a man is, and the greater his appropriate ability, the better able will he be to bring
forward whatsoever relevant arguments in support
of his declared opinions the nature of the case
affords : and, the stronger the reliance placed by
him on the effect looked for from his mere opinion,
the stronger the evidence of the consciousness of
the depravity of the system, and the weakness of
all arguments producible in favour of it.

16. To conclude. In this state of things, if,
from the pressure of the enormous and perennial
load of misery, from which relief is hereby endeavoured to be obtained; any such relief is to be
expected,—it must be at the hands of one or
other of three distinguishable descriptions of men
in the situation of legislators : one, in which a
sense of moral duty has place, and that same
sense strong enough to constitute an effective
cause of action : another, that to which it appears
that its own particular interest is so bound up

with the general weal, as to have more to gain than
to suffer, from the substitution of the good system
to the bad one : the third and last, that in which
a salutary fear, in sufficient strength, has place :
the fear, lest wearied by the oppression, and en-
lightened at length by the information received, as
to the causes and the authors of it,—the subject-
many should, in sufficient number, concur in doing
for themselves. what ought to have been done for
them, and in so doing cease to exhibit that compliance, by, and in proportion to which, all power
is constituted.

Still, before this Supplement is concluded, a few
more articles, particularly the fifth and last of them,
may it is hoped be found not altogether without
their use. As to the third and fourth, exhibiting
impunity given to murder, and right trampled
upon—both without the shadow of a reason—the
practice is of such continual occurrence, that these
instance of it would not have been inserted, but
that, at the moment of sending off the matter to
the press, the memorandums made of them happened to present themselves to view.

1. *Applying to Device* III.—*Written. Instruments,
where worse than useless, necessitated.*

From the *Examiner* for 30th November, 1828:—
" An action has been brought against the ' select'
" (of St Giles's and St George's Bloomsbury) to
" try their, title ; 200*l.* were therefore abstracted
" from. the funds raised for the support of the poor,
" and thus stimulated. his (the solicitor's) industry,
" was extraordinary, for he put in fifteen special
" pleas covering the surface of 175 folios !   On
" Tuesday week however the Court of King's-

" Bench *reduced* the number more than one half,*
" and thus the select have incurred personally the
" needless and vexatious expense to which they
" resorted for obvious purposes."

2. *Applying to Device V.—Oaths, for the estab-*
   lishment of the mendacity system, necessitated.

From the *Windsor Express,* August 2, 1828.
" At the Manchester quarter sessions, a woman
" was arraigned for stealing a shawl from a child
" in the street. A little boy was brought forward
" to give evidence of the fact; instead of being
" suffered to do this, however, the Chairman
" examined the child as to certain theological
" doctrines. After the child had said he knew it
" was a bad thing to tell lies, the Chairman said
" Do you know what becomes of those who tell
" lies ? ' No, I don't.' Chairman: ' Do you ever
" say your prayers ?' ' Yes, I said my prayers
" once.' Chairman : 'And what prayer was it you
" said ?' ' I said Amen.' Upon this the Chairman
" refused to receive his evidence, and the woman
" was set free."

3. *Applying to Device XI.—Decisions on grounds*
   avowedly foreign to the merits—exemplification of
   the crime-licencing system.

From the *Windsor Express* for July 19, 1828.
Exemplification of the crime-licencing system.

---

* In the reduction thus made, may be seen a sample of the
sort of law reform, which, were the matter left to them, would
be established by Judge and Co. As to the *reduction* made in the
gibberish,—what was the reduction made by it in the expense, or
what the expense of the *application* made for the reduction?
and therein, of the *saving* to the parties from these reductions,
what was the *net* amount?

"At the present Berkshire assizes, a woman
"was charged with murdering her child by wilfully
"suffocating it. Before any evidence, counsel
"submitted that the woman must be acquitted of
"this murder; *because at the coroner's inquest, the
"name of one of the jurors was stated to be Thomas
"Winter Borne, instead of Thomas Winter Burn.*

"Mr Baron Vaughan—'I cannot hold that
"Borne and Burn are the same name, and *I am
"clearly of opinion* that this objection *puts an end
"to the case.*' The prisoner must be discharged."

"Another case occurred on Tuesday in the
"King's Bench: Fisher *v.* Clement. It came
"out during the trial that the defendant who had
"been found guilty in the Common Pleas, was
"allowed a *venire de novo* by the King's Bench,
"*because* in one of the counts in the declaration,
"the words 'of and concerning' had been omitted."

4. *Applying to Device* XIV.—*Groundless arrest
for debt.*

From the *Examiner* of 11th January 1829, page
28.—"The *rules* embrace a suburb, immediately
"adjoining the King's Bench prison, of a circum-
"ference of about from two to three miles, and
"containing about six miles of open roads and
"streets. This advantage to debtors is somewhat
"similar to that accorded prisoners of war on their
"*parole d'honneur*, with the exception, that, in this
"instance, the law fixing the marshal for the debt
"of his prisoner, whenever the latter shall be
"found without the limits of ' the rules,' that offi-
"cer very properly takes care to receive sufficient
"security. It is by the privilege of granting ' the
"rules' to prisoners, that the marshal realises the
"greater portion of his income, which is said to

" amount in the gross, to from 10,000*l.* to 20,000*l.*
" The charge for the rules is in proportion to the
" amount of the debt, the rate demanded being 8*l.*
" for the first and 5*l.* for every other 100*l.* of the
" detainers lodged against a prisoner. The bonds
" are also prepared in the marshal's office, and
" leave their profit in his pocket.—*King's Bench*
" *Gazette.*"

The patronage of this office, whatever may be
the emolument of it, being in the hands of the
chief justice of the King's Bench, as the patronage
of a living is in the hands of the proprietor of the
advowson; and it being thus his interest, that oppression and depredation, at the charge of men thus
under affliction, should, in proportion as any increase in the amount of the emolument is the
result, be screwed up to the highest pitch possible,—
these things considered, what regard can be due,
to the *ipse dixit* authority, of anything which by a
man in *such* a situation, is ever said in favour of
the existing system, may be left to be imagined.

5. *Applying to Device* XIII.—*Jurisdiction split and
spliced: Abridged Petition, Article* 257.

Not by any means a matter of indifference is,
in this case, the appellation employed. To many
a functionary, by whom, as such, the power of a
judge is exercised, the appellation of *judge* is not
wont to be applyed. Instance, a *justice of the
peace.* Mind now the advantage taken of this
circumstance, for the never neglected purpose, of
excluding, from the practice of judicature, the light
of publicity, and thence the only check, to which
in various situations—and more especially in that of
a judge who is styled *judge,*—power, otherwise
completely arbitrary, stands exposed. Speaking

of the judicatory of the sort of judge styled a *jus-tice of the peace*, in the cases in which he acts, or may act, without any other with him,—so shameless have been judges of the sort styled *judges*—to such a degree shameless, as to declare—that it is *not* a *court of justice:* and that, this being so, he who presides is not under the obligation of carrying on the business otherwise than *in secret*. Is *not* a court of justice? What then *is* it? A court of injustice? this it must be, if anything; unless between the one and the other a medium can be found.

Other instances have been afforded by the sort of judge styled a *coroner*, who presides in the judicatory styled *the coroner's inquest*. To what purpose, unless it be that of sharing, in the privilege of giving impunity to past, and thereby encouragement to future murder, possessed and exercised; as above by judges styled judges?

Behold here an example, of the way in which the judge-made law styled *common law* is made. King, lords, and commons, altogether, would they dare do any such thing?

6. *Applying to almost the whole constellation of Devices*.

Under the Mosaic code, justice was administered at the city *gates*. Why at the *gates?* Even because *there* was the greatest affluence of passengers: affluence—not of paid, but of gratuitous observers, and thereby *inspectors*, on the principle above submitted to the Honourable House. Of factitious expense or delay, in no shape, under that system, is any trace visible. Exclusion of parties from judges' presence—unintelligible-language—useless written instruments—subordination and practice of lying—cessation of judge's service for six months and twelvemonths together—blind fixation of times for judicial operations—mechanical, substituted (as hath been seen) to mental judicature—useless transference in bandying: add—transference of suits from judicatory to judicatory—decision on grounds avowedly foreign to the merits—jurisdiction, when it should be entire, split and spliced,—of any one of all these abominations, not a vestige visible.

Whence now this difference?—Whence? but that the God of Moses was the God of Justice; the God of Judge and Co., the Dæmon of Chicane.

17. October the 3rd, 1829: one more last word: *facit indignatio verbum*—indignation, called forth by the occurrence of the moment, has produced it. But, the *very* last word this must be: for, if the like cause were constantly productive of this same effect, never would this publication find its close.

18. Two guineas for one minute occupied in bearing a part in the useless and mischievous ceremony—the swearing ceremony! fees to this amount extorted by a master *(ordinary)* in Chancery, for a business, which, by a solicitor arrayed in the title of MASTER EXTRAORDINARY, is done for half-a-crown! Five guineas, to the same extortioner for the bare *receiving*, of a paper styled *an answer;* besides travelling expenses, for a useless journey of from six to twenty miles.

19. Plunderage, to these amounts, extorted, or endeavoured to be extorted, from *paupers* whilst in *prison!* In prison,—during life. And for what? For no less a crime (it is true) than that of *rebel-*

lion. But, the proof of it is—what?—No other than the inability to pay costs: the costs, all factitious: tares, sown by the dæmon of chicane; crops, for the sowing and gathering in of which, the courts of iniquity, so miscalled *courts of equity*, are kept on foot.

20. Of this same eventually intended life imprisonment, in one case seventeen years already passed. Of this case, with six other similar ones, the disclosure produced by a visit to the Fleet prison; namely, the visit, forced from the foremost of the *anti-codificationists*, and anti-reformists in all shapes, in Honourable House—the new Solicitor-general, imported into it, with his minute scraps of reforms and sham reforms, for the special purpose of keeping the door shut against all adequate ones.

21. Behold the letter written by him—written to one of the victims of the oppression: giving him the assurance, that it would be "his own fault" if he continued to be thus oppressed. Behold in this letter a genuine English lawyer's sermon, on the text.—" I was in prison and ye visited me."

22. " Woe unto you lawyers! for ye have " taken away the key of knowledge; ye entered " not in yourselves, and them that were entering " in ye hindred." Luke xi. 52. Read this, ye Anti-codificationists!

23. " Woe unto you also ye lawyers! for ye " lade men with burdens grievous to be borne, " and ye touch not the burdens with one of your " fingers." Read this, ye fee-fed delayers, deniers, and sellers, of what ye call *justice!*

24. The power, given to judges by Lord Eldon and Mr Peel—the power of imposing, on the

indigent and already afflicted, taxes without stint; putting the produce into their own pockets— this power has already been over and over again held up to abhorrence; and, on each occasion that seems favourable, will be so again, so long as any blood remains in the hand which gives motion to this pen. Of the purpose and use of the creation and preservation of this *power*, this case presents an exemplification.—And this is called *government!* and this is called *justice!*

25. *Rebellion* forsooth? " *Durum est*" (says a maxim of their own)—Oh yes—*durum* enough— durum est torquere leges, ad hoc " ut torqueant homines.''

> To torture men, the tyrant words distorts:
> These are the fee-fed lawyer's cruel sports.

26. Of these sham convictions of *rebellion*,—if persevered in, with the practical consequences deduced from them,—what more apposite requital than a real and successful one?*

---

* Seen, for the history of this business, have been the documents following:—

1. Account of the Solicitor-general's visits to the Fleet prison on the 11th and 12th; headed CHANCERY REFORMS.— Morning Chronicle, 15th September 1829. " From the British Traveller."

2. Account of these same visits: one of seven cases mentioned in the above, the last four omitted.—Morning Herald 15th September; headed CHANCERY REFORMS, Visits, &c. " From the British Traveller."

3. Article, headed CHANCERY REFORMS, CONTEMPTS OF COURT.—Morning Herald, September 17th.

4. Masters in Chancery—their charges. In a letter signed, A Solicitor. Article, headed CONTEMPTS OF CHANCERY.— Morning Herald, October 2d.

5. Article, headed " CHANCERY PRACTICE. The Solicitor-

general and the rebel Pickering" containing a Bill of Costs.—
Morning Chronicle, October 3rd.

Not seen, the British Traveller—the original source of the information on this subject.

☞ A beneficial exemplification of public spirit would be a republication of the above matter in a cheap form.

PETITION FOR CODIFICATION.

The Petition of the Undersigned,

HUMBLY SHEWETH,

THAT, in so far as our respective consciences will allow, we entertain the sincerest disposition to conform ourselves in all things to the good pleasure of those who are set in authority over us.

That, when, by any of us, a wish is expressed to know what that pleasure is, he is bid to look to *the law of the land*.

That, when a man asks what that same law is, he learns that there are two parts of it : that the one is called *Statute Law*, and the other *Common Law*, and that there are books in which these same two parts are to be found.

That, when a man asks in what book the *Statute Law* is to be found, he learns that, so far from being contained in any *one* book, howsoever large, it fills books composing a heap greater than he would be able to lift.

That if, he thereupon asks, in which of all these books he could, upon occasion, lay his hands, and find those parts in which he himself is concerned, without being bewildered with those in

a

which he has no concern,—what he learns is— that the whole matter is so completely mixt up together, that for him to pick out the collection of those same parts from the rest, is utterly impossible.

That, if he asks in what book the *Common Law* is to be found, he learns that the collection of the books in which, on each occasion, search is to be made for it, are so vast, that the house he lives in would scarcely be sufficient to contain it.

That, if he asks who it is that the Statute Law is *made by,* he is told, without difficulty, that it is by King, Lords and Commons, in Parliament assembled.

That, if in continuation, we proceed, any of us, to ask who it is that the Common Law has been made by, we learn, to our inexpressible surprise, that it has been made by nobody : that it is not made by King, Lords and Commons, nor by anybody else : that the words of it are not to be found anywhere : that, in short, it has no existence ; it is a mere *fiction ;* and that to speak of it as having any existence, is what no man can do, without giving currency to an imposture.

When, upon observing that, by every *judge,* it is spoken of as a reality, and that he professes to be acting under it,—we ask whether it is not *he* that makes it ? We are told that this is what no judge ever does, and that, by any of the learned judges, a question what part of the law is of his making, would be received with indignation, and resented as a calumny.

That when, seeing men put to death, and otherwise grievously punished by order of judges, a man asks by what authority this is done, he learns that it is by the authority of Statute Law or Common Law, as it may happen : and if he thereupon asks whether, when it is upon the authority of the Common Law that the judge does this, it is not by this same judge that this same Common Law is made, he still receives the same assurance—that no judge ever makes law, and that a question what part of the law is of his making, would be received with indignation, and resented as a calumny: while the truth is—that, on each occasion, the rule to which a judge gives the force of law, is one which, on this very occasion, he makes out of his own head : and this—not till the act for which the man is thus dealt with has been done : while, by these same judges, if the same thing were done by the acknowledged legislature, it would be spoken of as an act of flagrant injustice, designated and reprobated, in their language, by the name of an *ex post facto* law.

All this while, we are told, that we have *rights* given to us, and we are bid to be grateful for those rights : we are told that we have *duties* prescribed to us, and we are bid to be punctual in the fulfilment of all those duties ; and so (we are told) we must be, if we would save ourselves from being visited with condign punishment. Hearing this, we would *really* be grateful for these same *rights*, if we knew *what* they were, and were able to avail ourselves of them : but, to avail ourselves of rights, of which we have no knowledge, being in the nature of things impossible, we are utterly unable to learn—for what, as well as to whom, to pay the so called-for tribute of our gratitude.

As to these same *duties*, we would endeavour at least to be punctual in the fulfilment of them, if we knew but what they were ; but, to be punctual in the fulfilment of duties, the knowledge of which is kept concealed from us, is equally impossible. That which is but too possible, and too frequently experienced by us, is the being thus punished for not doing that which it has thus been rendered impossible for us to do.

Thus, while the rights we are bid to be grateful for are mere illusions, the punishments we are made to undergo are sad realities.

Finally, thus it is that we, who, in so far as such oppression admits of our being so, are his Majesty's dutiful and loyal subjects, are dealt with as were the children of Israel under their Egyptian task-masters.

We hear of tyrants, and those cruel ones: but, whatever we may have felt, we have never heard of any tyrant in such sort cruel, as to punish men for disobedience to laws or orders which he had kept them from the knowledge of.

We have heard much of cruelties practised by *slaveholders* upon those who are called their *slaves*. But, so far as regards the mode of treatment we thus experience,—whatever be the cruelties practised upon *them*, never have we heard this to be of the number of those cruelties. The negro, so long as he does what he is commanded to do,. and abstains from doing that which he is forbidden to do —the negro—slave as he is, is safe. In this respect, his condition is an object of envy to us, and we pray that it may be ours.

We have heard not a little of the pains taken by the Honourable House, in the endeavour to put an end to those same cruelties. We cannot refuse to any such endeavour the humble tribute of our applause. But we hope we are not altogether unreasonable in our wish, to receive from the hands of the Honourable House, the benefit of the like endeavours.

. That which, for this purpose, we have need of (need we say it?) is a body of law, from the respective parts of which we may, each of us, by reading them or hearing them read, learn, and on each occasion know, what are his *rights*, and what his *duties*.

The framing of any such body of law cannot indeed but be a work of time. This is what we are fully sensible of. But the sooner it is begun, the sooner will it have been completed : and the longer the commencement of it is deferred, the more difficult will be the completion of it. Completed indeed it cannot be ; and of this too we are fully sensible, otherwise than by the King and the Lords, in conjunction with your Honourable House. But, to the taking in hand this most important of all works, there is *a preparatory operation*, which, we have been assured, and verily believe, is within not only the *power*, but the *practice* of the House—of the House—acting in its single capacity, and by its sole authority. This is what we hereby pray for, and it is as follows.

1. That the House, in and by its votes, may be pleased to give invitation to all persons so disposed, to send in, each of them, a *plan* of an all-comprehensive code, followed by the text thereof; this text, either the whole of it at the same time, or in successive portions, as he may find most convenient.

2. That, for indemnifying each such contributor from the *expence of printing*, the House may be pleased to give authority to him to send in, such his work, in manuscript, to any person authorised

by the House to print its proceedings : that is to say, for the purpose, and, subject to the limitation hereinafter mentioned, under the assurance that the same will be printed, along with the other proceedings of the House, in like manner as Acts of Parliament are at present.

3. As to the persons of such contributors, we humbly insist, that, from the liberty of sending in draughts for this purpose, no person should stand excluded. No; not any person whatsoever. For suppose, for example, a foreigner to send in a draught better adapted to the purpose than any draught sent in by any of his Majesty's subjects, —we see not why his being so should debar us from the benefit of it: and assuredly we see not any reason whatever for any such apprehension, as that, by the Honourable House, the circumstance of the draughtsman's being a foreigner should ever cause a less well-adapted draught to be employed and sanctioned, in preference to a better adapted one.

4. As to the expence that might be eventually attendant on the printing of such draughts, it is no more than we are perfectly aware of. But there are two arrangements, which taken together, we cannot but rely on, as sufficient to reduce within a moderate compass, the amount of that expence.

5. One is, that it be an instruction to every contributor, tha. no such contributor shall receive the benefit of the accommodation thus afforded, unless, to each article or set of articles in his proposed code, the *reason*, or *set* of *reasons*, by which it was suggested, on which it is grounded, and to which it trusts for its explanation and reception, be appended.

6. The other is—that, by the Honourable House,

power be reserved to itself, by the hands of any person or persons for that purpose, thereto appointed,—to put a stop at any time, to the printing of any such draught: after which, should the impression be continued, it will be at the contributor's own expense. But that, to assist him in the faculty of thus making a virtual appeal to public opinion,—such part of his draught as shall have been already printed, shall be delivered to him, to be disposed of as he shall think fit.

As to the obligation of attaching the abovementioned *rationale*, we trust to it as a powerful *incentive*, to the framing and sending in, well-grounded draughts, as well as a powerful instrument for keeping the service unincumbered with ill-grounded and ungrounded ones. To frame a proposed code of laws, with apt reasons all along for its support, is, in our eyes, the most arduous, as well as the most useful, of all purely human tasks that the human faculties can employ themselves upon: and, proportioned to this our persuasion, is of course our desire—that, without any exception, the door should remain open to all contributors, as above: while, on the other hand, to frame proposed laws, destitute of such support, is what no hand that can give motion to a pen would feel to be out of its power: it is what not we alone, but our mothers and our grandmothers likewise, would be capable of doing, and might peradventure be disposed to do: and it is (we have sometimes heard) no altogether uncommon sight, to see hands, little better qualified, thus occupied.

To each such contribution should be attached a *name* and address: this, not for the purpose of determing the *authorship* (for that might be left to each one's desire,) but for the purpose of *responsi-bility*, in the case of any inapplicable matter, sent in for the purpose of derision, by persons engaged by sinister interest in the endeavour to render the measure abortive.

As to *remuneration*, we humbly insist that none in any shape other than that of the eventual honour, of distinction and public approbation, with the benefits, which, in so many shapes, in amounts proportioned to the degrees of it, cannot but be among the fruits of such approbation,—ought to be allotted to any work so sent in : so far from promoting, any such remuneration could not but operate in countèraction to its proposed object, as above. It would operate as a notice of *exclusion*, to every man who could not regard himself as situated within the sphere of personal favour ; and, the higher the reward, the greater would be the number of those who would regard themselves as thus excluded.

We beg to be believed, giving as we do our assurance to the Honourable House, that it is not to any such purpose as that of seeing so much as proposed, much less effected, any change in the hands, in which the supreme power of government is lodged, that this our humble Petition is directed : and accordingly what we not only consent to, but wish and desire is, that, out of the field of the proposed otherwise all-comprehensive code, all those parts which regard the prerogative of the King, the privileges of the several Members of the two Houses of Parliament, collectively and severally possessed, and the consideration of the hands in which the elective function is placed, be excepted ; unless it be—that, for the sake of symmetry and complete-